BASIC ETHICS IN ACTION

Genetic Engineering
Science and Ethics on the New Frontier

MICHAEL BOYLAN
KEVIN E. BROWN

Prentice
Hall

Upper Saddle River, New Jersey 07458

Library of Congress Cataloging-in-Publication Data

Boylan, Michael, 1952–
    Genetic engineering : science and ethics on the new frontier / Michael Boylan., Kevin E. Brown.
      p.   cm. — (Basic ethics in action)
    Includes bibliographical references and index.
    ISBN 0–13–091085–6
    1. Genetic engineering—Moral and ethical aspects. 2. Medical genetics—Moral and
    ethical aspects. I. Brown, Kevin E. II. Title. III. Series.

QH442.B69 2002
174'.957—dc21
                                                2001034053

To our parents

Editor-in-Chief: Charlyce Jones Owen
Acquisitions Editor: Ross Miller
Assistant Editor: Katie Janssen
Editorial Assistant: Carla Worner
Senior Managing Editor: Jan Stephan
Production Liaison: Fran Russello
Project Manager: Linda B. Pawelchak

Prepress and Manufacturing Buyer:
  Sherry Lewis
Cover Director: Jayne Conte
Cover Design: Bruce Kenselaar
Marketing Manager: Ilse Wolf
Copy Editing: Chris Ruel
Proofreading: Ann-Marie WongSam

This book was set in 10/12 Palatino by Pub-Set, Inc.
and was printed and bound by Courier Companies, Inc.
The cover was printed by Phoenix Color Corp.

© 2001 by Michael Boylan and Kevin E. Brown
Published by Pearson Education, Inc.
Upper Saddle River, New Jersey 07458

Printed in the United States of America
10 9 8 7 6 5 4 3 2

ISBN 0-13-091085-6

Pearson Education LTD., *London*
Pearson Education Australia Pty. Limited, *Sydney*
Pearson Education Singapore, Pte. Ltd.
Pearson Education North Asia Ltd., *Hong Kong*
Pearson Education Canada Inc., *Toronto*
Pearson Educación de Mexico, S.A. de C.V.
Pearson Education—Japan, *Tokyo*
Pearson Education Malaysia, Pte. Ltd.

Contents

chapter two

PROFESSIONAL AND PRACTICAL PRINCIPLES
OF CONDUCT   12

Part II: The Science of Genetic Engineering

chapter three

WHERE WE ARE AND HOW WE GOT HERE   26

chapter four

THE BIOLOGICAL BASICS   30

Preface

This book hopes to introduce the reader to important ethical issues that arise in the realm of biomedical ethics. As such, it fits into that branch of ethics entitled applied ethics. *Genetic Engineering* is the fifth book in the series *Basic Ethics in Action*. The composition of this series is ongoing. The central poles are medical ethics, business ethics, environmental ethics, and social/political philosophy. The emphasis in this series is single-author books from various philosophers and practitioners in the fields. The books are presented in a normal or a condensed format. The former will run around 200 to 250 pages, while the latter will be 100 to 200 pages and will highlight a focused topic.

The series is anchored by *Basic Ethics,* an essay on normative ethics and metaethics. The combination of volumes offers many possibilities for instructors and students of ethics:

1. *Basic Ethics* alone or with other primary texts can be used in an ethical theory course.
2. *Basic Ethics* along with one of the applied texts in the series can be used in an ethics course that emphasizes an integration of theory and practice.
3. One or more of the applied texts can be used for courses that wish to concentrate upon practice.

Distinctive features of this book include (a) discussion of a "cutting edge" series of issues in a focused format; (b) presentation of both philosophical and biological issues in a way that allows each to maintain its disciplinary integrity (by practitioners in both philosophy and biology who are also "fellow travelers" of the other discipline); (c) background in both key biological and philosophical concepts so that the reader can make important connections; and (d) discussion of the principal issues facing genetic engineering today, giving weight to both the philosophical and the biological issues.

Like all interdisciplinary projects, this book will find audiences who are better versed in either philosophy or biology. To attempt to accommodate both audiences, certain key terms have been set out in bold and defined in the glossary, and the book is divided into three parts. Part One introduces some important ethical concepts that are tied into the mission of the series: to utilize personal and community worldviews and the ensuing *Personal Worldview* and *Shared Community Imperatives* as a molding influence upon how we render ethical judgments.

Part Two reviews certain fundamental concepts in cell biology and evolutionary theory that provide an overview of some basic mechanics necessary to understand the biology behind the procedures we are evaluating.

Part Three integrates biology and philosophy as we explore some key issues that have emerged in genetic engineering: (a) the limits of science, (b) genetic testing and screening, (c) somatic gene therapy, (d) cloning, (e) germline therapy, and (f) the intersection between business and science. In each case there is an attempt to integrate philosophy and biology in a way that offers a treatment of each that is rigorous and accurate.

For those readers who wish to explore the ethical issues in genetic engineering but are a little unsure about their background in science, we have staggered our presentation so that they might dip in and out of the text. The presentations in Part Two are made in an order of increasing complexity. Thus, the reader can begin with Chapter Three and proceed until he or she can go no further. For those students in medical school or students in advanced undergraduate programs in biology, Part Two should pose no difficulty. For humanities students with some biology background, we have compiled a list of questions that might give you a gauge on your scientific literacy.

SOME SAMPLE QUESTIONS FOR SELF-EVALUATION.

If you can respond to at least some of these, please attempt Part Two:

- How would you distinguish between a genotype and a phenotype?
- How do fitness and environment interact in evolutionary theory?
- What are viruses?

- What is a retrovirus vector?
- What is transcription and translation?
- What is polymerase chain reaction (PCR)?
- What are DNA and RNA and where are they found in cells?
- What are the steps in the process of protein formation?

For those readers who totally struck out on this set of questions or for those who consider themselves scientifically illiterate, there is still the option of dipping into this book in the following fashion:

1. Read Chapters One and Two.
2. Read as much as you can understand of Chapters Three through Six (and scan the glossary for scientific terms).
3. Read Chapters Seven through Twelve and consult only the shaded boxes (referencing scientific concepts) as they meet your needs.

We believe that the subjects raised in this book are of crucial importance for society to examine. We exhort our readers to stretch themselves to acquire as much philosophy or biology as possible to make this interdisciplinary exercise work.

For readers who are biologically competent but are philosophically challenged, we suggest dipping into *Basic Ethics* (the anchor volume for the series *Basic Ethics in Action*). This book goes into greater detail on various issues of worldview and its relation to the most prominent ethical theories.

As always in a project such as this there are many to thank: Edmund D. Pellegrino, Rosemarie Tong, Carol Taylor, John Bishop, Arthur Christian, Susan Brown, and Bernard Brown for reading the entire manuscript and providing useful comments for its improvement. We would also like to thank Susan Brown for her expert advice and assistance in preparing the manuscript. Last but not least, the authors are deeply grateful to our families who nurture us, support us, and put up with our many eccentricities.

Michael Boylan
Kevin E. Brown

chapter one

Worldview and Theory Choice

Genetic engineering has captured the imagination of many in recent years as science seems to be on the threshold of new and exciting therapies that will allow physicians to carry out their mission of healing in more effective ways. Along with the tremendous promise that genetic engineering offers are some potential practical and ethical difficulties that also need to be addressed.

For example, some researchers are also stockholders in companies that will benefit from their discoveries. This may involve a conflict of interest. Another set of problems revolves around the researcher as physician and his or her ensuing professional duties, as such. This involves the physician carrying out his or her role as a healer first. Still other critical issues involve the very subject matter itself—altering who we are as humans and the resulting impact upon nature. Genetic therapy in this sense is highly controversial. Debates range from issues involving somatic therapy (therapy affecting only the individual person) versus germ-cell therapy (therapy that will extend into one's reproductive capacities and future generations). Another issue concerns how to introduce the new genes into the cells. These "vectors" are often viruses that insert the desired changes into the cells of the patient. Obviously, the sorts of viruses involved (such as a "deactivated" AIDS retrovirus) can cause concerns in themselves.

In order to address as many of these problems as possible within the modest confines of this volume, it will be useful to examine some basic ethical principles concerning (1) worldview and ethical theory choice; (2) the ethical role of the physician; (3) the ethical role of the researcher; (4) conflict of interest; (5) duties to future generations; and (6) environmental duties. The first of these principles will be dealt with in this chapter while the others will be the subject of Chapter Two.

First, a brief overview is presented of some prominent ethical theories (Ethical Intuitionism, Virtue Ethics, Utilitarianism, and Deontology) with some exercises that will make them more understandable. Next, a model of theory evaluation is sketched that will aid a person in choosing that theory (or another) to guide her action.

I. Four Ethical Theories.

A. Ethical Intuitionism.

One can generally describe **Ethical Intuitionism** as a theory of justification about the immediate grasping of self-evident ethical truths. Ethical Intuitionism can operate on the level of general principles or on the level of daily decision making. In this latter mode many of us have experienced a form of Ethical Intuitionism through the teaching of timeless adages such as "Look before you leap" and "Faint heart never won fair maiden." The truth of these sayings is justified through intuition. Many adages or maxims contradict each other (such as the two above), so that the ability properly to apply these maxims is also understood through intuition.

A Quick Exercise to Understand Ethical Intuitionism.

In practice Ethical Intuitionism works from an established list of moral maxims that have no other justification other than they are immediately perceived to be true. In order to understand better how this ethical theory works, try the following exercise:

Step One: Set out a list of moral maxims that are general and that you believe will cover most moral situations (e.g., "Don't lie"). Choose at least three and no more than ten.

Step Two: Establish a hierarchy among your maxims that will apply "for the most part."

Step Three: Create a moral situation of your own that involves at least two moral maxims from your list. Set out which moral maxim best applies in the situation.

State the reasons for your choice. How would you respond to someone who disagrees with your choice?

B. Virtue Ethics.

Virtue Ethics is also sometimes called agent-based ethics. It takes the viewpoint that in living your life you should try to cultivate excellence in all that you do and all that others do. These excellences or virtues are both moral and nonmoral. Through conscious training, for example, an athlete can achieve excellence in a sport (nonmoral example). In the same way a person can achieve moral excellence as well. The way these habits are developed and the sort of community that nurtures them are all under the umbrella of Virtue Ethics.

Virtue Ethics works from an established list of accepted character traits called virtues. These traits are acquired by habit and guide the practitioner in making moral decisions. Aristotle described these character traits as being a mean between extremes. The Good man so habituates his behavior to these virtues that he will carry out the Good actions over and over again throughout his life.

A Quick Exercise to Understand Virtue Ethics.

To better understand what is meant by Virtue Ethics, try the following exercise:

Step One: Set out a list of traits you believe to be virtues. Make sure you have at least three virtues and no more than ten.

Step Two: Establish the mean by outlining how the virtues in step one are really somewhere in the middle of two extremes.

Step Three: Describe how one might ingrain this trait into his or her character. What consequences would it have?

Step Four: Create a moral situation of your own and show how the individual guided by Virtue Ethics would resolve it. How does Virtue Ethics make a difference in this situation?

C. Utilitarianism.

Utilitarianism is a theory that suggests that an action is morally right when that action produces more total utility for the group as a consequence than any other alternative. Sometimes this has been shortened to the slogan, "The greatest Good for the greatest number." This emphasis, calculating quantitatively the general population's projected consequential utility among competing alternatives, appeals to many of the same principles that underlie democracy and capitalism (which is why this theory has always been very popular in the United States and other Western capitalistic democracies).

A Quick Exercise to Understand Utilitarianism.

Since Utilitarianism is a moral theory that commends the moral choice that produces the greatest happiness for the greatest number of people, under this system we have to have a mechanism for determining: (a) the alternatives involved; (b) a list of possible outcomes of the alternatives; (c) a clear definition of the population sample to be affected by the alternatives; and (d) a way to measure the possible impact that each alternative would have on the population sample so that it will become clear which alternative will yield the most pleasure/utility.

It should also be noted that the test you choose must be one that can be carried out and have relatively uncontroversial units by which the happiness-impact can be measured and examined. In order to better understand this, try the following exercise:

Step One: Create a moral situation of your own that seems to involve a difficult choice of alternative actions. (Cases that pit the majority interests against rights of the minority are often good for this exercise.)

Step Two: Set out the possible alternatives along with their projected outcomes.

Step Three: Define the population that is affected by your case.

Step Four: Propose a way to measure the happiness of the parties involved. Be sure that your measuring system can be quantified. What sorts of attacks could people make against your test? How would you defend it?

Step Five: Run your test on your sample population and give the actual numbers of the happiness coefficients that each group will possess according to each alternative.

Step Six: Justify your choice from step five against possible attacks.

D. Deontology.

Deontology is a moral theory that emphasizes one's duty to do a particular action just because the action itself is inherently right and not through any other sorts of calculations—such as the consequences of the action. Because of this nonconsequentialist bent, Deontology is often contrasted with Utilitarianism, which defines the right action in terms of its ability to bring about the greatest aggregate utility. In contradistinction to Utilitarianism, Deontology will recommend an action based upon principle. "Principle" is justified through an understanding of the structure of action, the nature of reason, and the operation of the will. The result is a moral command to act that does not justify itself by calculating consequences.

The moral principle is derived from and justified by the nature of reason and the structure of human action. Since its justification is general, so also is its scope general. The principle defines duty concerning moral situations in general. One way to understand this level of generality is to liken it to a scientific law. It is universal and absolute covering all societies in all historical epochs.

One difficulty people often face with such a general principle is that moral cases are presented to us as "particulars." In logic general or universal propositions are contrasted to particular or individual propositions. They are different logical types and cannot be directly compared. What you have to do is "translate" your moral problem into the same level of general language as the moral principle. This will allow you to arrive at a definitive outcome. However, this translation is not so easy. For example, take the case of Sally contemplating an abortion. All the particulars of Sally's individual situation must be translated into the general form of a general moral principle or general moral law.

For this example, let us assume Kant's categorical imperative as our general principle. It states that we should "act only on that maxim through which you can at the same time will that it should become a universal law." This principle prohibits murder.[1] This is because a universal law of murder in any society is logically contradictory. (If everyone murdered everyone else, then there would be no society.) Logically contradictory universal laws are immoral, therefore; murder is immoral.

Autonomy, however, is also dictated by the categorical imperative and becomes the cornerstone of a formulation of the categorical imperative that addresses people as ends and not means only.

An example of the problem of moving from the particular to the general level (necessary for applying the moral laws/principles of Deontology) can be seen in the following: "How do we translate abortion?" Is abortion an instance of *killing* or of *autonomy*? If it is the former, it is prohibited. If it is the latter, it is permitted.

The real debate rests in the translation. Once a moral situation is translated, the application to the moral law is easy. The moral law determines our duty in the situation, and we must do our duty or else we repudiate our human nature: rationality.

---

[1] The mode of this prohibition is that all moral maxims generated from the notion of a universal society of murderers are shown to incoherent. This means that when you create a moral maxim such as "It is permissable to murder," such a maxim is found to contain a logical contradiction. Like Plato, Kant believes that logical contradictions indicate immorality. This is because morality means, "the right and wrong in human action." "Right" and "wrong" are determined by reference to logic. Illogic, therefore, is wrong. This is the driving force behind the universality of the categorical imperative in its various forms.

A Quick Exercise to Understand Deontology.

In order better to understand how Deontology works, try the following exercise:

Step One: Choose a universal moral principle (it can be Kant's or any other principle stated in general "lawlike" terminology).

Step Two: Create a particular moral situation of your own that seems to involve a difficult choice of alternative actions. (Cases that pit two moral duties against each other are often good for this exercise.)

Step Three: Set out the possible alternative ways to translate the particular case into more general language, that is, as an instance of truth telling, murder, or autonomy.

Step Four: Justify your translation while pointing out the flaws in alternative translations.

Step Five: Show how your translation fits a general corollary of the universal moral principle. Explain how you arrived at the corollary, and explain the outcome of translation to corollary. What sorts of attacks could people make against your translation, corollary derivation, or outcomes application? How would you defend yourself against these attacks?

II. THE PERSONAL WORLDVIEW IMPERATIVE AND THEORY CHOICE.

The Personal Worldview Imperative is a command that each of us should take our values seriously and try to fit all of our values into a coherent whole so that we can use these values in our daily lives: "All people must develop a single comprehensive and internally coherent worldview that is Good and that we strive to act out in our daily lives."[2] What the Personal Worldview requires is that we examine all the various values we hold. We have chosen to group these values into three groups (there may be others): ethics, religion, and aesthetics.

In the first group, ethics, one has personal maxims, which may or may not be coherent, of how to act in particular situations. Then there are professional maxims about how one ought to act at work and social maxims that operate in the family and the various communities in which we live. These various ethical values may or may not work in the same direction.

---

[2]The argument for the Personal Worldview Imperative can be found in Michael Boylan, *Basic Ethics* (Upper Saddle River, NJ: Prentice Hall, 2000), Introduction.

For example, it is not unusual for a person to hold a principle of beneficence in the family (that is, to act so that Good is brought about) and merely a principle of doing no harm in the professional sphere. These two principles, when viewed separately, can endorse a different range of actions. The former is a positive injunction to bring about Good, while the latter is satisfied by merely avoiding harm.

The point of the Personal Worldview Imperative is to engage the agent in a critical self-examination in order to organize his ethical values (under all his various descriptions and societal roles) in order that they work positively together through a unified front.

The same holds true when we consider moral maxims and religious values. These must also accord. If completeness and coherence are to be taken seriously as formal ways to judge systems—including value systems—then a person cannot live one life when she goes to church, synagogue, mosque, or dharma talks and another when she is a public person in the world.

Aesthetic values are also important, since much of what we do is determined by the beautiful. We believe that there are many normative connections between what each of us judge as beautiful and our commitments toward that object (artificial or natural).[3]

The principal way that the Personal Worldview Imperative acts to help us make our various values work together is through the process of projecting the various candidates forward into a single arena in which the agent can visualize them working in concert. This is what can be termed the dialectical process of understanding that can be put forward (along with traditional logical justification) as one of the two ways we evaluate ethical theories.[4] Each of us should go through such a process regularly (just as we defragment our computers so that they work properly). All of this follows rather generally from the Socratic dictum that the unexamined life is not worth living.

The criteria for deciding between ethical theories are elaborated by metaethics. Once a theory has been endorsed, then one of the principal issues is how it is to be applied. Let's go through an example of examining a moral maxim as a warm-up exercise in order better to understand some of these concepts.

---

[3]One such relationship is the "value-duty relation." In this relation it is held that "Whenever agent X values P (where P is an artifact, a natural object, an agent, or a human institution), then X takes on a corresponding duty to protect and defend P subject to the constraints of the Principle of Human Survival and the 'ought implies can' doctrine." For a defense of this position, see "Worldview and the Value-Duty Link to Environmental Ethics" in *Environmental Ethics*. Michael Boylan, ed. (Upper Saddle River, NJ: Prentice Hall, 2001).

[4]A more detailed exposition can be found in Michael Boylan, "Choosing an Ethical Theory" in *Gewirth: Critical Essays on Action, Rationality, and Community*. Michael Boylan, ed. (Lanham, MD, Boulder, CO, and Oxford, Eng.: Rowman and Littlefield, 1999).

One commonly held principle of application states that "like cases are to be treated equally." Let this principle be termed the "just implementation of rules."

This principle is a purely formal principle of distributive justice.[5] (Distributive justice is that subbranch of morality that provides criteria by which Goods and services may be parsed to recipients.) As a formal principle, this tells us that no matter what the content of the rule, it is formally just to treat like cases equally.

Upon reflection, we can see that the "just implementation of rules" maxim is a necessary but not a sufficient principle. For example, if we project the principle into the era of Nazi Germany, we know that the Nazis held that the consent to live is granted only to non-Jews. In this case the application of the "just implementation of rules" maxim (by itself) would suggest that all Jews be killed!

What is needed further are specifications on the *content* of the rule. When the content of the rule is included (as per the Personal Worldview Imperative), it is obvious that the imperative is inconsistent since there is no morally relevant difference between Jewish and non-Jewish agents. Since the Nazis contend that there is such a difference, they can be accused of being logically inconsistent.

Some might contend, "So what?" These bestial creatures could care less. The answer would be that they diminish themselves—whether they know it or not—by being violators of the Personal Worldview Imperative.

What further specifications might help the "just implementation of rules" maxim? Well, for starters one might set out and defend a system of distributive justice. Traditional candidates of distributive justice have included: *capitalism* (to each according to his production), *socialism* (to each according to his need), *egalitarianism* (to each equally), *aristocracy* (to each according to his inherited station), and *kraterism* (to each according to his ability to snatch it for himself).

There are other candidates, but this provides the flavor of various formulae, which are often brought forth to answer the question of how Goods and services are to be distributed.

Once one has argued for and accepted a theory of distributive justice, then according to the "just implementation of rules," he must apply it in a like manner to all similar cases.

In the previous example the sort of theory of justice one adopts constitutes the material element in the theory while the "just implementation of rules" represents merely a formal implementation tool.

This example is meant to illustrate the sorts of issues with which normative ethics concerns itself. In this domain we are interested in creating

---

[5]Distributive justice is only one form of justice. The other most prominent form is "retributive" justice, which outlines how we are to punish others and the conditions upon which these decisions are made and justified.

norms for conduct. This includes a justification and defense of all issues involved with the creation, understanding, or general application of such ethical norms.

There is one further moral maxim that will be important for us to examine and that is the "duty to rescue." It is often said that there are two classes of duties: negative duties (or prohibitions against doing such and such) and positive duties (imperatives to do such and such). Both are necessary in creating a moral theory. The duty not to murder someone is a negative duty. As long as you don't do it, you are an ethical individual.

The duty to rescue is somewhat broader. It refers in the most narrow sense to the duty to save someone's life and/or his Basic Goods of Agency when these are threatened and when the agent in question can perform his saving act without risking his similarly ranked Goods of Agency. For example, if I can save the life of a drowning man by throwing him a rope, rowing a boat to him, or handing him a stick, I risk only my time and effort. That man's life is more essential to the foundations of action than my time and effort (even if I am interrupting my work). Thus, according to the duty to rescue, any of us put into this situation must save this person's life. We do not deserve to be thanked or praised. We have merely executed our ethical duty.

However, if the person drowning requires that I swim out to him, and if in doing so I put my own life at risk, then I have no binding duty to jump in the water and attempt a rescue. This is because my own life is just as proximate to the fundamental character of action as is the drowning person's life. To say that the agent is obligated to risk his life to save another would be tantamount to saying that the drowning man's life is more important than the observer's. This is because a subtext of action suggests that the drowning person must be saved at all costs—including the observer's own life. This is false. All human lives are to count equally. No one's life is worth any more than another's. Thus, *if* the observer jumped into the water and saved the man's life, the observer would be going above and beyond his moral duty. This is the definition of a hero. A hero deserves to be thanked. He or she has gone above and beyond his or her duty.

The reason that no one's life is worth more than any other's is that all are equal. However, it is often the case that people fail to recognize this principle, and they see others as mere instruments to fulfill their personal needs. This is similar to Kant's second form of the categorical imperative.[6] If we agree with Kant here, then it is impermissible to treat people as means only. This includes one's relationship with one's self.

---

[6] "Act in such a way that you always treat humanity whether in your own person or in the person of another never simply as a means, but always at the same time as an end." Immanuel Kant, *Groundwork of the Metaphysics of Morals*, tr. H. J. Paton (London: Hutchinson, 1948), pp. 429/466–67.

However, a further issue needs to be addressed, and that is what goods are most proximate to action. This is a complicated question, but for our purposes let us set out the following table.[7]

For this book, let us assume that the foundations of human action are the most fundamental. Thus, whenever these Goods come into conflict with any other Good, the claim to basic Goods trumps all other claims. This is a moral principle that is also a Principle of Distributive Justice. Goods (be they material or immaterial) require an allocation principle. Without such a principle, kraterism will rule the day.

The following table illustrates how basic Goods compare to other Goods.

The Table of Embeddedness

Basic Goods

Level One: Most Deeply Embedded[8] (that which is absolutely necessary for human action): food, clothing, shelter, protection from unwarranted bodily harm

Level Two: Deeply Embedded (that which is necessary for effective basic action within any given society):
- Literacy in the language of the country
- Basic mathematical skills
- Other fundamental skills necessary to be an effective agent in that country (e.g., in the United States some computer literacy is necessary)
- Some familiarity with the culture and history of the country in which one lives
- The assurance that those you interact with are not lying to promote their own interests
- The assurance that those you interact with will recognize your human dignity (as per above) and not exploit you as a means only
- Basic human rights such as those listed in the U.S. Bill of Rights and the United Nations Universal Declaration of Human Rights

Secondary Goods

Life Enhancing: Medium to High-Medium on Embeddedness
- Basic societal respect
- Equal opportunity to compete for the prudential goods of society
- Ability to pursue a life plan according to the Personal Worldview Imperative
- Ability to participate equally as an agent in the Shared Community Worldview Imperative

---

[7]This table is argued for in Michael Boylan and James A. Donahue, *Ethics Across the Curriculum* (Lanham, MD, Boulder, CO and New York: Lexington Books, 2002), Chapter Five.

[8]"Embedded" in this context means the relative fundamental nature of the Good for action. A more deeply embedded Good is one that is more primary to action.

Useful: Medium Embeddedness
- Ability to utilize one's real and portable property in the manner she chooses
- Ability to gain from and exploit the consequences of one's labor regardless of starting point
- Ability to pursue goods that are generally owned by most citizens (e.g., in the United States today, a telephone, television, and automobile would fit into this class)

Luxurious: Low Embeddedness
- Ability to pursue goods that are pleasant even though they are far removed from action and from the expectations of most citizens within a given country (e.g., in the United States today, a European vacation would fit into this class)
- Ability to exert one's will so that she might extract a disproportionate share of society's resources for her own use.

The point in setting out this table is to indicate that the duty to rescue is predicated upon the notion that certain Goods are more fundamental to action than others. One is not required to sacrifice a Good of equal or higher level in order to promote an equal or lower Good of another. Such a calculus can only become clear once the Goods of Agency are set out.

We have sketched out some key moral distinctions and theories that will be useful in our exploration of the ethical issues involved in genetic engineering. The reader is encouraged to explore one of the traditional moral theories as well as a theory of justice in order to create a critical base upon which he or she might come to terms with some of the challenges that genetic engineering poses to us all. The writers of this book take the view of a deontological moral theory that sets the Basic Goods of Action as its centerpiece for determining whether some action is or is not morally justified.

In the next chapter we examine some more specific professional and ethical duties. Chapter Seven examines the limits of science from the ethical superstructure that we have suggested. Finally, in Part Three the specific topics of genetic engineering, including genetic screening, somatic therapy, genetic enhancement, cloning, germ-line therapy, and "where business and science intersect," are examined using these principles. This is a vast landscape to be treated in such an abbreviated form. It is hoped that inquisitive readers will use this book as an introduction to these topics that will spur them on to further study.

chapter two

Professional and Practical Principles of Conduct

This chapter moves from ethical theory and its interpretation via the Personal Worldview Imperative to issues concerning Professional Ethics and various related ethical issues that are important as we examine the limits of genetic engineering.

I. THE ETHICAL ROLE OF THE PHYSICIAN.

When a person considers the ethical role of the physician, he is involved in applied Professional Ethics, which gives a standard that mixes practical considerations of how to perform excellently in that profession according to some purely functional standard and how to integrate pivotal ethical concerns within that larger functional role. One classic standard for Professional Ethics in medicine is the Hippocratic Oath.

The Oath[1]

By Apollo (the physician), by Asclepius (god of healing), by Hygenia (god of health), by Panacea (god of remedy), and all the gods and goddesses, together

---

[1]The text we are using is Littre's. The translation is Boylan's, after a more modern, somewhat less literal and gender-neutral approach.

as witnesses, I hereby swear that I will carry out, inasmuch as I am able and true to my considered judgment, this oath and the ensuing duties:

1. To hold my teacher in this art on a par with my parents. To make my teacher a partner in my livelihood. To look after my teacher and financially share with her/him when she/he is in need. To consider him/her as a brother/sister along with his/her family. To teach his/her family the art of medicine, if they want to learn it, without tuition or any other conditions of service. To impart all the lessons necessary to practice medicine to my own sons and daughters, the sons and daughters of my teacher and to my own students, who have taken this oath—but to no one else.[2]

2. I will help the sick according to my skill and judgment, but never with an intent to do harm or injury to another.

3. I will never administer poison to anyone—even when asked to do so. Nor will I ever suggest a way that others (even the patient) could do so. Similarly, I will never induce an abortion. Instead, I will keep holy my life and art.

4. I will not engage in surgery—not even upon suffers from stone, but will withdraw in favor of others who do this work.[3]

5. Whoever I visit, rich or poor, I will concern myself with the well-being of the sick. I will commit no intentional misdeeds, nor any other harmful action such as engaging in sexual relations with my patients (regardless of their status).

6. Whatever I hear or see in the course of my professional duties (or even outside the course of treatment) regarding my patients is strictly confidential and I will not allow it to be spread about. But instead, will hold these as holy secrets.

Now if I carry out this oath and not break its injunctions, may I enjoy a Good life and may my reputation be pure and honored for all generations. But if I fail and break this oath, then may the opposite befall me.

There are many versions of professional codes.[4] We thought about including the American Medical Association Code, and the codes for various other health professions, but then decided that the Hippocratic Oath set the

---

[2]In other words, to those who would not be fit to practice medicine. To this day we maintain an elaborate "sorting mechanism" to eliminate those we do not believe to be academically or otherwise fit to enter into the practice of medicine.

[3]This is a rather odd clause that has disturbed many over the years. The question is, "Why shouldn't the physician engage in surgery?" Is surgery wrong? If so, then why not simply prohibit it. To leave it for another to do seems like passing the buck. Some have suggested that this passage refers to castration. But again, if this is the case, then why not prohibit the act itself. Others have suggested that one should not engage in surgery until one is a master physician. In this case the injunction is only directed toward new physicians who have just taken the oath. The problem with this interpretation is that there is no textual support for this. A final interpretation is that that surgery, being rather messy, is not for master physicians, but rather for less talented technicians. Though not totally satisfactory, this seems the best interpretation to me.

[4]The reader is encouraged to turn to the more extensive treatment of this subject in Chapter Seven of *Basic Ethics* by Michael Boylan.

standard of what a professional code is. Let us examine a few key features that will tell why we should accept or reject such codes.

We begin by saying that we think that among professional codes, the Hippocratic Oath is a Good one. It balances between very specific prohibitions such as not administering poison or not having sexual relations with one's patients, to more general principles such as "I will concern myself with the well-being of the sick" and "do no harm." These general principles are very useful because they govern a larger domain than simply prohibiting a particular action. These principles are not set out without context. Instead, they are put into the context—medicine's mission.

Beginning with number one, the tone is set that medicine is an art that is "given by the gods." It is an esoteric art that is to be reserved for those who are willing to commit to the provisions of the code. Thus, it is not open to everyone. This fulfills the condition of specialized knowledge mentioned earlier. Secondly, it is for the sake of doing Good to others and always avoiding harm. This fulfills the condition of providing a service for others.

Third, the code ties itself to the larger moral tradition: "I will commit no intentional misdeeds." Whereas "harm" has a direct link to the manner in which medicine is practiced, "misdeeds" links the physician to the larger moral tradition. There is no possible hiding in the Shared Community Perspective alone.

These three factors are the basis of any Good professional code.

Codes of professional ethics fail in overemphasizing one of these elements too highly or in ignoring an element entirely. If codes of ethics exist in order to remedy the "inward perspective" problem described earlier, then they must create links to more general "shared worldviews." This would put them in the realm of common morality.

This is the most important point from our perspective. So often the "practice" of the profession defines its excellence in an introspective way such that the achievement of these functional requirements is all that matters—divorced from any other visions (viz., moral visions).

In the modern arena, many professional codes have evolved from a legal perspective. The practitioners of the profession do not want to go to jail or to

---

A good professional code should contain:

1. A specific listing of common abuses.
2. A few general guidelines that tie behavior to the mission of the profession.
3. A link to general theories of morality.

FIGURE 2.1 **Elements in a Normative Professional Code**

be sued. Thus, they create certain codes that will make this possible situation less probable. These sorts of codes are defensive in nature and stand at the opposite end of the spectrum from the Hippocratic Oath. Their mission is not to set internal standards and link to common morality, rather they seek to "shave" as close as possible to maximizing an egoistic bottom line at the expense of the pillars of professionalism: one's specialized education and one's mission to serve others.

Any code that takes as its basis merely a negative approach designed to protect the practitioner from going to jail or being sued is fundamentally inadequate. This is not where we should set our sights. Rather, we should dream about what the profession may be—in the best of all possible worlds. This properly sets the mission that should drive all codes of professional ethics.

When adapting the Hippocratic Oath to the specific requirements of the biomedical researcher, we must affirm everything within the Oath and add the specific duties that attach to the researcher (in cases that involve the physician and researcher as the same person). Since the purpose of biomedical research is to benefit humankind, these extra duties will fall in line with those of the practicing physician. The difference is that everything is once removed from the proximate act of healing.

When the researcher is not in the professional role of physician or is not a physician at all, the situation is somewhat different. In this case, the researcher's professional responsibility is to pursue a program of study that will expand our understanding of nature and benefit humankind within the ethical limits of scientific inquiry (see Chapter Seven).

It is, in fact, probably a better situation that the physician and the biomedical researcher be separate. This is because their respective missions are not identical. The physician is concerned with the well-being of the patient and in doing no harm. The researcher is concerned with expanding our understanding of nature and benefiting humankind. This mission will lead him in one direction. The mission of the physician may lead her in another direction. When the physician and researcher are one and the same person, a conflict may occur.

We are not necessarily against a physician and researcher being one and the same person, but merely point out that since the missions of each are different, potential conflicts may arise.

In cases in which the researcher is also a physician but is not in the role of physician treating a patient, the dictum to do no harm must be seen not in the context of doing harm to the biological samples that the researcher is examining, but rather to the patients and potential patients who will be benefited or harmed by the results of this research. In this situation it is also the case that the biomedical researcher must maintain this sort of projection into his "potential" patients in a way that the nonphysician research may not (because she lacks that dimension of professional duty). However, in all of these cases, the ethical responsibilities remain the same.

The extent of those who must be considered in this ethical calculus ranges from those who will be immediately benefited to others in the society who may also be affected by the activity of altering some of the key mechanisms of nature. This is, indeed, an awesome responsibility.

II. The Ethical Role of the Researcher.

Scientific research involves an individual in a community of scholars seeking truths of nature. This community (as do all communities) has a worldview, or a collection of values about what is acceptable practice within the community. The mechanism by which individuals collectively create their community can be termed the Shared Community Worldview Imperative. It states: "Each agent must strive to create a common body of knowledge that supports the creation of a shared community worldview (that is complete, coherent, and Good) through which social institutions and their resulting policies might flourish within the constraints of the essential core of commonly held values (ethics, aesthetics, and religion)."[5] In the case of the scientific community, there are a number of competing worldviews at present. These include (a) I'm the smartest kid on the block and I'm going to win the prize; (b) I'm a part of a team that is the smartest on the block and the team will win the prize; (c) I'm part of a community dedicated to help others—I don't care who gets credit so long as we help people; and (d) I'm part of a team dedicated to help others—none of us cares who gets credit so long as we help people.

Obviously, there is a big difference in the choice we make. The first two are centered on a practical worldview that is self-interested and competitive. Researchers in these categories want to win prizes, prestige, and money for their scientific accomplishments. It is as if graduate school had been extended and they were still competing to be "top in the class."

But should this be what scientific research is all about? Why should the society (the Shared Community Worldview) support a bevy of individuals seeking to puff up their personal egos? Perhaps, one might say, it is because the selfish motivation that such a competition engenders leads to higher achievement in the shortest possible time frame. We all benefit from the higher achievement so that it is to everyone's practical advantage to play "smartest kid/group on the block." Put like this, one asks whether researchers will put in the long hours necessary to succeed in the shortest possible time frame *unless* they feel the pressure of a competitive situation.

This is possibly correct.

---

[5]For a justification of the Shared Community Worldview Imperative see Boylan, "Worldview and the Value-Duty Link to Environmental Ethics," *op. cit.*

It is our opinion that competition *can* bring out the best in people. But it is also true that it can bring out the *worst* as well. The result stems from whether the competitor views his fellow competitors as comrades engaged in a Good effort together—"may the best man/woman win" and all that—or whether the competitor views her fellow competitors as people who are striving for a limited pool of glory/money/and so forth that goes to whoever can garner it: "As long as we don't break the law, everything else is okay. After all, the common folk don't understand science much, anyway."

This is an important attitude in competition. On the one hand, there are individuals and groups intrinsically interested in what they are doing for its own sake. In this case the competition is merely a device to spur them on. On the other hand, the scientific endeavor is really a means to the more important ends of glory, prestige, and money. When this is the case, science is not valued for its own sake, and thus corners may be cut and established practices shortchanged all for the sake of the extrinsic ends of glory, prestige, and money.

What are we really about in our enterprise? Most science programs in schools are set up in a Draconian competition, with the underlying attitude that the system is so fair that it correctly picks out the very best; for the purpose of future reward, it is easy to see how the extrinsic prize-oriented competition is so prevalent.

Proponents of this model point to pure objectivity of the truth attained and dismiss concerns about the basis of competition among biomedical practitioners. The underlying thought is that the pureness of the phenomena and their rules purifies questionable means.

But the history of late twentieth-century philosophy of science has suggested that this model isn't so neat.[6] It is entirely possible that science serves social and political agendas. If this is true, then the ideal model of scientific researchers (like track athletes) competing on a level track against all comers is false. Rather, it may be that the needs of society dictate what research should be supported (à la the Shared Community Worldview Imperative). This is rather different from the cowboy mentality of alternatives (a) and (b). We are not talking about pioneers staking out the borders of truth against the din of the hoi polloi who don't know any better. This is the *Frankenstein* model.

Instead, we can posit a model of the scientist in a community of other scientists who embrace the (c) and (d) alternatives because they know that their research *must* be dominated by the imperative to serve the public Good (especially when it is funded by public money). This is not about fame, money, or prestige. In this way medical research is different from ordinary business. The underlying mission of the researcher is to strive for the sorts of truth that society (through the Shared Community Worldview Imperative) is willing to

---

[6]The classic example, of course, is Thomas Kuhn, *The Structure of Scientific Revolutions*, 2nd ed. (Chicago: University of Chicago Press, 1970).

support. (We assume an informed electorate that has recently fulfilled the dictates of the Personal Worldview Imperative.)

If these assumptions about the role and mission of science are correct, then (a) and (b) are false. Only (c) and (d) ought to be adopted. This will make a significant difference in the way we evaluate genetic engineering.

III. CONFLICTS OF INTEREST.

The problems involved in conflicts of interest are on the one hand very simple and on the other extremely complex. Let us begin with a simple maxim: "A conflict of interest occurs when an agent's prudential interests are not the same as her professional duties." Take the example of a judge in a civil hearing. The plaintiff in the case (ABC Corporation) is suing the defendant (XYZ Corporation) for copyright infringement. Now the judge, Ms. Goode, has a number of professional duties as a judge. She must listen to all relevant evidence, she must ensure a proceeding that abides by established practice, and she must remain impartial (among other duties). Now let us suppose that Judge Goode holds stock or sits on the Board of Directors of ABC Corporation. In this situation Judge Goode has a conflict of interest (Figure 2.2).

It is clear that there may be situations in which in order to do her professional duty, as in this case, Judge Goode will have to work against her own prudential interests. Likewise, if she wants to maximize her prudential interests (as most people do), then she will have to forgo her professional duty. This is because the two may be in conflict.

Now it may be the case that Judge Goode is just that sort of person who can forget her personal prudential interests and devote herself entirely to her professional duty. There are many who can. Say that she rules in favor of the defendant. In this case she has not let her personal interests corrupt her professional duty. But how do outsiders really know if this was the case? Perhaps she is just very *good* at covering her tracks? Or perhaps Judge Goode isn't even aware of her prejudices. In any event, the only way for the public to be sure a judge (or any other professional) is fulfilling her professional duty is for that judge to step aside and let another judge hear the case. This

Professional Duties	Personal Prudential Interest
1. Listen to all relevant evidence	A. ABC's profitability
2. Abide by established practice	B. Personal monetary gain
3. Remain impartial	C. Possible fiduciary responsibility

FIGURE 2.2 **Judge Goode's Conflict of Interest**

course of action avoids the possibility of acting to promote a personal prudential benefit at the expense of fulfilling professional duty. Thus, in this case, the proper course of action is for Judge Goode to recuse herself.

This is the simple and straightforward version of conflict of interest. In such cases there is a direct tie to an agent whose duties to self and profession are different. But there are other cases in which the ties are more remote or in which one's personal benefit is so trivial it can hardly be said to constitute a conflict.

In the first of these more complicated situations one may have only a remote tie to the situation at hand. For example, what if Judge Goode owned shares in a mutual fund for her retirement and the mutual fund owned shares of ABC Corporation. In this situation, it is probable that Judge Goode is unaware that she has a personal interest in the case. (This is because few people really know what stocks their mutual fund owns.) If Judge Goode is unaware that she has a conflict of interest, then she cannot be in a situation in which her judgment is divided between personal benefit and professional duties.

But how do we, the public, *know* that Judge Goode was unaware? Should she have been aware of the connection? These are difficult questions and can never be completely covered save by a blind trust in which the individual knows nothing about his or her personal financial interests. Since this option is costly, it seems rather extreme to force such an alternative on any save for very prominent public figures.

For the rest of the public it would seem that some sort of dialogue about what is reasonable to expect is in order. This is one of the tenets of the Shared Community Worldview Imperative. The public must create a "prudent" standard that is accepted as reasonable. Perhaps a judge should be accountable for knowing direct stock holdings but not mutual fund holdings. At some level the community will decide what constitutes the line between proximate Goods (which one is expected to be aware of) and remote Goods (which one is not required to be aware of).[7]

The second type of complicated case concerns the level of "trivial" conflicts, in which it is contended that when the prudential advantage is trivial, it hardly causes a tension with professional duty. Thus, there is no conflict of interest. This is obviously true in some cases. Consider a case in which Judge Goode forgot her watch and asks one of the attorneys what time it is. The attorney looks at his watch and responds.

Judge Goode has received a prudential benefit. It has allowed her not to call a recess just to retire to her chambers to retrieve her watch. However, everyone would agree that this benefit would in no way cause a conflict of

---

[7]Though obviously, *if* a person did know her holdings beyond the normal standard proximate holdings, then such knowledge would create a conflict subject to the conditions of proportionality about to be discussed.

interest such that Judge Goode's professional judgment might be clouded or even the suspicion of such.

The so-called trivial good argument has been often employed by individuals who wish to accept a certain give and take with those whom they have a professional relationship. This is indeed a slippery slope. Let's look at a few examples.

Lunch and Conflicts of Interest for a Physician in a Large Practice.

1. Physician P accepts an offer for lunch at a local restaurant from a pharmaceutical representative. The total cost of the lunch is $15 for some delicious oriental food.

2. Physician Q accepts an offer for lunch at a local restaurant from a pharmaceutical representative. The cost of the lunch is $50 for some delicious French cuisine and a modestly priced wine.

3. Physician R accepts an offer for lunch at a swank local restaurant from a representative from a pharmaceutical company. The cost of the lunch is $200 for fine food and excellent wine.

The cost of the lunch varies. But the key points are (1) whether the lunch was prudentially trivial from the physician's point of view and (2) whether the lunch might appear to be less than trivial from an outsider's point of view.

The intent of the pharmaceutical representative is to entice the physician to prescribe the company's product line whenever possible. Oftentimes there may be only a small difference between the way one drug works as opposed to another. If there is only a small difference, then who cares which drug you prescribe, right? After all, you really like this representative.

Wrong. Once the physician is enticed into forgetting her primary duty to the patient and his health, then she has violated her professional duty. But why? Maybe it was for something as simple as a lunch. Maybe it was for something as trivial as cultivating a personal friendship with someone who has an interest in your professional conduct.

The difficulty in the argument on triviality is that it really depends upon the person(s) involved. What might be trivial to one person might not be trivial to another. But *because* we are social beings who must and should interact with our fellow Homo sapiens, some degree of positive social interaction will and should occur. The question is where to draw the line.

As in the case of remote versus proximate prudential interests, the ultimate answer should be in the Shared Community Worldview. If it is thought that examples (1) and (2) are acceptable and (3) is too extreme, then that should be expressed explicitly so that all can agree on the rules. Some sort of Principle of Proportionality must play a part. This would take into account the relationship of the favor to the decision maker's financial state and would also place the favor in a proportion with the value of the project actually being considered. A $25 lunch concerning a $50 deal constitutes a large portion of what is under consideration and so would be illegitimate.

The eventual agreement that the community makes based upon some understanding of a Principle of Proportionality must be made in a way that all parties are sensitive to where the general line of triviality ends.[8]

But even this standard can be transgressed.

What the community must create is some sort of Principle of Proportionality that defines triviality in terms of the professional duty at hand and in terms of the financial position of the professional agent involved. Say you were a university professor in charge of a large genetics lab, and your university has asked you to choose a partner from industry to help fund your research to the tune of $40 million over four years. If you had an annual salary at the university of $80,000 plus various perks that made it seem like $120,000 per year, then certainly accepting a lunch on the lines of (1) above would probably count as trivial. Lunch (3) might count as extravagant. But what about (2)?

A CEO of a Fortune 500 company told one of the authors a story in which a client had given him an exquisite antique watch. The CEO's wife fell in love with the gift. The CEO asked his ethics office about how to handle it, and they told him to give it to the company and then buy it back from the company. In this way the CEO would not be indebted to the other party. However, it is our opinion that even after the CEO paid $5,000 to his company for the watch, he was still getting a benefit: an exquisite antique watch that was very rare indeed. The gift was merely access to such an item. The rarity of the item made it more than a trivial gesture.

Clearly other factors besides money can cause one to compromise professional duties. Even friendship—normally a per se good among humans—can be used to create a conflict of interest. There is no way of getting around it: a case of conflict of interest has two faces. On the one hand, we have the strict definition of personal interest compromising professional duties. On the other hand is the *appearance* to others that personal interest has compromised professional duties. The Principle of Proportionality regarding triviality must be applied not only from the point of view of the agent's actual motivations, but also from what they might appear to be from the vantage point of a cynical observer.

Clearly, conflicts of interest constitute a very difficult class of decisions. Sometimes people go to some length (like the CEO earlier) to remove the conflict and its appearance but may be unsuccessful. Only an absolutist position of receiving nothing would satisfy all, but this may be too strict. In practice, some sort of community debate on this is necessary so that all may believe that they are in accord with the Shared Community Worldview.

---

[8]This is extremely difficult to do because there is often deception at work. People will say that this particular perk is trivial, but if it is seen in the context of many such perks, then it is seen to be a real advantage that might create (at least) the illusion of a conflict of interest.

IV. DUTIES TO FUTURE GENERATIONS.

In discussions of genetic engineering one of the most important principles is that of a person's duty to future generations. If we tinker with the natural order and damage it, as we have time and time again in the past, then we have harmed people in times to come.

One way to better understand this is by reference to a theory of human rights.[9] Let us begin with several key distinctions. First, an intricate relationship exists between duties and rights.[10] This relationship can be explained by the following sentence:

    I.   X has a right against Y to Z in virtue of P.

X is a person, Y is a person, Z is a good (such as the liberty to vote, to have adequate health care, to maintain ownership of the automobile that is titled under your name, or to be able to purchase a new consumer product), and P is a legitimating moral institution.

This rights claim implies a correlative duty:

    II.   Y has a duty to provide X with Z in virtue of P.

Let us put some examples into this formula to see how it works. In the first, it becomes the following example: John Doe has a right to vote against the Citizens of the United States in virtue of the Constitution of the United States and the Moral Principles upon which it stands. Assume that John Doe is an African American in a southern state in 1963 (in which governmental and nongovernmental authorities employed various devices to deny voting privileges to many African Americans).

The correlative duty statement would read: The Citizens of the United States have a duty to provide John Doe his voting privileges in virtue of the Constitution of the United States and the Moral Principles upon which it stands.

The Voting Rights Act of 1965 might be considered as a moral response to this correlative duty. A law was passed that created safeguards for citizens against spurious devices (such as poll taxes and various citizenship/civics "tests" that served to deny universal suffrage).

---

[9]There are a number of theories of human rights to which the reader can refer. For the purposes of this volume let it suffice that we are following Alan Gewirth, *Reason and Morality* (Chicago: University of Chicago Press, 1978); Wesley N. Hohfeld, *Fundamental Legal Conceptions* (New Haven, CT: Yale University Press, 1919); and S.I. Benn and R.S. Peters, *Social Principles and the Democratic State* (London: George Allen and Unwin, 1959) concerning the correlative nature of rights and duties and the foci upon goods as a critical element in determining a rights claim. Compare Henry Shue, *Basic Rights: Subsistence, Affluence, and U.S. Foreign Policy* (Princeton: Princeton University Press, 1996), pp. 32ff.

[10]Wesley N. Hohfeld, *Fundamental Legal Conceptions* (New Haven, CT: Yale University Press, 1919).

All things being equal, each of us must uphold his duties to others when they have a legitimate rights claim. To fail to do so would be immoral.

One factor that complicates mutuality in the case of future generations is that it is hard to define a generation, since the term is rather slippery. There is no clear point of demarcation whereby we have a new generation. This problem of identifying what a generation is (much less a future generation) leads to a second point. Future generations do not exist, so that to say that they have rights or duties is rather a stretch (keeping in mind the requirement for mutuality). Does this mean we do nothing? No. Any discussion of duties toward future generations must assume the following:

1. *An assumption that though future generations do not presently exist, they will (all things being equal) come to be.* This means that unless there is a catastrophic event (such as a cataclysmic nuclear war or life-ending disease), future generations *will* be born and have a right to expect that their forefathers and foremothers acted prudently with respect to nature. This includes ecological duties not to damage the ecosystem and any of the life forms within it—including *Homo sapiens.*

2. *The adoption of a transgenerational orientation that distinguishes two sorts of basis for positing duties to future generations.* The first is humanistic because its first concern is the interests of human beings and their moral rights (both present and future). This sort of claim resembles the rights-duties formula sketched out earlier.

The second is naturalistic in that it posits nature as having an intrinsic claim on being left no worse than when we found it. This is a particularly difficult command since nature seems to be rather delicately balanced. A change here or there might have many unforeseen consequences.

When we are working well within the frame of what we think we know about nature, we may have a greater epistemological justification that we are fulfilling this duty. However, when we are working on the edge of scientific knowledge, adhering to this duty becomes more difficult. Many scientists, in their zeal to be "the smartest kid on the block," will turn a blind eye to what they may be doing to nature. After all, the principal imperative that they heed is merely prudential glory, status, and money. These concerns can certainly work against the interests of morality.

We thus contend that we do possess a duty to future generations not to despoil nature (including the human genome). This is particularly acute for those working at the frontiers of knowledge (such as those involved in genetic engineering) because they are not entirely sure about the effects of their efforts. Such an admonition will certainly slow down the pace of research, but speed should never be our goal. Even when the outcome is saving human life (e.g., through gene therapy), we cannot forget the countless others in the future who may be harmed if we do not observe every possible precaution. This can include stopping entire projects when we cannot proceed cautiously.

V. ENVIRONMENTAL DUTIES.

In addition to duties to future generations that also include care of the environment, there are direct duties to the environment. We ground these in what we term the "value-duty relation."

We contend that whenever agent X values P (where P is an artifact, a natural object, an agent, or a human institution[11]), then X takes on a corresponding duty to protect and defend P subject to the constraints of the Principle of Human Survival and the "ought implies can" doctrine.[12]

Figure 2.3 shows the import of the value-duty relation.

Thus, according to this argument, whenever we perceive anything, we undergo a process whereby we value it (positively or negatively) according to the standards of our personal worldview. If we value it to be good, then we have a duty to protect and defend it. The extent of this duty is proportional to the gradation of positive value that we assign to it.

The last section accorded ethical duties on the basis of potential rights claims that may be made by future generations. This section grounds environmental duties upon our valuing nature. This valuing can be aesthetic or some other class of value. The point is that whatever the ground of value, whenever we value something, we incur a duty to protect it. This would include protecting the biome against any possible deleterious effects from genetic engineering.

This chapter began by exploring the professional duties of the physician-researcher in terms of the traditional code of Hippocrates. This was meant to be suggestive of the ways we might formulate a professional code of conduct that also includes the activities of the biomedical researcher. Next we examined several critical maxims concerning the practice of genetic engineering today. These include the ethical role of the researcher, conflicts of interest, duties to future generations, and duties to the environment.

These tools, along with the ethical theories presented in Chapter One, will guide us as we try to evaluate some of the complex conundrums that genetic engineering presents to us.

---

[11]This listing is meant to be suggestive and not exhaustive of the entities that might fall under this principle.

[12]The "ought implies can" doctrine is generally attributed to Kant (though there is some dispute about this). It is a straightforward doctrine that says that no one can command you to do what is impossible for you to do. However, this becomes rather slippery when you analyze what is meant by "impossible." Often, this transforms to "inconvenient" and thus guts the force of the doctrine.

1. X apprehends P (where X is an agent and P is an artifact, a natural object, an agent, or a human institution—among other things/processes/activities)—Fact

2. All apprehensions involve the internal value filter of the personal worldview—Fact

3. The act of valuation assesses a negative, neutral, or positive value according to a gradated scale that begins with disapproval, moves by steps to neutrality, and finally moves by steps of approbation to total approval—Assertion

4. When X apprehends P, X engages in a process of valuation according to the standards set by her personal worldview—1–3

5. The act of valuing anything means that one is giving some gradated approval to it—Assertion

6. Giving approval to anything means that you think it is good that that thing/process/activity exists—Assertion

7. Whenever you encounter a thing/process/activity that is good, an interaction with that thing/process/activity occurs—Assertion

8. The act of valuing anything creates an ongoing interaction between the subject and that which the subject judges to be good—5–7

9. Ongoing interactions with that which is judged to be good constitute striving to act out that which is good in our lives—Assertion

10. The Personal Worldview Imperative commands that all people must develop a single comprehensive and internally coherent worldview that is good and that we strive to act out in our daily lives—Fact

11. The Personal Worldview Imperative commands that whenever we value anything, we create an ongoing interaction with that thing/process/activity in our daily lives—8–10

12. One cannot have an ongoing interaction with something that is destroyed or no longer exists—Fact

13. When one is commanded to maintain an ongoing interaction with something, then one must maintain that something's existence (as much as it is in one's power)—Assertion

14. Maintaining the existence of something (as much as it is in one's power) is to protect and defend that thing—Fact

15. The Personal Worldview Imperative commands us to protect and defend that which we value—11–14

16. When X is commanded to do Y, then X has a duty to do Y—Fact

17. Whenever X apprehends P and judges it to be good (i.e., positively values P), then X incurs a duty to protect and defend P—4, 8, 11, 15, 16

FIGURE 2.3 The Value-Duty Relation

chapter three

Where We Are and How We Got Here

Since the discovery that many **diseases** had a genetic component, the focus of genetic research has been to identify the genetic defect. Once the genetic defect is identified, assays can be developed for either postnatal or prenatal diagnosis, and some form of therapy, such as diet modification, medication, or blood transfusion, may be sought to alleviate the impact of the gene defect. More recently, with the progress in research in **DNA** manipulation and molecular biotechnology (Table 3.1), it is possible to insert whole genes into novel biological **vectors** and potentially "correct" the biological defect. In addition, we are learning how to control these inserted genes and are developing techniques that may allow correction of the defective genes *in vivo*. Such is the promise of **gene therapy.** Although much is promised by these methodologies, the science is relatively young, and to date no one has been cured by these methods. This is reflected by the increasing current emphasis to call this practice "gene transfer" rather than gene therapy, since therapy is a misleading term to patients and families. We still have much to learn!

I. HISTORICAL PERSPECTIVE.

The first human gene therapy trial was initiated in September 1990 at the National Institutes of Health, Bethesda, Maryland, although a study beginning the previous year had investigated the feasibility of giving **cells** modified by

TABLE 3.1 Historical Developments in Gene Therapy

Date	Event
1869	Miescher isolated DNA for the first time
1944	Avery, MacLeod, and McCarty demonstrated that DNA is the genetic material
1953	Watson and Crick determined the structure of DNA
1957	Kornberg discovered DNA polymerase
1966	Nirenberg, Ochoa, and Khorana elucidated entire genetic code
1967	Gellert discovered DNA ligase
1970	First restriction endonuclease isolated
1973	Cohen and colleagues constructed a functional bacterial plasmid
1975	Southern developed DNA transfer and hybridization techniques
1976	Efficient techniques developed to sequence DNA
1978	Commercial company (Genentech) produced human insulin in *E. coli.*
1981	First commercial automated DNA synthesizers sold
1982	First commercial animal vaccine produced by **recombinant DNA technology**
1985	Mullis invented polymerase chain reaction (PCR)
1990	First human gene therapy trial initiated at NIH
1990	Human Genome Project officially initiated
1996	Complete DNA sequence of a eukaryotic organism (*S. cervisiae*) determined
1997	Nuclear cloning of a mammal (Dolly, the sheep) from a differentiated cell nucleus
1999	First human chromosome completely sequenced
1999	First human death following gene therapy treatment

a **recombinant virus** back to patients. In this original study, no therapeutic gene was administered, but modified cells had a novel gene inserted as a marker and the fate of these altered or "marked" cells was monitored.[1] The first patient to be treated by administration of a therapeutic gene was Ashanti de Silva, then, in 1990, a four-year-old child with adenosine deaminase (ADA) deficiency, a rare genetic disorder resulting in profound immune deficiency. Samples of blood were obtained from the patient, and the **lymphocytes** purified, then modified with a **retrovirus** containing the ADA gene, and transfused back into the patient at regular intervals.[2] At the same time the patient continued on regular drug replacement therapy with **exogenous** adenosine deaminase. She received a total of 11 infusions over the next two years and has shown improved immune function with increased T cell numbers and ADA levels and no toxicity, although the vigor of the immune response has gradually diminished in recent years.[3]

---

[1]Such studies are known as **marker studies.**
[2]R. Michael Blaese et al., "The ADA Human Gene Therapy Clinical Protocol," *Human Gene Therapy* 1 (1990): 327–62.
[3]W. French Anderson, "The Best of Times, the Worst of Times," *Science* 288 (2000): 627–29.

The use of peripheral blood lymphocytes as targets has its own problems, however. The cells have a limited life span, and the number of lymphocytes that can be corrected by this method is limited. To overcome these problems, similar studies have been performed using **hematopoietic stem cells** or CD34+ cells. Unfortunately, the majority of ADA-deficient patients treated with gene-corrected stem cells have not been significantly helped. The reasons for this lack of success are multifactoral but are due primarily to the fact that the **transduction** efficiency of human hematopoietic stem cells by the original retroviral vectors was inefficient, especially compared to the data from murine models. More recently, with both modified retroviral vectors and modifications to the way stem cells are grown and transduced in culture, there has been a marked increase in the number of stem cells that can be genetically modified, leading to the recent reporting of three cases of severe combined immunodeficiency (SCID-X1) that, following gene therapy (at least for 10 months), were able to lead normal lives and were not receiving any additional therapy.[4] Thus, ten years after the first patient was treated with gene therapy, as vectors improve and we learn more about using this new treatment, we are beginning to see patients who show the promise of being "cured" of their genetic disease by gene therapy.

II. CURRENT GENE THERAPY STUDIES.

Despite the limited number of successes to date, since 1990 a large number of studies have been initiated worldwide. In the United States more than 300 clinical protocols have either been approved or are currently under review. Thirty of these studies are marker studies, but the rest are for experimental treatments. Perhaps surprisingly, fewer than 40 of these studies are for the treatment of **monogenic disorders,** such as **cystic fibrosis** and **hemophilia,** for which the aim is to replace a mutated or deficient gene. The majority of the protocols (more than 200) are for the treatment of cancers by either directly targeting the malignant cells or by heightening the immune response to the cancerous tissue. A smaller number of studies treat AIDS (~20), vascular disorders, multiple sclerosis, and rheumatoid arthritis. Most studies have used modified viruses, generally retroviruses, as the vector to introduce the gene into cells, but other viruses, including modified **adenoviruses, parvoviruses,** and **herpesviruses** have been used. Similarly, different strategies have been used to manipulate the target cells, including *in vitro* cell culture of target cells, or direct administration of the vector to the tissue of interest.

---

[4]Marina Cavazzana-Calvo et al., "Gene Therapy of Human Severe Combined Immunodeficiency (SCID-X1) Disease," *Science* 288 (2000): 669–75.

III. Risks of Gene Therapy.

The first decade of gene therapy has seen not only the first successes of the new treatment but the first death due to the therapy itself. In September 1999, Jesse Gelsinger, a relatively fit 18-year-old with an inherited **enzyme** (ornithine transcarbamylase, or OTC) deficiency, died after the administration of a modified adenovirus directly into the liver. His death, a personal tragedy for his family and friends and a salutary reminder of the risks that are involved in any new/research protocol, has raised many questions regarding how we are currently conducting clinical research in gene therapy.

Ornithine transcarbamylase, an enzyme usually produced in the liver, is needed to remove ammonia from the blood, and many infants with this deficiency become comatose and die shortly after birth. In patients with mild deficiency, such as Jesse Gelsinger, the disease can be controlled by diet and drug treatment. The hope was to develop a gene therapy vector to treat acutely ill comatose infants, who after the initial treatment could then be treated with either a second—different—gene therapy vector or liver transplantation. When the protocol was discussed during review at the institution, the researchers believed it was inappropriate to test vectors in sick children; instead, it was decided to perform initial toxicity studies in adults. However, because the vector to be used, a modified adenovirus,[5] produces such a potent immune response, the vector can only be given once, and thus these volunteer adults would have limited, if any, benefit from the treatment (although at the initiation of the trial it was hoped that future modification to the adenovirus could be developed to allow readministration).

There are several concerns here. First, is it appropriate for relatively fit individuals, even if they do have genetic enzyme deficiencies, to be enrolled in experimental protocols with so little potential benefit?

Second, there has been much discussion in the scientific literature about whether the known liver toxicity of adenoviruses, and previous studies with adenovirus or adenoviral vectors in primates, should have precluded the study taking place at all. In particular, animal toxicity studies had relied to a great part on the use of mouse studies. Primate studies are expensive, and controversial in their own right, but should all these studies be conducted in monkeys, baboons, or chimpanzees before trials in humans?

Third, the case has brought to light the tangle of relationships between physicians/scientists managing clinical gene therapy, companies that are producing the vectors, and often the scientific institutions themselves, creating huge conflicts of interest (see Chapter Twelve).

Although none of these concerns is unique to gene therapy, they all need to be addressed, so that the full potential and promise of this technology can be used to improve human health.

---

[5]See Chapter Six for more details about adenovirus vectors.

chapter four

The Biological Basics

I. GENES, CHROMOSOMES, AND DNA.

From the dawn of time it has been known that biological characteristics have been transmitted from generation to generation, and humans have attempted to modify that process to breed better crops, fiercer guard dogs, or more beautiful flowers.[1] The genes that individuals inherit from their biological parents determine many of their biological characteristics. But what are **genes** and how are they transmitted from one generation to the next?

The concept of a gene is somewhat tricky because it implies an inherent reductionism. This has been a contentious issue in the philosophy of science during the twentieth century. Many among the logical empiricists (who were mostly physicists) declared a largely **reductionistic** strategy. This meant that the lowest level of organization (such as the arrangement of DNA bases)

---

[1]There is a rich source of literature in these and associated explorations. See G.E.R. Lloyd, *Magic, Reason, and Experience* (Cambridge, UK: Cambridge University Press, 1979); G.E.R. Lloyd, *Greek Science After Aristotle* (New York: Norton, 1973); Ludwig Edelstein, *Ancient Medicine* (Baltimore, MD: Johns Hopkins University Press, 1967); Michael Boylan, "The Galenic and Hippocratic Challenges to Aristotle's Conception Theory," *Journal of the History of Biology* 17.1 (1984): 83–112; and "Galen's Conception Theory," *Journal of the History of Biology* 19.1 (1986): 44–77.

would necessarily determine the phenotypic traits. Such a reductionistic strategy is problematic because many intermediate levels of organization between the **genotype** and the **phenotype** can affect the final outcome.[2] For our purposes in this book we define a gene as incorporating both the lowest level of organization (such as the DNA sequences) as well as intervening levels—such as protein synthesis, **epigenetic** interactions with the environment, biofeedback with existing cells in the organism, and so forth. Thus, though we may concentrate upon terminology that may sound reductionistic (such as the ensuing discussions on biochemistry), it is our contention that many intervening levels of organization are important in the expression of a genotype. In addition, our definition of a gene has changed as our understanding of DNA and inheritance has broadened.

Genetics as we know it, the scientific study of patterns of inheritance, was initiated by the monk Gregor Mendel with his studies on the inheritance of peas.[3] He studied seven different characters or traits, each of which occurs in two distinct forms.[4] From the results of his cross pollination studies he hypothesized that these characters or traits were determined by a pair of "factors," one from each parent, and in addition one of these factors, at random, was passed on to each of the offspring. If an offspring inherited two different factors for the same trait, then one masked the effect of the other: thus one trait is said to be **dominant,** and the other **recessive,** and the recessive trait will be manifested only if both factors are for the recessive trait.

Mendel's paper on genetics was published in 1866, but for many years the significance of his observations was not realized. It was William Sutton, studying the chromosome movement during gamete formation in 1901, who

---

[2]The literature on reductionism is very large. For some of the central issues, see Rudolf Carnap, "The Logical Foundations of the Unity of Science" in *International Encyclopedia of Unified Science: Volume I,* ed. O. Neurath, R. Carnap, and C. Morris (Chicago: University of Chicago Press, 1938–55), pp. 42–62; and Paul Oppenheim and Hilary Putnam, "Unity of Science as a Working Hypothesis," *Minnesota Studies in the Philosophy of Science,* Vol. II, ed. H. Feigl, M. Scriven, and G. Maxwell (Minneapolis: U. of Minnesota Press, 1958), pp. 3–36. These two essays set the logical empiricist position from which most of the "reactions" have been from biology. See especially Alan Garfinkel, *Forms of Explanation* (New Haven, CT: Yale University Press, 1981), pp. 49–74; and J. Sterelny and Philip Kitcher, "The Return of the Gene," *Journal of Philosophy* 85.7 (July 1988): 339–61. In the philosophy of biology (as in the logical empiricist account), biology is really a shorthand account for chemistry, which is a shorthand account for physics. However, in biology the contention is that there is causation from "top" to "bottom" and vice versa as opposed to the logical empiricists who claim only "bottom" to "top" causation. This means that the genotype-phenotype relation is not a simple one. To speak of a gene, *simpliciter* as merely the DNA base combinations, is too simplistic. Rather, one should refer to all the intervening mechanisms when describing this sort of relationship. For a sketch of this process in the context of human cloning, see Richard C. Lewontin, "Cloning and the Fallacy of Biological Determinism" in *Human Cloning: Science, Ethics and Public Policy,* ed. Barbara Mackinnon (Urbana, IL: University of Illinois Press, 2000), pp. 37–52.

[3]Although plant hybridists worked before Mendel, the idea of a simplistic reductionist factor or gene was Mendel's.

[4]Red or white flowers; long or short stems; axial or terminal flowers; green or yellow pods; inflated or constricted pods; smooth or wrinkled seeds; yellow or green seeds.

realized that it was the chromosomes separating during gamete production and recombining at fertilization that contained Mendel's genetic "factors" or genes. There are 22 pairs of **homologous chromosomes** in human cells and an additional pair of **sex chromosomes,** either two X chromosomes in females or an X and a Y chromosome in males. And as each pair of homologous chromosomes carries genes for the same trait in the same location, each cell has a pair of genes for each trait.

Alternative forms of the same gene are known as **alleles,** and there can be many different alleles (**multiple alleles**), but an individual can only have one pair of alleles. If the alleles are both the same, the individual is said to be **homozygous** for that allele, and if they are different, **heterozygous.** However, because some alleles may be dominant and others recessive, it is not possible to tell the genotype (genetic makeup) of an individual, merely by observation (looking at the phenotype). In addition, both an organism's genotype and environment contribute to the final phenotype of an organism: either starvation or "short" genes may lead to plants or animals with below average height.

It is now known that genetic information is encoded in DNA (deoxyribonucleic acid) molecules present in all living organisms. In cells the DNA molecules are tightly organized around a **histone** protein core to form the **chromosomes:** a single chromosome is formed from one enormously long DNA molecule, and on average encodes for a series of several thousand genes. As we describe later in this chapter, the DNA sequence not only stores and is able to transfer genetic information from one generation to the next, but also expresses this information in the cells of the body by the **proteins** that the DNA encodes for. Thus, more often in molecular biology, *gene* is used to denote a segment of DNA that codes for, and controls expression of, a **polypeptide** or protein.

A. DNA Structure.

The biochemical nature of DNA had been studied since the nineteenth century, but it was only with the discovery of the structure of DNA in 1953 that it was understood how DNA could encode genetic information. DNA is made up of a long chain of individual units known as nucleotides. Each **nucleotide** consists of an organic base (**adenine, cytosine, guanine,** and **thymine**), attached to a pentose (5 carbon) sugar (deoxyribose) and a phosphate group, with the phosphate group linking the 5' carbon of one sugar with the 3' carbon of the next sugar on the DNA chain (Table 4.1; Figure 4.1, p. 34). A **polynucleotide** strand has a 5' phosphate group on one end of the chain (5' end) and a 3' hydroxyl (OH) group on the opposite end (3' end).

In 1953 James Watson and Francis Crick discovered that native DNA consists of two strands of DNA that twist around each other in a double-helix structure, with the bases extending into the helix like rungs on a ladder (Figure 4.2, p. 35). The DNA strands run in opposite directions, and each base

TABLE 4.1 Bases, Nucleosides, and Nucleotides in DNA and RNA

	BASE	BASE + PENTOSE = NUCLEOSIDE	BASE + PENTOSE + PHOSPHATE = NUCLEOTIDE
A	adenine	adenosine	adenosine triphosphate, ATP
C	cytosine	cytidine	cytidine triphosphate, CTP
G	guanine	guanosine	guanosine triphosphate, GTP
T[a]	thymine	thymidine	thymidine triphosphate, TTP
U[b]	uracil	uridine	uridine triphosphate, UTP

[a]T is only in DNA; [b]U is only in RNA

pairs with the base on the opposite strand. This "base-pairing" is very specific, with an adenine base only pairing with thymine, and guanine only pairing with cytosine. Thus if one strand has the nucleotide sequence 5'-ACTGGAC-3',[5] then the opposite strand will be 3'-TGACCTG-5'. The order of the bases in any DNA strand is used to encode genetic information, and it is the precise complementation of the two strands of DNA that allows the genetic information encoded within the molecule to be accurately copied and hence transmitted to daughter cells or organisms.

B. DNA Replication.

As predicted by the Watson-Crick model, each strand of DNA acts as a template for the production of a new strand. Thus, after one round of **replication,** two daughter DNA molecules are produced. Replication of a DNA molecule begins with the local separation of the double-stranded helix by DNA helicase enzymes, and the unwound DNA stabilized by single-stranded DNA-binding proteins. In bacteria, or **prokaryotes,** replication is initiated at a specific region of the chromosomal DNA known as the **origin (of replication).** In **eukaryotes,** chromosomes have many different sites of initiation of replication. Because of the Y-shaped appearance of the separated strands at the site of active replication, the structure is known as a DNA replication fork (Figure 4.3). In both bacteria and eukaryotes, the substrates for the new chain are **deoxynucleotide triphosphates.** The appropriate incoming nucleotide triphosphate (**dATP, dCTP, dGTP,** or **dTTP**) is aligned with the template DNA nucleotide base and added to the 3' end of the newly synthesized daughter strand by cleavage of two of the phosphate groups. This reaction is catalyzed by the enzyme **DNA polymerase.** Thus DNA replication occurs

---

[5]By convention the sequence of a strand of DNA is denoted by the sequence of nucleotide bases, beginning with the nucleotide with the 5' phosphate group (5') to the nucleotide with the 3' hydroxyl (OH) group.

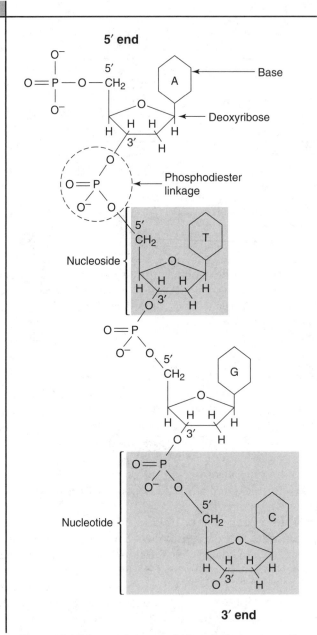

5′ end

Base

Deoxyribose

Phosphodiester linkage

Nucleoside

Nucleotide

3′ end

FIGURE 4.1 Nomenclature and chemical structure of DNA. Single strand showing linkage between the different bases, sugars, and phosphate groups.

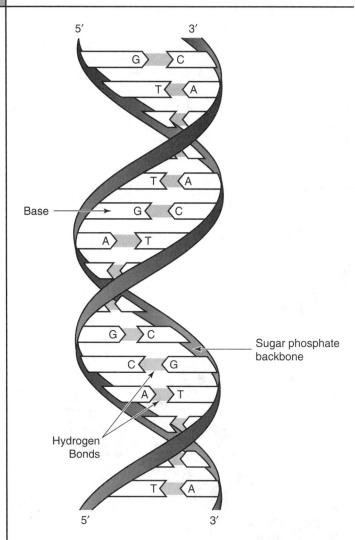

FIGURE 4.2 Schematic of the structure of the double-stranded DNA helix, illustrating pairing of the complementary bases, A with T and C with G.

only in a 5′–3′ direction and *always* requires a primer sequence for initiation. These two features ensure highly accurate second-strand synthesis, as the strand cannot be extended if there is no primer or an incorrect nucleotide is incorporated. For new DNA synthesis in cells, this primer is a short length

(~10 nucleotides) of **ribonucleic acid (RNA)** synthesized by the enzyme DNA primase. Once the primer has been synthesized, DNA chain polymerization can theoretically continue indefinitely. However, because the chains of DNA run in opposite directions, DNA synthesis at the replication fork is asymmetrical (see Figure 4.3). On one of the strands, the leading-strand template, DNA synthesis once initiated can continue uninterrupted. On the other strand, the lagging-strand template, however, only short lengths of DNA can be synthesized in the 5'–3' direction, and after removal of the RNA primers the individual DNA pieces are then joined together by **DNA ligase.** The short intermediate lengths of DNA have about 1,000 to 2,000 nucleotides in bacteria. In eukaryotes they are only 100 to 200 nucleotides long and are known as **Okazaki fragments.** In addition, in eukaryotes a special replication enzyme (known as telomerase) is required for synthesizing the ends, or **telomeres,** of

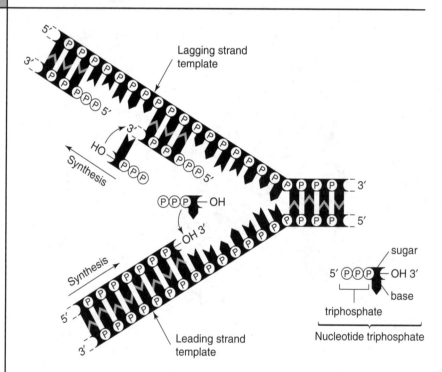

FIGURE 4.3 **Schematic of the asymmetric DNA replication fork. DNA synthesis is always in the 5'–3' direction, and this synthesis of one strand is always slower (lagging strand) and requires the production of short DNA fragments (Okazaki fragments) that are ligated together.**

the chromosomes. Even from this simplistic description it is clear that many different reactions and proteins are required for DNA replication. In reality, most of the proteins are held together in a large multiprotein complex that moves down the DNA as it replicates.

C. DNA Sequence Information.

The order, or sequence, of the nucleotide bases in the DNA molecule encodes the genetic information. Thus, specific sequences of DNA enable DNA binding proteins to bind to DNA to initiate replication. Many of the structures in a cell and complex organism are made up of proteins, however, and proteins control virtually all the metabolic processes required for life, and the information for making these proteins is encoded within the DNA nucleotide sequence. Not only is the information required for the amino-acid sequence of the proteins, but also for the control or **promoter regions,** which govern whether the protein is made or not. In addition, in eukaryotic DNA, but not bacteria, within the DNA sequences required to encode proteins (known as **exons**) are intervening pieces of DNA, known as **introns.** Together, the piece of DNA that includes the entire **amino acid** coding sequence for a protein, the noncoding **regulatory sequences,** and intervening introns is known as a gene.

D. Mitochondrial DNA.

The nuclear DNA is not the only DNA in eukaryotic cells. **Mitochondria,** the energy-producing organelle in the cell where most oxidative phosphorylation takes place and ATP is produced, also contain DNA (mtDNA). Most cells contain many hundreds of mitochondria, with each containing between two to ten copies of a small (16.5 kilobases in mammalian cells) circular DNA molecule.[6] Mitochondrial DNA accounts for only 1 percent of the total DNA of a mammalian cell. The DNA encodes for some of the proteins involved in aerobic metabolism (the rest are encoded by the nuclear DNA), and as in prokaryotic DNA, the genes do not contain any introns.[7]

---

[6]In yeast the mDNAs are larger. In plants the chloroplasts contain genetic material.

[7]Mitochondria are similar to prokaryotes in a number of ways, indicating that they probably evolved from an engulfed aerobic bacteria: they have a similar size to bacteria, with a similar DNA structure and protein synthesis to prokaryotes. In addition, like bacteria they reproduce by fission.

II. RNA.

Closely related to DNA is ribonucleic acid, RNA. As suggested by the name, it has the same basic structure as a single strand of DNA, with a **ribose** sugar substituted for the deoxyribose in the sugar-phosphate backbone. In addition, **uracil** (U), which pairs with adenine, is substituted for thymine as one of the nucleotide bases. In contrast to DNA, however, most RNA is single-stranded, and the molecules are relatively short compared to DNA, generally encoding information for only one or a few proteins or functions. The single-stranded nature of RNA means that it does not have a double-helix structure, but instead, the RNA is much less rigid, and parts of the chain that have runs of complementary nucleotides bind to each other to form local double-stranded regions, and a complex secondary structure.

There are several different types of RNA in the cell, although all seem to have a direct role in translating the DNA genetic information into functional proteins. RNA transcripts that encode the amino acid sequence of a protein are known as **messenger RNA (mRNA)** and comprise ~3 to 5 percent of the cellular RNA. In addition there are **transfer RNA (tRNA)** that directly translate the nucleotide sequence into amino acid sequence (4 percent of the cellular RNA), and **ribosomal RNA (rRNA)** (the coding strand), which in a complex of over 50 different proteins comprise the **ribosome,** the molecular machinery for synthesizing proteins from mRNA. The complex secondary structures that RNA can form enables RNA to act as a catalyst to cut and splice either itself or other RNA molecules, and such catalytic RNAs are known as **ribozymes.**

A. RNA Synthesis/Transcription.

Although in evolutionary terms RNA is the older genetic material, apart from material in some viruses and rare ribonuclear proteins,[8] RNA is synthesized from DNA in a process known as **RNA transcription** (Figure 4.4). In the cell, only about 1 percent of the genomic DNA is transcribed into functional RNA molecules. RNA transcription is very similar to DNA replication, with one strand of DNA (the **coding strand**) acting as a template for RNA synthesis. Transcription begins with a large, multipeptide enzyme, RNA polymerase, binding to a specific sequence of DNA, known as the promoter sequence, and the chains of DNA separating locally. Once the template strand is exposed, complementary ribonucleotides are aligned with the DNA template and joined together by the RNA polymerase. Additional ribonucleotides are attached

---

[8]Such as the active unit of telomerase, the enzyme that synthesizes the telomers, or ends of chromosomes.

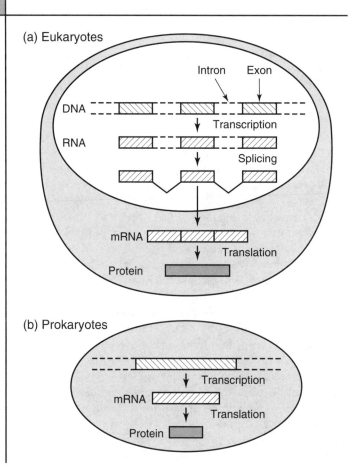

FIGURE 4.4 **Production of proteins from a DNA template. (a) In eukaryotes the DNA is transcribed to produce RNA and the RNA modified to remove introns in the nucleus, transported to the cytoplasm, and the mRNA translated into proteins. (b) In prokaryotes there is no post-transcription modification of the RNA.**

stepwise, and the RNA polymerase moves down the DNA molecule as the RNA is synthesized. All RNA synthesis is in the 5′–3′ direction only, and continues along the DNA until the polymerase reaches a termination (or stop) signal, at which point the nascent RNA and polymerase are released from the DNA. In eukaryotes different types of RNA are synthesized by different **RNA polymerases:** mRNA is synthesized by RNA polymerase II; large ribosomal RNA by RNA polymerase I; and small ribosomal RNA and tRNA by polymerase III.

B. Post-RNA Synthesis Modifications.

Following the synthesis of mRNA precursors by RNA polymerase II, the transcripts are modified in three different ways. First, even as the RNA transcript is being produced, after the synthesis of ~30 nucleotides, the 5' end (start) of the transcript is modified by the addition of a methylated G nucleotide in a process known as **capping.** This cap is important for protein synthesis, and appears to protect the RNA from rapid degradation within the cell.

Second, the RNA is cleaved at a defined place in the sequence, and a long tail of 100–200 nucleotides of adenine **(poly-A tail)** are attached by an enzyme poly-A polymerase. Together these two modifications produce the **primary RNA transcript.** Following cleavage of the RNA transcript, the RNA polymerase may continue synthesizing RNA for many hundreds of nucleotides, but these transcripts without the 5' cap are rapidly degraded.

The final modification is the removal of the intron sequences. These introns (intervening sequences) vary in size from ~80 nucleotides to several thousand nucleotides or more: sequences at the boundaries of each intron are relatively conserved and are known as the 5' splice (or donor) site and 3' splice (or acceptor) site respectively. The RNA primary transcript is cleaved at these sites, and the RNA spliced together by a large multiunit **ribonucleoprotein** known as a **spliceosome.** Multiple intron sequences are generally removed from each primary transcript and the final product is mRNA. In eukaryotes DNA replication and translation occurs in the **nucleus.**

After modification, the finished/spliced mRNA molecules are recognized by receptor proteins and actively transported through pores in the nuclear membrane into the **cytoplasm,** where they bind to ribosomes for immediate protein synthesis.

III. PROTEINS.

Proteins make up more than 50 percent of the dried weight of a cell and are critical for cell function: in many ways they can be considered the building blocks of life. Thus different proteins (a) determine the shape and structure of a cell, (b) are involved in transport and storage of molecules in the cell, (c) are enzymes (which apart from ribozymes are all proteins) that catalyze reactions in cells, and (d) are hormones that signal between cells in an organism. Proteins are also key components in immune surveillance, and as we have already learned, many of the processes involved in DNA replication and transcription are controlled by DNA- or RNA-binding proteins that recognize specific nucleotide sequences or motifs. It has been learned recently that proteins are also more versatile than we once appreciated and that the same protein may have multiple functions in a cell or organism.[9]

A. Protein Structure.

Proteins consist of one or more polypeptides, linear chains of amino acids. There are 20 different amino acids, and although they have the same basic structure, a carboxylic acid group, an amino group, and a side chain (R) linked to a single carbon (α-carbon) molecule, the different chemical structures of the side chain lead to very different chemical properties. Thus the 20 amino acids can be grouped into four families: those with acidic side groups; those with basic side groups; those with nonionic polar, or uncharged polar, side chains; and those with nonpolar side chains (Table 4.2). These properties allow interaction of the side chains of different amino acids both within the same polypeptide chain and from other molecules. The amino acids are joined together through an amide linkage of the carboxyl group and amino groups of adjacent amino acids, known as a peptide bond. Thus, although proteins are long, unbranched chains of amino acids, they can fold up to form complex shapes, which are stabilized by the interactions of these side chains.

A protein's **primary structure** is the sequence of amino acids, and this can be determined by biochemical means or, more often today, by knowing the nucleotide sequence of the mRNA that it is synthesized from (see p. 43). Local regions of the polypeptide sequence may fold to form specific structures, and this is known as the **secondary structure.** The two most common types of secondary structure are the alpha helix and beta pleated sheet.[10] These local areas of structure can often be predicted from the protein primary structure using computer algorithms.

In contrast, the overall or **tertiary structure** is usually extremely complex and is often fundamental to the function of the protein. It is maintained by the ionic bonds, hydrogen bonds, and hydrophobic bonds between the different R side chains of the amino acids. In addition, there may be covalent bonds due to the linking of the sulfur molecules of cysteine. In contrast to the secondary structure, the tertiary structure usually cannot be predicted from the primary structure, unless the structure of a closely related protein is already

---

[9]For example, glucose-6-phosphate isomerase (GPI), a protein that catalyzes the conversion of glucose-6-phosphate to fructose-6-phosphate, a key enzyme in glycolysis, also acts as a lymphokine produced by stimulated T cells (known as neuroleukin), and also as a motility factor in cancer cells (autocrine motility factor).

[10]An alpha helix is when a polypeptide chain turns upon itself to form a cylinder structure, with hydrogen bonds between neighboring amino acids stabilizing the structure. In beta sheets, as the name suggests, the polypeptide chains align either in parallel or (more commonly) antiparallel to form a sheet structure, with hydrogen bonding between the amino acids in the aligned peptide strands.

Table 4.2 Amino Acid Structures

Amino Acid	Abbreviation	Symbol	Codons	Side Chain Family
Alanine	Ala	A	GCA GCC GCG GCU	Nonpolar
Arginine	Arg	R	AGA AGG CGA CGC CGG CGU	Basic
Asparagine	Asn	N	AAC AAU	Uncharged polar
Aspartic acid	Asp	D	GAC GAU	Acidic
Cysteine	Cys	C	UGC UGU	Nonpolar
Glutamic acid	Glu	E	GAA GAG	Acidic
Glutamine	Gln	Q	CAA CAG	Uncharged polar
Glycine	Gly	G	GGA GGC GGG GGU	Nonpolar
Histidine	His	H	CAC CAU	Basic
Isoleucine	Ile	I	AUA AUC AUU	Nonpolar
Leucine	Leu	L	UUA UUG CUA CUC CUG CUU	Nonpolar
Lysine	Lys	K	AAA AAG	Basic
Methionine	Met	M	AUG	Nonpolar
Phenylalanine	Phe	F	UUC UUU	Nonpolar
Proline	Pro	P	CCA CCC CCG CCU	Nonpolar
Serine	Ser	S	AGC AGU UCA UCC UCG UCU	Uncharged polar
Threonine	Thr	T	ACA ACC ACG ACU	Uncharged polar
Tryptophan	Trp	W	UGG	Nonpolar
Tyrosine	Tyr	Y	UAC UAU	Uncharged polar
Valine	Val	V	GUA GUC GUG GUU	Nonpolar
Stop sequence			UAA UAG UGA	

known (and often not even then) and has to be determined empirically. A substitution of a single amino acid may lead to a completely different tertiary structure and render a protein completely nonfunctional.

B. Protein Synthesis.

The turnover of many proteins in a cell is rapid, and the synthesis of new protein is one of the major functions of a cell. The primary structure, or sequence of amino acids in a polypeptide chain, is determined by **triplets** of nucleotide sequence in the mRNA, and the polypeptides are manufactured from the mRNA in a process known as **translation.** Each set of 3 nucleotides, known as a **codon,** specifies either an amino acid or a stop sequence (see Table 4.2). Theoretically 3 nucleotides could encode 4^3 or 64 amino acids; however, there are only 20 different amino acids so the **genetic code** often has several different triplets encoding the same amino acid. For several, only the first two nucleotides in the codon are critical, with any base in the third position encoding the same amino acid. The genetic code is said to be **degenerate.** This degeneracy also provides some flexibility, as often alterations of the third codon nucleotide will not affect the primary structure (and hence tertiary structure) of a protein. However, the genetic code is conserved across all living species, including bacteria, plants, and mammals.[11]

The translation of the mRNA into proteins occurs in the ribosomes in the cell cytoplasm. Each ribosome is made up of a small and a large subunit and consists of a complex of more than 50 different proteins and several RNA molecules. Translation is facilitated by tRNA, which act as adapter molecules. Each type of amino acid is linked through its carboxyl group to a specific tRNA to form an amino acyl-tRNA. The tRNA have a cloverleaf structure, resulting from base pairing within the RNA molecule, and critically the **anticodon** sequence, a sequence of three nucleotides complementary to the amino acid's codon.

During translation, the small ribosomal subunit binds to the mRNA and tRNA, and the large subunit catalyzes the formation of the peptide bond. There are two binding sites for tRNA, the peptidyl-tRNA binding site (P-site) and the aminoacyl-tRNA binding site (A-site). In eukaryotes, translation is initiated by the binding of the small ribosomal subunit to a specific initiator tRNA, Met-tRNA in the P site, and together with several initiation factors binding to the 5' cap of the mRNA. The complex then moves down the RNA to the first AUG start codon. After the start codon has been found, the large subunit binds to the complex. The vacant A-site aligns with the next codon immediately adjacent to the start codon, allowing an aminoacyl-tRNA with the correct anticodon sequences to bind. RNA in the large ribosomal unit separates

---

[11]The only exception is the DNA in mitochondria, and even in mitochondrial genomes, only 4 of the 64 codons have different meanings than in the universal genetic code.

the amino acid in the P-site from its tRNA and catalyzes the formation of the peptide bond with the aminoacyl-tRNA bound to the A-site. Once the tRNA in the P-site no longer has its amino acid attached, it dissociates from the ribosomal complex and is recycled into the cytoplasmic tRNA pool. The new peptidyl-tRNA is then translocated into the A-site, leaving the P-site vacant for the next incoming aminoacyl-tRNA. Elongation continues in this manner until a stop codon is reach, when cytoplasmic "release factors" bind to the codon and terminate elongation, with the separation of the ribosomal subunits and release of the nascent protein into the cytoplasm.

Theoretically, with a genetic code comprising three nucleotides in a codon, each mRNA could code for three different proteins, depending on the **reading frame** chosen. However, in eukaryotes, only one type of peptide chain is synthesized from each mRNA **(monocistronic),** with the reading frame being set by the first A-U-G sequence that is found during the initiation process. However, many ribosomes can bind to a single mRNA at any time, each sequentially synthesizing the same polypeptide.

Translation of proteins in bacteria prokaryotes is basically similar, although there is no nuclear or cytoplasmic localization of DNA/RNA synthesis and protein translation. In addition, bacteria do not cap the 5′ end of mRNA and therefore have a different method for selecting a start codon and the reading frame. Instead, they contain a specific ribosomal binding sequence[12] immediately (4–7 nucleotides) upstream from the start codon. In addition, bacterial mRNA are often **polycistronic,** encoding several polypeptides on the same mRNA transcript. Frequently, bacterial genes that encode proteins in a single metabolic pathway are contiguous, and the sequence or **operon** is transcribed in a single polycistronic mRNA.

C. Post-translation Modification.

In most proteins the polypeptide chains are modified in a variety of different ways before becoming a functional protein. In many proteins the initial methionine is removed. In addition the peptide may need to be cleaved into smaller pieces, or modified by the addition of other functional groups such as carbohydrate molecules **(glycoproteins)** or phosphate groups **(phosphoproteins),** or complexed with other peptide chains to form functional proteins. Proteins are also required in many different components in the cell and often contain **signal sequences** directing the new polypeptide to different compartments such as the nucleus, the cell membrane, or an organelle such as the mitochondria, endoplasmic reticulum, or Golgi apparatus in the cell. These signal sequences may be in the form of a peptide sequence, often at the amino end of the poplypeptide, or a signal patch that is generated when the peptide assumes its correct tertiary structure.

---

[12]Known as the **Shine-Delgarno sequence.**

Many proteins spontaneously fold into their correct tertiary shape, with the amino acids with nonpolar side chains tending to be internal, and those with polar side chains on the protein surface. In addition covalent bonds, such as disulfide bonds between cysteine residues, can stabilize the resultant structure. However, many proteins need the assistance of other proteins to correctly fold, and this is provided by molecular chaperone molecules, also known as **heat shock proteins,** because their concentration in a cell increases dramatically when the cells are heated above their natural temperature (i.e., 42° C in human cells). Incorrectly folded proteins or proteins in the wrong compartment of the cell are rapidly recognized and tagged by a protein (ubiquitin) and then degraded by proteases, and the amino acids are recycled into newly synthesized proteins.

D. Control of Protein Transcription.

Although every cell in an organism contains the genetic material to encode all the different proteins, in multicellular organisms only a subset of proteins is synthesized in any cell. Thus, only cells destined to become red cells synthesize **hemoglobin.** In addition, although a set of basal proteins maintains regular (household) cellular functions in cells, different amounts of many proteins are synthesized at different times in the **cell cycle.** Control of protein synthesis is primarily at the level of transcription, and in eukaryotes many DNA–protein-binding proteins or **transcription factors** bind to the promoter region to enhance transcription. In addition there are sequences or response elements that proteins and other chemicals can bind to and inhibit transcription, and a huge number of protein-protein interactions act as activators or repressors to fine-tune the system.

Synthesis of protein transcription in prokaryotes also needs to be tightly controlled, and a variety of regulatory systems have evolved. As noted earlier, proteins in a single metabolic pathway are often contiguous (an operon) and controlled by a single promoter. The sequence between the promoter sequence and the start of transcription is critical and plays an essential role in whether or not the operon is transcribed. The sequence is known as the **operator** or activating site, depending on the effect on transcription: binding of **repressor** protein to the operator sequence leads to a block of RNA polymerase traveling down the DNA, and hence no transcription of the operon. However, effector molecules, often low molecular weight substrates or metabolites, can bind to the repressor protein, changing the conformation of the repressor so that it can no longer bind to the operator sequence, and transcription will occur.[13] Conversely, binding of activator protein to the activating site promotes

---

[13]In some systems the native repressor is inactive and cannot bind to the operator sequence. Binding to the effector molecule renders the repressor active, allowing binding to the operator and blocking of transcription.

trancription, but this effect can also be blocked or activated by the binding of substrates to the activator.

IV. CELL CYCLE, DIVISION, AND EARLY EMBRYOGENESIS.

A. Mitosis.

Most cells in a multicellular organism need to grow and divide for either growth, repair, or maintenance. Before division can take place, cellular proteins have to be synthesized and the DNA duplicated. In all cells, the cell cycle is divided into the same four main phases, although the length of time in each phase can vary markedly. Entry into different phases of the cell cycle is controlled by two families of proteins: the **cyclin-dependent protein kinases (Cdk)** that become phosphorylated and dephosphorylated at critical points in the cycle; and the **cyclins** that bind to the Cdk molecules.

Immediately after division the newly formed cells enter G_1 **phase.** This is a time for consolidation and growth. During G_1 the cell monitors its internal and external environments prior to committing to the next round of DNA replication. Some cells such as neurons can enter a specialized resting state or G_0, in which they can remain for days, months, or even years. Once the conditions are right, the cell commits to DNA replication and initiates a chain of events leading to completion of the cell division cycle. After commitment, the cell enters the **S (synthesis) phase** of the cell cycle. During this phase, the DNA is replicated and the amount of DNA in the nucleus doubles. The twin copies of the chromosomes remain closely associated at first and are called sister **chromatids,** linked together at the **centromere.** In most cells[14] the S phase lasts between three and six hours. It is followed by G_2, a second time of growth and metabolism, during which proteins, RNA, and other **macromolecules** are synthesized prior to cell division. G_2 is also relatively constant in duration, lasting about two to five hours.

The final phase of the cell cycle is **M (mitosis) phase.** During the first stage of **mitosis,** called **prophase,** the nuclear membrane breaks down, and the nuclear contents condense into discrete chromosomes. In addition the cell's microtubules assemble into a diamond-like structure known as the **mitotic spindle.** During the next stage, **metaphase,** the duplicated chromosomes become attached to the microtubules at the centromere and are arranged in a plane perpendicular to the pole of the spindle in the center of the cell. Then as **anaphase** proceeds, the paired chromosomes are separated and pulled to the spindle

---

[14]This can vary widely, even within the same organism. Some erythroid precursor cells can cycle in seven hours.

poles, where they decondense and form intact nuclei. The cell body is then divided into two by a process called **cytokinesis.** This is the end of mitosis, and the cell reenters G_1 phase.

In contrast, mitochondrial replication is independent of mitosis and occurs by duplication of the mtDNA and division of the mitochondrium in a similar manner to that seen in bacteria. However, the relative amount of mtDNA in a cell remains fairly constant. With cytokinesis random segregation of the cytoplasmic mitochondria between the two daughter cells occurs.

B. Meiosis.

Although mitosis is the way most cells divide, higher organisms reproduce by sexual reproduction, which necessitates the formation of germ cells that are **haploid** (contain half the genetic material). Apart from the sex chromosomes, a normal human **diploid** nucleus contains 22 pairs of homologous chomosomes: one chromosome from each member of the pair is derived from the male parent and the other from the female parent. In contrast to mitosis, during **meiosis,** there are two divisions of the chromosomes, and thus meiosis produces four haploid cells. As in mitosis, the chromosomes duplicate. However, both homologous chromosomes line up together on the mitotic spindle. This pairing allows **genetic recombination** to take place, whereby a fragment of maternal chromatid may be exchanged for the corresponding part of the paternal chromatid. At the first division, the homologous chromosomes separate into different cells. However, the homologous chromosomes are independently sorted into the daughter cells, so in each cell some of the chromosomes will be paternally derived and some maternally derived. Immediately after the first division a second division occurs, during which the sister chromatids are separated into different cells as during normal mitosis. Thus during meiosis, genetic recombination within the homologous chromosomes and genetic assortment of the maternal and paternal chromosomes occurs.

During oocyte production, both divisions of the egg cell during meiosis are asymmetrical with the production of one large cell and another much smaller, as the polar body. These polar bodies eventually degenerate. Meiosis also arrests at the metaphase of the second division, perhaps for many years in the prospective mother, and proceeds only after fertilization.

C. Fertilization and Early Development.

Fertilization is the fusion of the male and female **gametes;** in mammals these are the highly specialized egg and sperm cells. In humans natural fertilization occurs in the fallopian tubes of the mother, but since the late 1950s it has been possible to fertilize mammalian eggs *in vitro,* with the first "test tube" baby conceived this way being born in 1978.

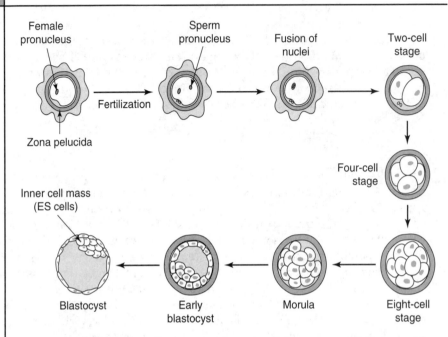

FIGURE 4.5 **Stages of early embryogenesis. After fertilization of the egg, the zygote divides by a series of cleavages through a 2-cell, 4-cell, 8-cell, 16-cell stage to form a morula. Between the 32–64 cell stage a blastocoele forms and the structure becomes polarized with the formation of the inner cell mass containing the embryonic stem cells.**

Following binding of a sperm with an egg (oocyte), the sperm penetrates the surrounding protective **zona pellucida,** and the sperm **pronucleus** enters the cytoplasm to form a **zygote.**[15] At this stage the pronuclei remain distinct, and in mammalian zygotes the pronuclei do not fuse directly. Instead as the zygote prepares for the first mitotic division and enters prophase, the pronuclei migrate to the center of the cell, and the two pronuclei membranes interdigitate and then break down. The chromosomes from both pronuclei align on a single mitotic spindle and proceed to segregate into two daughter cells as in regular mitotic division.

The zygote then proceeds through a series of mitotic cell divisions, known as cleavage, all within the protective coat of the zona pellucida. Initial cleavages lead to the formation of a **morula**[16] (Figure 4.5), initially a mulberry-shaped

---

[15]It should be noted that there is no contribution of mitochondria from the male gamete to the cytoplasm of the zygote, and thus all the mitochondria in the embryo are derived from the maternal cytoplasm. Thus mutations in the mtDNA will only be passed on through the maternal line.

[16]For mouse and human cells, this is about two to three days after fertilization.

structure, but with further divisions the morula becomes more spherical. Shortly after this, a fluid-filled cavity develops in the center of the morula, with the cells forming a layer around this blastocoele. The **blastocyst,** as the structure is known, is asymmetrical, with one pole having a much thicker layer of cells, known as the inner cell mass. It is this inner cell mass that grows, and after implantation of the blastocyst into the uterus, differentiates and goes on to develop into the embryo by processes of gastrulation, neurulation, and so forth.[17]

Until the 8-cell stage, any of the individual cells can be separated away from the rest of the embryo, and both will develop into normal adults. Conversely, two 8-cell stage morula can be combined to form a giant morula, which will develop into a single healthy adult animal. In this way, chimeric animals **(chimeras)** can be made. Alternatively, **embryonic stem (ES) cells,**[18] especially in mice, can be taken from the inner cell mass of embryos prior to implantation, and cultured and manipulated in the laboratory. When such cells are introduced into a fresh blastocyst, they will recombine with the inner cell mass and contribute to cells in the resulting offspring.[19]

V. Mutations, Genetic Variation, and Population Biology.

As discussed at the beginning of this chapter, DNA has two major functions as the genetic material within both the individual cell and in the organism as a whole. It must be able to store and transfer genetic information from one generation to the next, and it must be able to express this information in the cells of the body. To do this, DNA must be accurately replicated, especially as the haploid human genome contains about 3×10^9 nucleotide pairs, all of which need to be duplicated during cell division. DNA synthesis is remarkably accurate, and DNA polymerase makes approximately only one nucleotide substitution error every 10^9 base pairs. Part of the reason for the high fidelity of DNA replication is that the polymerase has its own proofreading process: in contrast to RNA polymerase, DNA polymerase requires a primer or previously synthesized strand of DNA to add new nucleotides to. If the 3' nucleotide is not correctly base-paired, DNA polymerase will not only be unable to extend the strand, but it catalytically removes the nucleotides in the 3'–5' direction until a correctly paired nucleotide is reached, and then chain extension continues.

---

[17]Implantation usually takes place five to six days after fertilization. The embryonic period is the first eight weeks post-fertilization (tenth week of pregnancy), with organogenesis occurring during weeks five to eight. For more information see any of a number of texts, i.e. Henry Gray, Lawrence M. Bonnestes, Martin M. Barry, Peter L. Williams, *Gray's Anatomy: The Anatomical Basis of Medicine and Surgery* (New York: Churchill Livingstone, 1995) or Ulrich Drews, *Color Atlas of Embryology* (New York: Thieme Medical Publishers, 1993).

[18]So-called due to their potential to form all different types of cell.

[19]See Chapters Ten and Eleven for more details.

Despite the high fidelity of DNA synthesis, replication errors, or **muta-tions,** in the DNA sequence will occur and can have a variety of consequences. In addition, DNA can become damaged not only by errors in DNA synthesis, but by chemical changes (thermal energy, reactive metabolites including re-active oxygen, especially in the mitochondria[20]), X rays, and ultraviolet radi-ation. The DNA, however is, protected by a large and efficient array of DNA repair mechanisms that can repair the damage if one of the strands remains intact. These repair mechanisms include enzymes that can replace dam-aged/denatured nucleotides or broken **phosphodiester bonds.** Despite these protective mechanisms, changes in the DNA can occur. And damage can occur to the repair mechanisms, so that increased rates of mutation may arise due to exposure to mutation-causing agents **(mutagens).**

Several different types of mutation arise. **Point mutations** occur with a single base substitution. Because of the redundancy in the genetic code, not all point mutations lead to alteration in the amino-acid sequence. Those that do may make only minimal changes to the protein tertiary structure and make little or no change to the protein function. However, an amino-acid substitu-tion or stop codon may severely alter the structure leading to a nonfunctional protein. Potentially more deleterious are additions or deletions of single base pairs that lead to **frame-shift mutations,** whereby a different set of codons is read for the amino-acid sequence, resulting in a completely different polypep-tide sequence. These proteins are often nonfunctional or may even block the effect of other proteins.

Depending on the protein affected, mutations may have serious conse-quences to the cell. Mutations in critical control proteins may lead to a non-functional cell, which will then die or be at such a selective disadvantage that the mutations will not be passed onto the next generation. Alternatively, mu-tations in some proteins may give the cell a selective advantage or allow un-controlled proliferation, as is seen in cancerous cells. Some mutations do not lead to cell death and will be passed on to future daughter cells. However, mutations in somatic cells will be passed on only to daughter cells derived from the damaged cell. In contrast, mutations in the gametes can potentially be passed on to new generations. Mutations in mtDNA will be distributed randomly in daughter cells and will be passed on to future generations only through the maternal line.[21]

In addition to point and frame-shift mutations, damage may occur to whole chromosomes due either to mutagenesis or to errors during homologous

---

[20]The mutation rate in mtDNA is 10–20 times greater than nDNA in part because of the exposure to reactive oxygen radicals, the lack of a protective histone core, and greater rate of replication.

[21]An increasing number of diseases are now recognized to be due to mutations in mtDNA, including blindness (Leber's hereditary optic neuropathy) and neurological disorders. See Patrick F. Chinnery et al., "Clinical Mitochondrial Genetics," *Medical Genetics* 36.6 (1999): 425–36 for more information.

recombination, leading to **deletions** of part of the chromosome sequence. Incorrect repair may lead to duplication of chromosome sequence, **inversions** (where the sequence is reattached in the incorrect orientation), and **translocations** (parts of one chromosome become attached to another chromosome). The **duplication** of a whole chromosome is known as trisomy, and the deletion of a chromosome as **monosomy.** The most common is trisomy 22, leading to Down's syndrome in humans.

A. Mutations and Evolutionary Theory.[22]

Although mutations can have serious consequences for the cell, with the production of abnormal proteins, smaller changes may lead to only minor modifications, and it is this genetic variation, or **genetic drift,** that is the raw material of **evolution.** Many genes have multiple alleles, that is, different gene products with slightly different functions, which have arisen by mutations in the gene. These mutations act not only at a cellular level, but on the organism as a whole, so that mutations that give an organism a selective advantage are more likely to be reproduced, and the genes to be passed to the next generation.

Mutations, and the large number of different alleles, are one of the principal causes of variation within the species. It is a given in most forms of evolutionary theory that the genetic population within the species exhibits genetic variation. If we assume a somewhat reliable relation between genetic variability and fitness, then genetic variability is a per se good as far as the species is concerned.[23] In brief, if a species is diverse in the genetic variability among its population, then as environments change it is in a better position to continue than a species that has less diversity. Variability of the genetic population, therefore, will enhance the species' chances of survival in situations of environmental change. For example, if one were to gloss Kettlewell's classic experiment with moth wing color, it would go like this. Subspecies (a) has variegated wing color. Subspecies (b) has black wing color. In environment-1

---

[22]There is, of course, some controversary about what constitutes evolutionary theory. This is linked both to the reductionistic question noted earlier and the units of selection controversy. The wide-ranging nature of these debates puts them beyond the scope of this volume. However, the reader may wish to consult the following for a taste of some of these issues: Elliot Sober, "The Two Faces of Fitness" in R. Singh, D. Paul, C. Krimbas, and J. Beatty, eds. *Thinking About Evolution: Historical, Philosophical, and Political Perspectives* (Cambridge, UK: Cambridge University Press, 1999), pp. 26–51; Elliot Sober, "Screening Off and the Units of Selection," *Philosophy of Science* 59 (1992): 142–52; Philip Kitcher, "Species," *Philosophy of Science* 51 (1984): 308–33; David Hull, "A Matter of Individuality," *Philosophy of Science* 45 (1980): 311–32; K. Sterelny and P. Griffiths, *Sex and Death: An Introduction to Philosophy of Biology* (Chicago: University of Chicago Press, 1999); and Richard Lewontin, "The Units of Selection," *Annual Review of Ecology and Systematics* 1 (1970): 1–14.

[23]H. Kettlewell, *The Evolution of Melanism* (London: Oxford University Press, 1973); George Williams, *Adaptation and Natural Selection* (Princeton, NJ: Princeton University Press, 1966); Michael Ruse, "Charles Darwin on Group Selection," *Annals of Science* 37 (1980): 615–30. For an opposing view—N. Eldredge and S. Gould, *The Units of Evolution: Essays on the Nature of Species* (Cambridge, MA: MIT Press, 1992).

the trees that constitute the habitat of the moths are variegated in color. In environment-2 pollution has made the trees black with soot.

Kettlewell noticed that the normally populous subspecies (a) in environment-1 were giving way to subspecies (b). This was due to industrial pollution creating environment-2. By cleaning the trees, Kettlewell was able to reverse the trend [making subspecies (a) more populous again by re-creating environment-1].

Does this mean that subspecies (a) is *better* than subspecies (b)? Certainly not. For in environment-2, subspecies (b) flourished and dominated subspecies (a). All that it shows is that no traits are "good" or "bad" per se, but are only so within certain environmental contexts.

Another example is the gene that expresses sickle hemoglobin. Hemoglobin is the oxygen-carrying protein in red cells, and a specific mutation in the beta polypeptide chain of hemoglobin leads to sickle hemoglobin, so-called because the erythrocytes assume a sickle shape in conditions of low oxygen. Not only are such cells more rapidly cleared from the circulation than normal cells, leading to sickle cell anemia, but especially in individuals who are homozygous for the gene, such sickle cells can aggregate, and block blood vessels and organs, leading to the extremely painful and life-threatening sickle cell crisis. However, having erythrocytes that contain the sickle hemoglobin in an environment that contains malaria is beneficial. When such cells are infected with malaria, the red cells sickle and the parasites die. In addition, the parasite proteins are released to the circulation and the body can mount an immune response and abort the infection before full-blown malaria ensues. Thus, although being homozygous for sickle hemoglobin is deleterious, in an environment in which there is malaria, those who are heterozygous for the sickle hemoglobin gene will have a selective advantage and be superior reproducers to those without the gene. However, in an environment in which there is no malaria, the sickle hemoglobin gene will make those who have it less fit for reproduction. Thus genetic fitness is seen to be a function of a particular gene in a particular environment.

From the perspective of philosophy, phenotypic traits are not "good" or "bad." They simply "are." Variation in any species is a dogmatic given. This is what allows the species to survive in changing environments.

For our purposes, let it suffice that genetic diversity is per se good for the population. Anything that works against genetic diversity will necessarily harm the species' chances to adapt. Harming the species means that it is more likely to become extinct. Surely from the point of view of any species, becoming extinct is a per se evil. From the point of view of Homo sapiens, the value-duty relation requires that humans do all that they can to protect the species. At the very least this would include not engaging in conduct that would threaten the species' existence—such as diminishing the genetic diversity within the species. This is an important cautionary principle as we venture forth into the realm of genetic engineering.

chapter five

From Cell to Test Tube

The previous chapter described how DNA, RNA, and proteins were coded and produced in living cells. Many of the enzymes involved in replication, transcription, and translation have been identified and **cloned** and can be either synthesized or purified for *in vitro* use. This chapter considers how these components can be manipulated and analyzed in the laboratory.

I. DNA.

A. DNA Synthesis.

DNA is a relatively simple macromolecule made up of a sequential chain of nucleotides. Short lengths of DNA, or **oligonucleotides** (< 50 nucleotides), can be readily synthesized in most laboratories using DNA synthesizers. These machines consist of a series of pumps and valves that sequentially add chemically modified nucleosides in a predetermined order: in contrast to DNA polymerase, the synthesizer adds the **nucleosides** to the 5' end[1] of the

---

[1] The 5' end is the nucleotide that would conventionally have a 5' phosphate group. (See Chapter Four.)

synthesized chain. The finished product does not contain a phosphate group at the 5′ end.

Production of synthetic oligonucleotides has revolutionized molecular biology and **nucleic acid** characterization. Oligonucleotides can be used as **primers** for DNA synthesis and amplification, and as probes for detecting DNA and RNA, as well as for introducing specific mutations into DNA, and for producing linking sequences (linkers or **adapters**) for DNA cloning. In addition, artificial bases, such as **inosine** that can pair with any of the natural nucleotide bases, can be introduced into the oligonucleotide sequence to facilitate degeneracy in the nucleotide sequence or to increase stability of base pairing.

Although synthesizers can be useful for production of short DNA chains, and addition of each nucleotide is 98–99 percent efficient, the yield drops as the length increases. Even with an efficiency of 99 percent, the yield for an oligonucleotide of 60 bases is only 55 percent (0.99^{60}). Longer DNA sequences can be produced by the synthesis of overlapping short oligonucleotides, annealing, and ligation of the oligonucleotides with DNA ligase. In this way, small pieces of double-stranded DNA can be produced, and these can also be joined together to produce longer sequences. However, this is time-consuming, inefficient, and generally used only if no other method is available.

B. DNA Replication and Amplification.

A simpler way is to use a DNA template sequence to generate the DNA, analogous to the method used *in vivo*.[2] DNA can be purified from cells (by phenol-chloroform precipitation or resin/silica-based purification) and the strands separated by heat **denaturation.** With the addition of a mix of all four nucleotides, buffer (including magnesium ions that are critical for polymerase function), DNA polymerase, and a suitable oligonucleotide primer to initiate synthesis, a second DNA strand can be produced.

This method will produce only one second strand of DNA, but this double-stranded DNA can again be denatured, the strands separated, and the procedure repeated. The addition of one type of oligonucleotide results in a linear increase in DNA with each cycle (Figure 5.1a). The addition of two different oligonucleotides, at the 5′ and 3′ ends of the sequence to be synthesized, leads to exponential amplification of the DNA sequence and is the basis of the **polymerase chain reaction** or **PCR** (Figure 5.1b). DNA polymerase is itself denatured at the temperatures used for strand separation, so thermostable polymerases, such as **Taq polymerase** (originally isolated from *Thermus aquaticus*) are used for PCR. Thus, a typical PCR reaction has three steps in each amplification cycle: denaturation (~94° C), as the strands are separated; annealing

---

[2]*In vivo*—in living cells. From the Latin, literally meaning "in the living." Used in contrast to *in vitro*, literally meaning "in glass" but meaning "in the test tube" or another artificial environment.

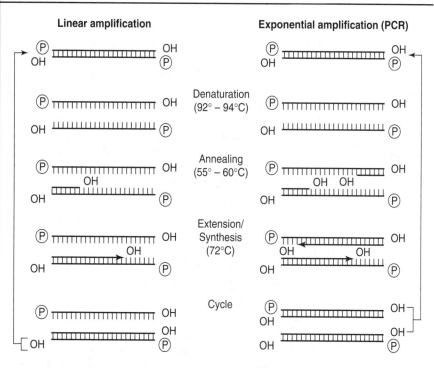

FIGURE 5.1 (a) Linear and (b) exponential amplification (polymerase chain amplification, PCR) of double-stranded DNA. The cycle begins with denaturation, with separation of the strands of double-stranded DNA. The temperature is dropped to allow annealing of the primers (one in linear amplification, and two in PCR) to the corresponding DNA sequence. Extension or synthesis of new DNA commences from the 3′ end of the primers to produce a complementary strand of DNA. The cycle then repeats with denaturation during which the newly synthesized strands are separated from the template. In PCR the newly synthesized DNA can also be a target for the future rounds of amplification leading to an exponential increase in the DNA template.

(~60° C), as the oligonucleotides bind to the complementary DNA sequence; and extension (~72° C) for DNA synthesis. Each cycle generally lasts 2–4 minutes and is repeated 25–40 times. Modifications of this protocol can be made to amplify long pieces of DNA (> 2 kilobases), to introduce mutations into a DNA sequence, or to amplify DNA using degenerate oligonucleotides. A recent advancement allows the production of the double-stranded DNA to be measured while the amplification cycles are progressing—so-called real-time PCR.

C. Cutting and Joining Double-Stranded DNA.

In order to manipulate DNA, methods are needed not only to synthesize DNA, but to cut the DNA at discrete sites and join the pieces together: DNA can be randomly broken into smaller pieces by mechanical means, such as sonication, but the sites of breakage are not reproducible. In 1970, a **restriction endonuclease,** EcoR I, was isolated from *E. coli.* This enzyme recognizes a palindromic sequence of double-stranded DNA, GAATTC, and cuts each strand between the G and A, to leave a staggered, or "sticky," DNA end (Table 5.1). Since the discovery of EcoR I, hundreds of similar type II restriction endonucleases[3] have been recognized; they are designated by the organisms in which they were first described. Most recognize a 4, 5, or 6 nucleotide palindromic DNA sequence and cleave the DNA within this site to produce "sticky" ends with 5' overhangs, 3' overhangs, or blunt ends. Provided that two DNA ends have complementary overhangs (or are both blunt ends), the DNA sequences can be joined together with DNA ligase to create new pieces of DNA.

D. DNA Analysis and Sequencing.

One of the simplest ways of analyzing a piece of DNA is to cleave it with different restriction enzymes, singly or in combination, and determine the size of the fragments by **gel electrophoresis:** either in horizontal agarose gels or vertical polyacrylamide gels (PAGE). Similar techniques can be used to separate proteins and RNA. The sample is mixed with a suitable loading buffer (usually containing a tracking dye) and loaded into a well at the top or one end of the gel. An electric current is applied across the gel, and the DNA fragments move along the gel toward the anode. For (linear) double-stranded DNA, the distance that the DNA moves into the gel is proportional to the logarithm of the DNA size/length. Markers of known size are run in parallel, and from these the size of the DNA can be estimated. The DNA is visualized by staining the gel with dyes that bind specifically to DNA, such as crystal violet, or more commonly, by examining the gel by ultraviolet (UV) light after staining with ethidium bromide. After separation of the bands, the DNA can be transferred to a nitrocellulose or nylon membrane (**Southern blotting**[4]) and probed with radio-labeled oligonucleotides or DNA.

More specific information about the DNA can be obtained by knowing the nucleotide sequence. Originally the sequence was obtained by chemical

---

[3]Type I restriction enzymes are less specific in their site of cleavage and therefore much less useful to molecular biologists.

[4]Named for Dr. Ed Southern who first described the technique of binding sized DNA to nitrocellulose.

TABLE 5.1 Recognition Sequences and Cleavage of Several Common Restriction Enzymes. The | indicates the position of cleavage.

ENZYME	ORIGINAL SOURCE	SEQUENCE AND CLEAVAGE	COMMENTS
EcoR I	*Escherichia coli* RY13	G|AATT C C TTAA|G	5′ overhang
Hind III	*Hemophilus influenzae*	A|AGCT T T TCGA|A	5′ overhang
Pst I	*Providencia stuartii*	C TGCA|G G|ACGT C	3′ overhang
Sma I	*Serratia marcesens*	CCC |GGG GGG|CCC	Blunt cutter

degradation (Maxam and Gilbert sequencing); these days, enzymatic or dideoxysequencing is more commonly the method of choice. A **dideoxynucleotide** is a nucleotide lacking the hydroxyl group on the 3′ carbon, and therefore, once incorporated into a DNA strand, chain extension is terminated. Dideoxynucleotides can be chemically modified so each dideoxynucleotide (ddA, ddT, ddC, and ddG) has a different fluorescent marker attached. For sequencing, linear cycle amplification is performed with a single oligonucleotide primer, the four standard nucleotides, and a smaller concentration of the marked dideoxynucleotides. During each round, the second DNA strand is synthesized until a dideoxynucleotide is incorporated. At this point, chain extension ceases and the chain is tagged by the appropriate fluorescent marker. At the end of the cycle-sequencing reaction, the pool of marked DNA fragments are separated by gel electrophoresis or **chromatography,** and the dideoxynucleotides that are incorporated into the DNA fragments in ascending order of size reflect the sequence of the template DNA.

E. Bacteria and Plasmid DNA.

Plasmids are pieces of circular self-replicating extrachromosomal double-stranded DNA that are found naturally in many bacterial species. They can carry genetic information for a variety of functions including their transfer between cells, antibiotic resistance, and utilization of unusual metabolites; in some cases, they may have no known function (cryptic plasmids). Some plasmids have 10–100 copies per bacteria, and their efficient autonomous replication and amplification in bacterial cells make them useful tools for molecular cloning. Although some plasmids can transfer naturally between bacteria, in the laboratory the bacteria (generally *E. coli*) are grown under special conditions to make them **competent** to receive the plasmid either by heat shock and high calcium concentration or **electroporation.**

All plasmids need an origin of replication and, as used in research, usually encode at least one antibiotic resistance gene for selection purpose (Figure 5.2);

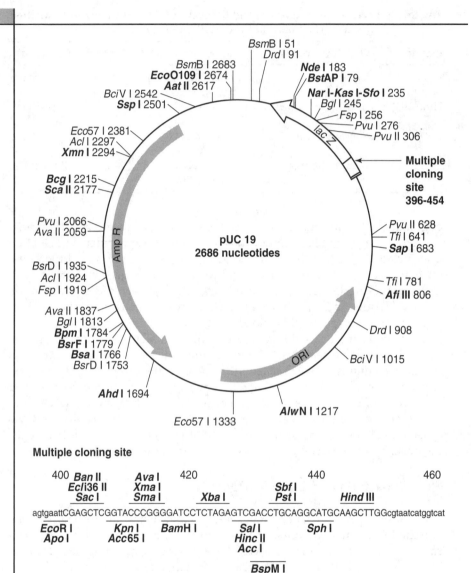

FIGURE 5.2 Schematic of a typical plasmid, pUC19. Plasmids are extrachromosomal DNA that replicate independently of the host genome. pUC19 is a small, high copy number plasmid, 2,686 base pairs in length. The schematic indicates the sites of the origin of replication *(ORI)*, the ampicillin antibiotic resistance gene (AmpR), the β-galactosidase marker gene, *lacZ*, and the multiple cloning site for insertion of the gene of interest. The sequence is accessible from GenBank, accession number X02514.

when bacteria are **transformed** with the plasmid, and cultured on agar plates containing the antibiotic, only those bacteria containing plasmid will be able to grow. Many also have been engineered to contain a multiple cloning site, with a selection of different restriction enzyme sequences to ease insertion of foreign DNA, and bacterial promoters to either express the inserted DNA sequence (expression vectors) or to express genes such as **β-galactosidase** or suicide genes if the vector recircularizes without incorporation of the cloned DNA. A common promoter includes part of the *lac* operon, which is active if isopropyl-β-D-thiogalactopyranoside (IPTG), a lactose analogue, is present in the media. In the presence of β-galactosidase, produced from the *lac* operon, the colorless chemical X-gal is cleaved to a blue pigmented chemical. X-gal is thus added to the bacterial growth medium, and the entire colony will turn blue if the β-gal gene remains intact.

Plasmids can be used to clone DNA sequences up to 10 kilobases (kb). For larger genes, DNA is cloned into either **bacteriophage,** a virus that infects *E. coli,* or **cosmids,** large circular DNA vectors that combine the properties of both plasmids and bacteriophage.

II. RNA.

A. Analysis.

In contrast to DNA, RNA is much more problematic to work with in the laboratory, not least because of the ubiquity of RNAses in the environment that rapidly degrade RNA unless extreme caution is maintained. Thus all equipment and reagents must be fastidiously cleaned and maintained, with careful attention to technique to prevent RNAse contamination.

Similar techniques can be used for analyzing RNA as DNA. However, because of the single-stranded nature of RNA, electrophoresis is generally performed with formaldehyde-agarose gels to prevent secondary structure formation. Transfer to nitrocellulose or nylon and probing is known as **northern blotting.**[5]

Although done much less often, RNA can be directly synthesized in a manner analogous to DNA synthesis, and this method is used to produce antisense RNA. More frequently, RNA probes and transcripts are produced from DNA templates using RNA polymerases originally isolated from bacteriophage. These polymerases, named SP6, T7, or T3, after the phage they were originally isolated from, bind to specific promoter sequences and produce long, single-stranded RNA molecules, complementary to the DNA sequence.

---

[5]It was not described by a Dr. Northern, but was named because it was analogous with Southern blotting for DNA—the molecular biologists' idea of a joke.

Frequently, the SP6 and T7 promoters are included in plasmids, so that by insertion of the gene of interest downstream from the promoter RNA, probes or transcripts can be readily obtained.

B. Reverse Transcription.

Eukaryotic DNA contains introns in the coding sequence that are removed after the production of the primary transcripts to produce mRNA. Prokaryotes do not have the molecular machinery to remove these introns. Therefore, in order to correctly transcribe and translate eukaryotic DNA in prokaryotes, the introns have to be removed prior to cloning. This is done by **reverse transcribing** mRNA into DNA. Although in eukaryotes, transcription is always from DNA to RNA, some viruses, such as the retroviruses (e.g., HIV), have an RNA genome and use this as a template for the production of DNA, using a virally encoded **reverse transcriptase.** As in DNA synthesis, a primer is required to initiate the DNA synthesis: if the template is mRNA, a poly-T sequence can be used as a primer; alternatively, either random **hexamers** or a specific primer complementary to the mRNA can be used. After production of the DNA strand, the RNA can be removed by denaturation or by RNA digestion. DNA that has been obtained from reverse transcription of mRNA is known as **complementary DNA,** or cDNA.

III. PROTEINS.

A. Protein Expression.

Once the cDNA has been obtained, it can be cloned into a number of different expression vectors and used to produce protein. Bacterial expression systems are widely used to produce recombinant protein. The systems are easy to use, and a number of purification strategies are available for obtaining pure protein. However, obtaining the correct amino-acid sequence does not necessarily mean that the correct protein will be produced: protein produced in prokaryotes does not have the same post-translational modifications. Because of this, and because prokaryotes do not have the same chaperone molecules for folding, poypeptides made in prokaryotes may not have the correct conformation (tertiary structure) required for a functional protein. For these reasons expression systems have been developed in yeast and in insect cells that more closely mimic mammalian translation and folding. Both systems have been used to produce large-scale recombinant protein yields for therapeutic and vaccine use.

In addition, vectors for direct expression of proteins in mammalian cells are available. In order to express proteins, promoters active in the target cell must be chosen, and often a poly-A addition sequence is included to get correct and efficient termination of transcription and translation.

B. Protein Detection.

Protein detection and analysis is much more complex than DNA detection and analysis. A number of different techniques can be used to measure proteins: some proteins, such as enzymes can be assayed by measuring their activity. However, although this will allow measurement of a functional protein, not all proteins have easily applied assays. More commonly, proteins are detected and measured by utilizing their binding to protein-specific antibodies. Antibodies can be chosen that will bind only to proteins with the correct tertiary structure (conformational epitopes), or to the primary structure (amino-acid sequence; nonconformational epitopes) alone. Proteins can then be detected by "capturing" the proteins with antibody and precipitating the antibody-protein complex (immunoprecipitation), or capturing the protein onto the surface of polystyrene microtiter plate wells and detecting the bound protein with a second antibody linked with a detectable marker (immunoassay). Alternatively, proteins can be separated by polyacylamide gel electrophoresis (PAGE), and/or transferred to a membrane, and detected with a specific antibody, a procedure known as **western blotting**[6] (cf. Southern and northern blotting).

The amino-acid sequence of a protein can be determined by chemical means and mass spectroscopy, but it is not easily accomplished in most molecular biology laboratories. Determining the tertiary structure is even more complex and is usually determined by X-ray crystallography and other complex methods.

---

[6] A continuation of the Southern/northern joke. Southern blotting is to detect DNA, northern blotting to detect RNA, and western blotting to detect proteins.

chapter six

The Biology
of Genetic Therapy

At its simplest, the general aim of gene therapy is the introduction of a fully functional and expressible gene into a target cell, resulting in permanent correction of a specific genetic disease: when the target is a tissue or organ within an organism, this is somatic gene therapy; targeting the eggs or sperm to affect all the cells in the offspring of an organism is germ-line gene therapy. Monogenic diseases are treated by either repair of the mutated gene (i.e., by ribozymes or oligonucleotides) or, more commonly today, by addition of fully functional genes (see Chapter Eight). For other nonmonogenic diseases, especially cancer and **AIDS,** gene therapy may have a number of different approaches: the addition of genes to enhance the immune response or to express proteins as a type of vaccination technique against either pathogens or cancer cells; the addition of suicide genes to kill targeted cells, especially tumor cells; or the addition of genes to protect healthy cells from the effects of chemotherapy. Although not technically gene therapy, cells may be **"marked"** using gene-therapy techniques so that the fate of individual cells can be followed, either as a research technique or for tracking the fate of tumor cells.

I. INITIAL QUESTIONS.

Before considering the strategy or vector for introducing any gene or protein into a cell, a number of other questions need to be addressed.

First, what is the target cell? Most genes are expressed only in a subpopulation of cells, and ideally the target would be the cells in which the gene to be introduced is normally expressed. However, this may not only not be possible but also (in the case of cells that are rapidly turning over, i.e., red blood cells or epithelial cells in the gut) targeting these cells would not lead to a permanent correction of disease. Instead, tissue **stem cells** that divide indefinitely, or cells such as muscle cells that have a long half-life, may be the preferred target, even though these are not the physiological sites of gene expression. Alternatively, an organ such as the liver, which contains a large number of potential cell targets, may be a more suitable tissue for gene transduction.

Related to the choice of target cell is how the cell will be accessed. Some cells, such as bone marrow cells, can be readily accessed, grown in culture, and manipulated *ex vivo*. After the genes have been inserted or corrected, the cells can then be returned to the body by the same techniques used in bone marrow transplantation. For other tissues or organs, the target cells either cannot be removed or cannot be grown/maintained in culture, and all manipulations must be performed *in vivo*. Often this is done by direct injection of the vector into the organ or into the bloodstream.

What proportion of cells needs to be corrected? In some diseases, correction of only a small percentage of cells may be curative, as in the case of ADA deficiency in the first case of gene therapy. In other illnesses, such as muscular dystrophy, it may be important to try to correct as many cells as possible.

Is the amount of protein produced by the cell critical, and will overexpression of the protein lead to disease? Control of protein levels may be important for expression of hormones and may require control of transcription. This can be performed by a number of different methods, including incorporation or use of the natural promoter, blocking promoter activity by the administration of antisense oligonucleotides (RNA or DNA), or inclusion of a promoter inducible by oral agents or drugs.[1] Alternatively, suicide genes can

---

[1] A popular system is based on tetracycline-inducible gene expression. This uses a modified bacterial tetracycline repressor protein that interacts with seven multiple tandem copies of the tet-operator sequence linked to a mammalian promoter sequence. In the original configuration, removal of tetracycline led to induction of the promoter and transcription of the downstream gene. With further modifications it is now possible to get the converse effect, with the addition of tetracycline inducing transcription, or even to get transcription turned both on or off depending on the tetracycline concentration.

be incorporated into the vector so that if too much protein is produced (or other untoward side effects of the gene therapy occur), transduced cells can be killed.[2] This same strategy can also be used to directly kill transduced cells, as in the gene therapy for cancer.

Over what period of time does the new protein need to be expressed or be functional? For most monogenic diseases, the answer is probably for the life of the patient. However, especially in these patients, the newly added gene may encode a protein that has not been seen by the body's immune system before and may be recognized as "foreign." Then the cells producing the protein either are killed or may induce an immune response. In addition, in some vectors, especially in retroviral vectors, protein expression appears to be shut off after some time because of the poorly understood process of transcriptional silencing.

Finally, there is the choice of vector. A number of different methods are being developed as a way of inserting the gene into the cell. Most of these are based on modified viral vectors (Table 6.1). At their simplest, **viruses** are pieces of DNA or RNA within a protein or lipid envelope that very efficiently enter cells and reproduce themselves. They possess no functional organelles and are entirely dependant on the host cell machinery for energy production and macromolecule synthesis. As part of their replication strategy, some viruses insert their viral genome into the host cell DNA, and it is this integration strategy that is exploited in gene therapy. Other viruses efficiently infect nondividing cells and transform them into viral protein production factories. Again, this can be exploited to transduce nondividing cells to produce genes of interest. Each modified viral vector has different advantages or shortcomings, hence the development of alternative vectors.

II. CHOICE OF VECTOR.

A. Retroviral-Based Vectors.

The first viral vector to be used in human gene therapy was based on the Moloney retrovirus, a mammalian "type C" retrovirus that naturally infects mice and integrates its viral sequence into the host cell genome. Exogenous wild-type retroviruses are found in a wide variety of mammals, in which they can be nonpathogenic or can lead to a variety of diseases, including leukemias, lymphomas and other cancers, or immunodeficiencies. They can be transmitted

---

[2]Currently a popular suicide gene is the thymidine kinase gene from the virus *Herpes simplex* (HSV*tk*). When the drug ganciclovir is administered, HSV*tk* phosphorylates the ganciclovir to monophosphate-gancyclovir, which can then be phosphorylated by host cell kinases to the triphosphate form, a potent inhibitor of DNA polymerase, thus blocking DNA synthesis and killing proliferating cells.

TABLE 6.1 Comparison of Different Viral Vectors Generally Used for Gene Therpy

Vector	Nondividing Cells	Maximum Insert Size	Pathogenic Progenitor	Integration	Major Disadvantage
Retrovirus	No	~10 kb	Yes	Random	Nondividing cells/random integration
Lentivirus	Yes	~10 kb	Yes	Random	Random integration/replication competent virus formation
Adenovirus	Yes	7–8 kb	Yes	No	Highly immunogenic/complicated vector
AAV	Yes	~4 kb	No	Episomal/random[a]	Small insert size
HSV	Yes	30 kb	Yes	No	Highly immunogenic/complicated vector

[a]Although wild-type AAV has a preferred integration site on chromosome 19, in the absence of the *rep* gene, integration is random.

by a variety of routes (exogenous). **Endogenous** proviruses that have entered the germ line are inherited in the same way as other genes, although in humans they do not appear to be associated with disease.

Wild-Type Retrovirus Infection.

Retroviruses are 80–100 nm enveloped viruses (enclosed in a lipid membrane), enclosing a protein capsid and containing two identical strands of RNA that each contain the viral genome. The viral genome is divided into a number of discrete regions: a unique 5′ (U5) region; a noncoding packaging signal, psi$^+$ (ψ^+); the *gag* (from **g**roup-specific **a**nti**g**en) or capsid coding region; the *pol* (from polymerase, but including reverse transcriptase and integrase) coding region; the *env* (envelope) coding region; and a unique 3′ region (U3), the poly-A tail (Figure 6.1).

During wild-type infection, the virus binds to the host cell by the interaction of the *env* proteins and specific host cell receptors and enters the cell by either fusion or **endocytosis.** A cDNA copy of the RNA genome is produced using the virally encoded reverse transcriptase and a tRNA specific primer that are also carried within the virus particle. The final product of reverse transcriptase is a double-stranded **provirus** sequence with a repeated U3-R-U5 sequence at both the 5′ and 3′ end[3]: sequences within the U3 region have strong enhancer/promoter activity. The provirus is transported to the nucleus and integrated into the host cell DNA at random sites in the genome by the virally encoded integrase. This involves the removal of two nucleotides from the ends of the proviral DNA and the generation of a short duplication of cell sequences at the duplication site.

Once integrated into the host cell DNA, the provirus is transcribed by cellular RNA polymerases to produce viral RNA and by alternative splicing shorter mRNA species: most of the viral proteins are produced as polyproteins that require **proteolytic cleavage** with a viral protease in order to become functional. Although the details of assembly and encapsidation are not well understood, capsids assemble at the plasma membrane, with viral RNA containing the ψ^+ signal, and are released from the cell by budding.

Retroviruses as Vectors.

For use as a gene therapy vector, a defective retrovirus is produced that contains the 5′- and 3′-LTR required for integration and the therapeutic gene/s within a viral envelope. The *gag, pol,* or *env* genes that are required to make replication competent viruses are not included. This is generally accomplished by using a "packaging" cell line (Figure 6.2). The packaging cell line has the *gag, pol,* and *env* genes inserted into the chromosomal DNA, but not the packaging

---

[3]Known as the 5′ long terminal repeat (5′-LTR) and 3′-LTR respectively.

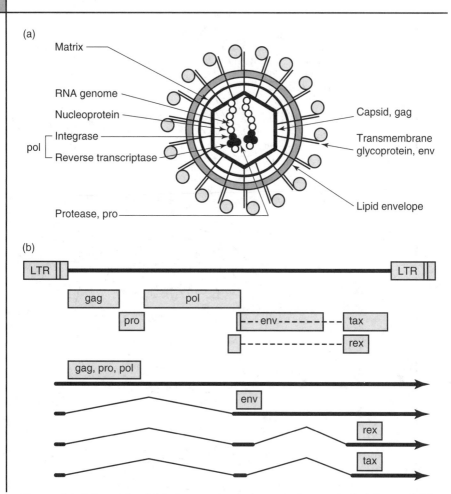

FIGURE 6.1 Schematic of (a) the structure of a typical retroviral virion and (b) the viral RNA transcription map, indicating the position of the key proteins in the retroviral structure.

signal, ψ^+, so although viral proteins are produced, no infectious virus particles are assembled. As an additional precaution, the viral genes are often inserted into different chromosomal sites, and the amount of homology between the gene sequences in the vector and the host is kept to a minimum to reduce homologous recombination.

A second "vector" plasmid is constructed with the therapeutic gene, often with a selectable marker such as neomycin resistance or **green fluorescent protein (GFP),** the viral LTRs, and the packaging signal sequence ψ^+. When this plasmid is transfected into the packaging cell line, viral particles are

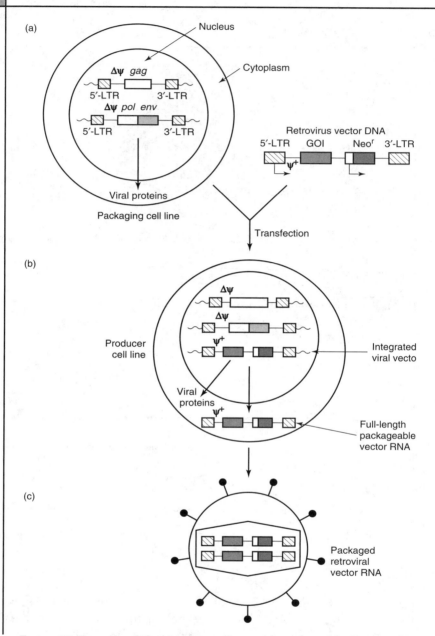

FIGURE 6.2 **Example of the strategy used to produce recombinant retroviruses using a packaging cell line containing the** *pol* **and** *env* **genes but no packaging sequence. (a) A packaging cell line with integrated copies of the** *gag, pol,* **and** *env* **genes but with no packaging sequence is produced. (b) This is transfected with vector DNA (generally a plasmid) containing (c) the retroviral LTRs, gene of interest, and the packaging signal. This sequence can be packaged into a recombinant viral vector by the packaging cell line** *pol, gag,* **and** *env* **proteins.**

produced, encapsidating the vector sequence. These viral particles are replication defective but can be used to deliver the vector sequence to permissive target cells at high efficiency.

As infection is initiated by the binding of the *env* proteins to specific host cell proteins (or receptors), different retroviruses are able to infect different types and species of cell, depending on the *env* proteins present. Thus, a number of different retroviral packaging systems are currently being used, and the viruses are divided into ecotropic viruses, those that will only infect or transduce mouse cell lines; xenotropic, those that will infect other species but not mouse lines; and amphotropic, those that will infect mouse and other cell lines. In addition, recently it has become popular to use completely different envelopes, from other types of viruses, to package the recombinant virus, known as pseudotyping: commonly vesicular stomatitis virus (VSV) envelopes are used as these viruses can bind to and therefore transduce a much wider range of cells than standard retroviruses.

One of the disadvantages of Moloney-based retrovirus vectors is that they will only transduce dividing cells. Recently, the related **lentiviruses** have been proposed as promising vectors, as they can infect both dividing and non-dividing cells. Members of the lentivirus genus, which includes human immunodeficiency virus, HIV, the cause of AIDS, differ from type C retroviruses in having additional gene products that are involved in the regulation and synthesis of viral RNA. In addition, there are no known endogenous lentiviruses, and all appear to be pathogenic in their host species. By deleting or mutating some of the gene products, vectors have been developed that retain the ability to transduce nondividing cells but without the pathogenicity,[4] and initial trials in animal models look promising.

B. Adenoviral Vectors.

Adenoviruses are nonenveloped viruses with a 80-nm protein capsid enclosing a single linear molecule of double-stranded DNA of ~36,000 base pairs, and with a virally encoded terminal protein attached to each 5' end. The capsid has an icosahedral symmetry, with fibers extending from each vertex, producing the so-called "cannonball with spikes" appearance (see Figure 6.3).[5] The protein coat and fibers not only protect the DNA from nuclease degradation but also are important in binding to host cell receptors and internalization. There are more than 47 serotypes of human adenovirus, classified by antigens on the fiber proteins. Adenoviruses 1–8 are the most common, with a worldwide distribution, and are responsible for ~5 percent of acute

---

[4]Gary L. Buchschaer Jr. and Flossie Wong-Staal, "Development of Lentiviral Vectors for Gene Therapy Diseases," *Blood* 95 (2000): 2499–504.
[5]Eliot Marshall, "Gene Therapy on Trial," *Science* 288 (2000): 951–57.

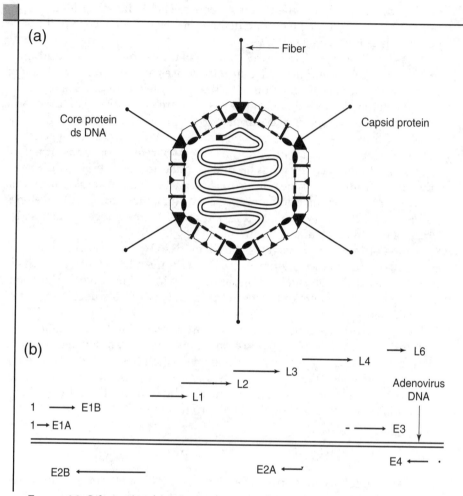

FIGURE 6.3 Schematic of (a) the structure of an adenoviral virion and (b) a simplified transcription map.

respiratory illness in children. In addition, wild-type human adenovirus infection may cause enteric infection, gastroenteritis and (rarely) hepatitis, eye infections, and genitourinary infection. Infection generally remains localized, and the virus does not spread beyond the draining lymph nodes, although in immunosuppressed patients, such as individuals with AIDS, life-threatening generalized infections may develop. Following infection, the virus persists asymptomatically in the tonsils and adenoids (hence the name *adeno-*) and may be shed intermittently for years, probably kept from active replication by the potent neutralizing antibody induced by infection.

Adenoviruses have a complex genome, with seven early, intermediate, and late promoters.[6] After binding to the host cell receptor via the fiber, then internalizing and uncoating, the DNA is transported to the cell nucleus for mRNA transcription. The early gene products E1 and E4 alter the host cell's transcriptional machinery, upregulating adenoviral transcription and blocking cellular repressors. The E1 gene product is absolutely required for adenovirus replication. E2 is required for formation of the adenoviral DNA replication complex, and E3 inhibits the transportation of MHC class I molecules to the cell surface, thus reducing the host's cytotoxic immune clearance of infected cells. Intermediate and late gene products (L1–L5) are involved in assembly and maturation of the virion.

The ability to infect a wide range of cells, dividing and nondividing, makes adenoviruses attractive for gene delivery. The deletion of E1 genes renders the virus replication incompetent, and for production of recombinant virus, virions are packaged in a cell line that has an integrated copy of E1 in its genome.

A number of ways to produce recombinant adenovirus have been developed. For the first-generation adenoviral vectors, the gene of interest was inserted into the E1 region of a plasmid containing the 3′ region of adenovirus. This was then transfected into an E1-containing cell, with a truncated adenoviral genome, and a full-length recombinant adenoviral genome was formed by homologous recombination. Alternatively, the gene of interest was directly ligated into a cosmid containing an E1-deleted adenoviral sequence, and this cosmid was transfected into the E1-containing packaging cells.

However, when transduced into cells, these first-generation vectors were highly immunogenic, particularly due to the expression of the adenovirus early gene products. More recently, second-generation adenoviral vectors have been produced that also have deletions in E2 and/or E4 genes or increased expression of the immune-modulating E3 product. Unfortunately, these approaches have not reduced the potent neutralizing antibody response to the virion capsid proteins, especially as many patients have preexisting immunity to adenoviruses prior to vector administration.

C. Adeno-Associated Virus Vectors.

Adeno-associated viruses (AAVs), so-called because they were first identified as contaminants of adenovirus preparations, are small (20–25 nm) nonenveloped viruses belonging to the parvovirus family. AAVs are sometimes

---

[6]See a standard virology text for more information.

characterized as defective viruses, as they require helper viruses such as adenovirus or herpesvirus for efficient replication. Several serotypes have been described, but all appear to be nonpathogenic in humans, and most studies have been performed with AAV serotype 2.

The virion capsid encloses a linear single-stranded DNA genome, with inverted terminal repeats (ITRs) at each end. The genome has three promoters, and encodes four *rep* proteins (nonstructural proteins) and three *cap* proteins (capsid proteins) by alternative **splicing.** In the presence of helper virus, efficient viral replication takes place, with production of infectious progeny. However, in the absence of helper virus, the viral genome is integrated into the host chromosome, particularly into a region on the short arm of chromosome 19.[7]

Recombinant AAVs are produced by insertion of the therapeutic gene between the ITR sequences. Together with a second plasmid containing the *rep* and *cap* genes, the DNA is transfected into a susceptible cell line infected with helper virus (Figure 6.4). The therapeutic gene, flanked by ITR sequences, is packaged into AAV capsids and released from the cells by cell lysis. However, helper virus is also produced, which has to be purified away from the virus vector. As a modification, the helper functions of adenovirus have been delineated, which can be incorporated into the *rep/cap* helper plasmid, or an additional third plasmid containing the critical adenoviral structures can be constructed.[8] Using these plasmids containing the adenoviral helper sequences, adenoviral-free stocks of recombinant AAV can be produced.

Recombinant AAV vectors have the advantage of being able to transduce a wide range of cell types, including dividing and nondividing cells, and to produce long-term gene expression. Unlike adenoviruses, AAV vectors have low immunogenicity. However, transduction of hematopoietic cells is relatively inefficient, especially compared with retroviruses.[9] In addition, although integration does occur, in the absence of *rep* expression, the insertion site is at random. Despite these limitations, and the small genome size that can be encapsidated, AAVs are being increasingly considered as the vector of choice for some diseases.

D. Herpes Simplex Virus Vectors.

Herpesviruses are large (120–200 nm) enveloped viruses, enclosing a 110-nm capsid and a linear double-stranded DNA. The herpes simplex virus (HSV) genome is 152 kb in length and encodes more than 70 genes, including most of the enzymes required to generate deoxynucleotides and replicate viral

---

[7]Robert M. Kotin et al., "Site-specific Integration by Adeno-Associated Virus," *Proceedings of the National Academy of Sciences U.S.A.* 87 (1990): 2211–15.

[8]Forrest K. Ferrari et al., "New Developments in the Generation of Ad-free, High-Titer rAAV Gene Therapy Vectors," *Nature Medicine* 3 (1997): 1295–97.

[9]Yutaka Hanazono et al., "In Vivo Marking of Rhesus Monkey Lymphocytes by Adeno-Associated Viral Vectors: Direct Comparison with Retroviral Vectors," *Blood* 94 (1999): 2263–70.

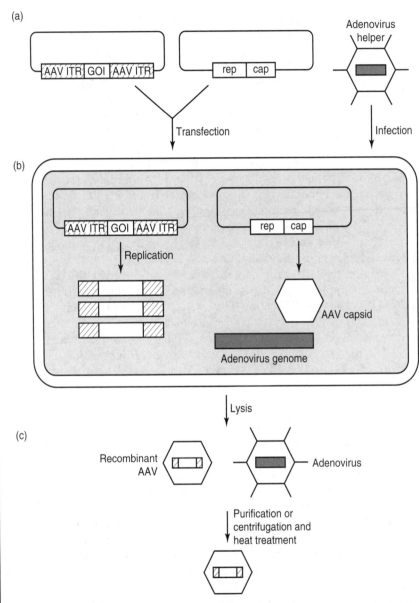

FIGURE 6.4 Example of the strategy used to produce recombinant AAV with adenovirus as the helper virus. (a) Two plasmids are constructed, one containing the AAV *rep* and *cap* proteins, and the second with the gene of interest flanked by the AAV ITRs. (b) When both plasmids are transfected into a cell line in the presence of helper virus (generally adenovirus, but herpesvirus can also be used, or the helper functions can be provided by a third plasmid), (c) the gene of interest flanked by the ITR sequence is spliced from the plasmid and encapsidated in AAV capsids.

DNA; viral gene expression is tightly regulated into a series of immediate early (α mRNA), early (β mRNA), and late (γ mRNA) gene products. The ability to synthesize all the enzymes for viral replication means that HSV can infect resting cells, such as neurons, that never make DNA and do not divide. Wild-type HSV infection is a common pathogen that causes periodic cold sores, genital herpes, and, rarely, encephalitis. Following initial infection, the virus becomes latent in neurons and can be reactivated by stress and hormone changes. The DNA does not integrate but remains episomal.

The large size of the HSV genome makes genetic manipulations of the virus difficult. One of the ways to produce recombinant HSV is to construct a plasmid with the therapeutic gene flanked by HSV DNA from a nonessential part of the genome. This plasmid can be transfected into cells, and after homologous recombination the therapeutic gene will be inserted into the HSV genome. Recombination is inefficient, so both recombinant and wild-type virus that can be screened for the prescence of the therapeutic gene will be produced, plaque-purified, and amplified for use.

Alternatively, recombinant virus can be produced by the HSV amplicon system. An amplicon plasmid is constructed with the therapeutic gene flanked by an HSV origin of replication (HSV *ori*) and the HSV packaging signal. This plasmid is transfected with a defective HSV helper virus whose genome cannot be packaged. The amplicon is replicated by a method known as rolling circle DNA replication to produce tandem copies of the therapeutic gene, and lengths of 150 kb are packaged into recombinant HSV particles.

E. Alternative Vector Systems.

Virtually any virus that infects human cells could be modified to be used as a viral vector, but the systems described are the ones that currently show the most promise for the treatment of monogenic disease. In addition, nonviral vectors are being assessed, mainly plasmids mixed with cationic liposomes, DNA-protein complexes, and DNA carried directly on ballistic metal particles (gene gun). These systems are easy to manipulate, do not appear to be toxic, and are not limited by insert size, allowing large DNA molecules to be delivered. In addition, there is no danger of replication competent virus being produced. However, so far these approaches have shown low transfection efficiency and only transient gene expression.

For gene therapy strategies in which immunogenicity is not a problem or is even being induced by the treatment,[10] other viral vectors can be utilized. The vaccinia virus is highly immunogenic and has a large genome. Recombinant vaccinia viruses have been extensively used to express proteins in

---

[10]That is, in cancer treatment or in immunization strategies.

cells in molecular biology and to produce novel vaccines. Similarly, a number of studies have been performed using the related fowl pox virus as a gene therapy vector.

III. In Vivo Gene Modulation.

Gene transfer usually involves the addition of a gene to targeted cells, but in some cases modulation of protein expression, although not necessarily curing the disease, may be therapeutic. Gene expression can be down-regulated by oligonucleotides that bind to DNA, preventing transcription, or bind to a specific RNA sequence, preventing translation. Such antisense oligonucleotides can be directly administered to cells or synthesized *in vitro* from a plasmid or gene therapy vector.

An alternative way of modifying gene expression is through the administration of ribozymes. Ribozymes are naturally occurring catalytic RNA molecules that have separate binding and catalytic cleavage domains. The binding is through base pairing with a complementary sequence of RNA, and as such it can be modified to directly bind to specific mRNA sequences and cleave the bound RNA.

IV. Correction of Genetic Mutations.

Many monogenic genetic diseases result from single nucleotide mutations. The ability to correct these sequences in the genome would have obvious advantages, not the least of which is that the control sequences surrounding the gene would be intact so that appropriate control of the gene would be maintained. A strategy using a modified RNA-DNA chimeric oligonucleotide has been developed,[11] based on the observation that RNA-DNA molecules are better targets for homologous recombination than duplex DNA. In addition, the chimeric RNA-DNA molecules are constructed with hairpin ends and modified ribose sugars to prevent degradation by RNAses. The strategy has been shown to be useful in correcting both episomal and chromosomal DNA *in vitro* and shows promise for further applications.

---

[11]Kyonngeun Yoon et al., "Targeted Gene Correction of Episomal DNA in Mammalian Cells Mediated by a Chimeric RNA-DNA Oligonucleotide," *Proceedings of the National Academy of Sciences U.S.A.* 93 (1996):2071–76.

chapter seven

The Limits of Science

Parts One and Two of this book sought to introduce ethics and science separately. Thus, the mission of Part Three is to merge the two. The structure of Part Three is a little different from that of the first two parts. Few technical words will be introduced. Also we are adding a new convention of setting down short, self-contained scientific examples in shaded boxes, especially for the reader who wants to take the biological application to another level. Others who are less proficient at science may want to skip these boxes altogether.

The chapters in Part Three are relatively short and concise to allow the reader to get through a number of issues very efficiently. Obviously, the drawback is that some issues must be presented in rather broad and quick strokes. For readers who want to take a particular topic further, there are footnotes and suggested readings.

Let us begin our interdisciplinary excursion by examining the very limits of science itself. The structure of our short exploration revolves around a foundational concept called the Principle of Plenitude. This concept is fundamental to our value-directed exploration of genetic engineering.

I. The Principle of Plenitude.

Many readers will be familiar with the Principle of Plenitude as discussed by Arthur O. Lovejoy in his classic work, *The Great Chain of Being*.[1] Lovejoy intended a kind of "possibility implies normative assent" thesis: What can be known should be known. When one applies this to the scientific realm, it rings almost like religious dogma: Whatever can be known about the physical world should be known.

Boylan once quizzed some scientist colleagues about this principle and could not find a single objector to the proposition.

Who could argue with such a thesis? There have been some. In the seventeenth century, it was an issue of contention. John Milton expresses this view in *Paradise Lost:*

> Heaven is for thee too high
> To know what passes there; be lowly wise:
> Think only what concerns thee and thy being. (Bk 8, ll 172–4)

The seventeenth century was the age of scientific revolution. Entire paradigms of thinking were altering.[2] As in all changes, there was an upside and a downside. Some of the benefits had to do with more accurate scientific theories that had greatly expanded explanatory power. From Galileo to Newton, the century was alive with discovery.

The downside had to do with the social unrest that may have been a consequence of challenging established authority. The English civil war and increased turbulence on the Continent are only two examples of such unrest. The age of the magisterium of the Roman and English Catholic/Anglican Churches was matched by a corresponding emphasis upon the individual.[3] John Locke wrote about individual human rights that were logically prior to those that the state chose to recognize. The seeds of the American and French Revolutions were sown here.

---

[1] Arthur O. Lovejoy, *The Great Chain of Being* (Cambridge, MA: Harvard University Press, 1936), p. 52ff. Our exposition of the Principle of Plenitude is not meant to be a faithful representation of Lovejoy's. Rather, we have a more narrow and limited purpose here.

[2] There has been much written about scientific revolutions. One starting point is with Thomas Kuhn, *The Structure of Scientific Revolutions* (Chicago: University of Chicago Press, 1962). Two prominent critiques of Kuhn's notions are Imre Lakatos and Alan Musgrave, eds., *Criticism and the Growth of Knowledge* (Cambridge, UK: Cambridge University Press, 1970) and Karl Popper, *Conjectures and Refutations: The Growth of Scientific Knowledge* (New York: Harper and Row, 1965), p. 232ff.

[3] The rise of individualism and its corresponding corollaries (such as the depiction of private property) has been documented by Matthew H. Kramer, *John Locke and the Origins of Private Property: Philosophical Explorations of Individualism, Community and Equality* (Cambridge, UK: Cambridge University Press, 1997).

Now many would say that such movements were very positive events in the grand scope of history. They may have been. But there was much that was lost as well. Rapid change tends to reward first those opportunists who have established themselves in the vanguard. The ordinary people are often left in an onerous holding pattern (that may be worse than it was before) as society adjusts.

II. THE LIMITS OF SCIENCE.

It is characteristic of many scientists that they are consciously or unconsciously blind to the possible consequences of their actions. Since the mission ("What can be known should be known") dangles before their eyes, they often believe that whatever it takes to get there (the means) is justified by the lofty goal (the ends). Few moral theories will say that the end always justifies the means. Not even Utilitarianism professes this in every case (since such an action creates a precedent that, itself, can have severe negative utility).[4]

It is entirely plausible that the thesis of plenitude is not always true. There may be instances in which we should refrain from exploring certain research strategies. These include instances in which the means of obtaining the scientific ends are immoral and instances in which the ends themselves may clearly be seen to be involved in a larger action that is, itself, immoral.

Let us examine these in order. First is the instance of *immoral scientific means.* This, in turn, comes in two varieties: relative immorality and per se immorality. In relative immorality, one may not have the technological means to do something humanely at the moment, but "in principle" it may be possible in the future. An example of this is the observation of human organs as they function within a living organism. In ancient times the only means available to obtain this scientific end was vivisection. Celsus reports that vivisection was performed by Erasistratus and Herophilus upon condemned prisoners.[5] The explicit purpose of vivisection (the surgical exposure of the internal organs of a live person without anesthetics of any kind) was to learn more about how the human organs functioned. This scientific end is indeed a valuable one. Under the plenitude principle, what can be known should be known; ergo, let us cut up another poor soul.

---

[4]Unless one is an extreme act Utilitarian.

[5]"Herophilus and Erasistratus are asserted by some to have acted in by far the best way: they cut open living men—those who were condemned criminals released by the king for such purposes. These prisoners were observed while they still breathed: their body parts previously hidden were now exposed. . . . [However, I disagree.] [To] cut open a living man is cruel and unnecessary, but to cut open the dead is essential for medical students." Celsus, *De Medicina*, ed. F. Marx (Leipzig: Teubner, 1915), *Prooemium* 23, 74. Translation is Boylan's.

Of course, vivisection is cruel and inhumane—even when performed upon people condemned to death. This is because inflicting severe pain upon another human at will produces (from the agent's point of view) gratuitous suffering. Inflicting gratuitous suffering upon any human, at will, is to fail to respect that person's dignity. This is because tied up with dignity is a fundamental sense of rights to primary Basic Goods of Agency (food, clothing, shelter, and freedom from dehumanizing and degrading violence).[6] All humans have a claims right to the primary Basic Goods of Agency.[7] Thus, to either fail to provide or to deny another person the primary Basic Goods of Agency (when it is in your power to do so) is to fail to respect that person's human dignity. Since all people have a moral claims right to the primary Basic Goods of Agency, then to deny this to another is immoral. Thus, since to deny another the primary Basic Goods of Agency is to fail to respect human dignity, and since performing vivisection in ancient times was an instance of denying another the primary Basic Goods of Agency, then vivisection was an instance of failing to respect human dignity and thus is immoral.

If performing vivisection is the only means of obtaining the scientific end, then that end should be forsworn. Scientists should decide that they will *not* pursue the end (contrary to the Principle of Plenitude) because the only way that they can do so is to employ immoral means.

However, in this instance the immoral means are relative. That is, they are relative to a particular stage of scientific development. From the Greek physician Galen's time to a little more than a century ago, it would have been impossible safely and humanely to surgically examine a patient in order to understand the physiology of his organs. Once the technology progressed to the point at which surgery could proceed without being cruel and inhumane (thus failing to respect the human dignity of the subjects),

---

[6]The basic structure of this analysis is taken from Alan Gewirth, *Reason and Morality* (Chicago: University of Chicago Press, 1978). Boylan has been steadily making modifications to Gewirth. His latest attempt is in his essay, "Justice, Community, and the Limits to Autonomy" in James P. Sterba, ed. *Social and Political Philosophy: Contemporary Perspectives* (London: Routledge, 2002).

[7]The word "primary" here denotes one subclass of the Basic Goods of Agency. The primary Goods of Agency are universal and can be defined scientifically according to the parameters of human necessity. For example, humans generally die when their core temperature drops below a certain temperature for a given interval. Humans also, for the most part, die when they do not receive x amount of calories per kilogram of weight. Likewise, humans generally lose their ability to maintain mental health when they are subject to y amount of gratuitous violence and fear. All of these can (within certain ranges) be defined for all humanity. Secondary basic goods, are relative to each society. These are the goods necessary to be an effective agent within that society. For example, in the United States today it is hard to be an effective agent without at least a high school education—probably edging toward some college, too. In other societies this may not be the case. Thus, secondary basic goods are relative to the society, while primary basic goods aspire to a more universal, primitive description of the conditions for action.

then surgery could become a legitimate means of pursuing the end of physio-logical discovery.[8]

An example of a per se immoral means occurs in cases in which the scientific end inextricably entailed pain and suffering. For example, if a scientist wished to know the stages in which a disease killed people (in a controlled setting), then the means would necessarily require taking a group of humans inflicted with a fatal disease and watching them die without providing them with any real cures or significant palliative care (since such "intervention" might skew the pure view of the disease's progression and the effects upon humans). The researcher distances herself from the project and merely observes and records people in the various stages of death.

This scenario is not too far removed from the infamous Tuskegee experiment in which patients inflicted with syphilis were not properly treated so that they might be observed in their pain and suffering.[9] The scientific end of understanding the "natural" progressions of a fatal disease among a large controlled sample group is a valuable one. But it can be achieved only through immoral means. Thus, the scientists should have forsworn this research plan.[10]

Similar infamous research designs were carried out by Nazi Germany, Tojo's Japan, and Stalin's Soviet Union. In each case, scientific ends that could be carried out *only* by immoral means should have been avoided. This is yet another instance in which the Principle of Plenitude is flawed.

Some may contend that the different roles of physician and researcher could contribute to these sorts of problems at some level. The argument goes as follows. The physician is an advocate for her patient. She must abide by the professional dictum of promoting the best interests of the patient and doing no harm. However, the scientific researcher has a different imperative. He is concerned with expanding our understanding of nature and in benefitting humankind.

It is, in fact, probably a better situation that the physician and the biomedical researcher be separate. This is because their respective missions are not identical, as just noted. This mission will lead the researcher in one direction, while the mission of the physician may lead her in another direction.

---

[8]Of course, as further advances in technology have occurred, investigators have been able to use even less invasive techniques so that patient risk has dropped substantially. This is always important, since risk to patient health is a relative snapshot of the state of the art that researchers should always strive to improve.

[9]Two contemporary discussions of the Tuskegee experiment that fill out the horrific details are James Howard Jones, *Bad Blood: The Tuskegee Syphilis Experiment* (New York: Free Press, 1993) and Susan Reverby and James H. Jones, eds., *Tuskegee's Truths: Rethinking the Tuskegee Syphilis Study* (Chapel Hill, NC: University of North Carolina Press, 2000).

[10]There are, unfortunately, many such examples. The United States asked military personnel to act as guinea pigs during atomic bomb testing in order to determine the effect of radiation upon unprotected human subjects. This was an inhumane and immoral action, comparable to the vivisection cases discussed earlier. Similar atrocities have been committed by many different countries who have tested biological and chemical warfare agents upon their own citizens.

When the physician and researcher are one and the same person, a conflict may occur.

However, we are not against a physician and researcher being one and the same person, but merely point out that since the missions of each are different, potential conflicts may arise.

The second category of exceptions to the Principle of Plenitude involves instances *in which the ends themselves may clearly be seen to be involved in a larger action that is, itself, immoral.* This second category seeks to examine the character of the proposed end of the scientific principle being explored. Fundamental to the exploration of this second category is the admission that science does not exist in a vacuum. As much as many researchers might like to think of themselves as being in a protective cocoon of pure intellectual speculation, this is really a pernicious fantasy that often blinds scientists to the actual uses of their research.

One paradigm case of immoral ends is the research into chemical and biological agents that can be used in warfare. In the United States, the former Soviet Union, and many smaller countries around the world, such as Iraq, there has been research into chemical and biological warfare.[11] Sometimes the country says to its scientists that they are investigating ways of deploying nerve gas or anthrax as a way to create defenses against such weapons that might be used against them. This is the ploy of many leaders: We only want to create an effective *defense*. No leaders want to admit that they are engaged in anything that might be construed as *offensive*. Nazi Germany invaded Poland on the pretext that it was responding to earlier injustices. Later conquests were also linked to past grievances that needed to be settled. Likewise with many other countries, such as Iraq; the Northern Ireland conflict; the Middle East conflict; the south central African conflict; and the southeast Asian conflict—all of the aggressive actions in those conflicts were sold to their peoples as being somehow defensive.

Who, after all, is going to approach his people and say, "Today we are about to engage in a grand offensive land/property heist because I, as your leader, think it my manifest destiny to garner as much money and power as possible because that is my personal mission in life"?

If you were a scientist asked to head the Manhattan atomic bomb project in the early 1940s, what would you say to yourself and what should you say to yourself?

On the one hand, you might think that here is a chance to be funded to perform basic research that will alter how particle physicists understand the nature of matter. What a grand opportunity! We now have a chance to

---

[11]The literature on chemical, biological, and germ warfare is immense. However, two contemporary treatments give a good snapshot of where we are: Allan B. Cobb, *Biological and Chemical Weapons: The Debate over Modern Warfare* (NewYork: Rosen Publishing Co., 2000) and Richard Buthe, *The Greatest Threat: Iraq, Weapons of Mass Destruction and the Growing Crisis in Global Society* (New York: Public Affairs, 2000).

demonstrate that the very word "atom" (meaning in ancient Greek "un-cutable") is wrong. The atom can be split, and you are on a research team that will do it. This is a chance to extend the boundaries of science: to know whatever can be known (the Principle of Plenitude).

On the other hand, you might realize that this research is for the purpose of creating a bomb that will kill people. This bomb is so devastating that it could never be used in accordance with the recognized "rules of war" that assert that armies attack only armies. Civilians are not fair game in the rules of war. But since the atomic bomb's effects were so pervasive, it would not be possible to deploy it without violating these rules of war. Whenever it was used, it would be a weapon of mass destruction. As such, it would be a vehicle of killing that would redefine warfare. The way warfare would be redefined is through the inclusion of mass killing of civilians on a scale that the world has never known before. Figure 7.1 shows what this means.

1. Warfare is morally justified only on the principle of generalized self-defense—Assertion
2. Self-defense is defined as committing minimal effective force against an aggressor to protect oneself—Fact
3. In the case of war the aggressor consists of the army of the attacking army and/or those civilians actively engaged in fabricating armaments—Assertion
4. Warfare only morally justifies the killing of soldiers in the army and/or those civilians actively engaged in fabricating armaments—1–3
5. Civilians living in the countries engaged in war are (except for armament workers) materially separated from the act of aggression—Assertion
6. Anyone materially separated from an act of generalized aggression is to be considered innocent—Fact
7. Civilians living in the countries engaged in war (except for armament workers) are morally innocent—5–6
8. Murder is defined as the killing of an innocent without just cause—Fact

9. The killing of soldiers or civilians engaged in armament fabrication can be morally justified in a defensive war, but the killing of other civilians is murder—4,7,8[12]

FIGURE 7.1 **The Argument Against Killing Innocent Civilians Even in a Defensive War.**

[12]This argument depends upon an understanding of traditional Just War theory. For a survey of some important issues at stake, see Richard B. Miller, *Interpretations of Conflict: Ethics, Pacifism, and the Just War Tradition* (Chicago: University of Chicago Press, 1991) and A.J. Coates, *The Ethics of War* (Manchester, UK: University of Manchester Press, 1997).

The practical end of the Manhattan Project was to create a weapon of mass destruction. A weapon of mass destruction will necessitate the deaths of thousands of innocent civilians. Thus, the practical end of the Manhattan Project was murder (according to the argument set out in Figure 7.1). Is being a part of the Manhattan Project as a contributing physicist something that *you*, as a scientist, should accept? You may pretend that you do not see the real end, but it is there nonetheless. One possible reason a scientist might blind himself to this intersubstitution of ends in the causal chain is that the scientist may view the proposition as opaque. However, this does not wash because we are not talking about mere substitution of terms, but of logical relationships that exist when anyone enters a causal process.[13]

This point can be illustrated by the following example. If Mary is an accountant for a pharmaceutical company that is adulterating its products with impotent fillers in order to make more money, and Mary knows this (or could have reasonably figured it out), then she cannot throw up her hands and claim innocence when someone dies from taking the medication. She cannot say that all she was doing was keeping the books according to the highest standards of accounting practice and that she cannot be connected to the ultimate end because the context is opaque. No, Mary is responsible for understanding that she acts in a context and bears some responsibility for the reasonably foreseeable outcomes of that context. If the end is immoral, then scientists should not join. On this line of analysis (instances in which the ends themselves may clearly be seen to be involved in a larger action that is, itself, immoral), no scientist should have signed on to the Manhattan Project (or other projects that had immoral ultimate ends). Under this line of argumentation, the second limit of science is not to participate in research projects that have immoral ends.

There are, however, two rejoinders to this argument: (a) What if the immoral ends are less immoral than some other end? (b) What if an individual joined in the project that had an immoral end with the purpose of sabotaging it?

Both of these suggestions are challenging. Let us address each in order. The first suggestion is that there are gradations of unethical conduct. If one were to do *x* (where *x* is an unethical action), then *x* might be *less* unethical than some other consequence *y*. In this situation, one might be confronted with a dilemma situation (meaning that without any prior wrongdoing on the agent's part he might be put in the situation in which he must perform an unethical action). If one holds that dilemma situations can occur,[14] then performing the lesser of two evils may be the most moral alternative.

---

[13]Most philosophers consider the work of Willard Van Orman Quine to be pioneering with respect to opaque contexts. Basically, an opaque context is created when a construction resists the substitutivity of identity. Quine uses the example, (1) " 'Tully was a Roman' is trochaic." (1) is a true proposition. Now Tully is identical to Cicero, so it would seem as if you could create the proposition (2) " 'Cicero was a Roman' is trochaic." But (2) is false since "Cicero" is a dactyl. For a more complete discussion, see Willard Quine, *Word and Object* (Cambridge, MA: M.I.T. Press, 1960), pp. 141ff.

[14]See *Basic Ethics*, pp. 54–57.

Returning to our example, if creating an atomic bomb will kill more than three hundred thousand people,[15] but a land invasion will mean the aggregate deaths of two million people, then (if human life is additive) it would be better to drop the atomic bomb than to attempt a land invasion.

This style of analysis is highly dependent upon consequentialist calculation. It assumes that the rightness or wrongness of any given human action depends upon the net result of utility consequences as seen over a reasonable time period.[16] Some would see this as an instance of the Trolley Dilemma. In the Trolley Dilemma one is asked whether it is more ethical to kill a fewer number of people than a greater number of people.[17] This speaks to the question of whether or not human life is additive. If human life is additive, then clearly dropping the atomic bomb is morally justified. But if human life is not additive (meaning that it is just as horrific to kill one immorally as to kill ten immorally), then there is no moral criterion by which to choose between killing one or killing a thousand. Human life is so precious that all killings are equally wrong no matter what the number.

However, even if one were to take this position, it would still be possible to argue that there might be other value criteria (such as aesthetics or religion) that *could* be decisive in such a dilemma situation.

One might effectively ask whether any scientist recruited at the beginning of the Manhattan Project would have the sort of information that President Harry Truman did when he made the executive order to drop the bombs. For all these scientists might have known, the death toll could have been in the tens of millions. All that they knew was that they were engaged in the creation of a weapon of mass destruction. How many people might be murdered or killed in violation of the rules of war was entirely unclear. Be this as it may, the first rebuttal against the sanction of scientists on the Manhattan Project would be one of consequential comparative advantage.

The second rebuttal centers on a person who joined the project with the purpose of sabotaging it (at least from the most evil excesses). This "fifth column" approach works as follows: Mr. X is invited to be a part of the

---

[15]According to the *Encyclopedia Americana* (Danbury, CT: Grolier, 1995), the number of people killed at Hiroshima was 271,000 and at Nagasaki, 71,000. For further background on this devastation, see John Hersey, *Hiroshima* (New York: Vintage, rpt. 1989); Robert Jay Lifton and Greg Mitchell, *Hiroshima in America: A Half Century of Denial* (New York: Avon, 1996); and Kyoko Selden and Mark Selden, eds., *The Atomic Bomb: Voices from Hiroshima* (Armonk, NY: M.E. Sharpe, 1997).

[16]For a discussion of the advantages and disadvantages of a Utilitarian viewpoint, see *Basic Ethics*, Chapter Three.

[17]The situation of the Trolley Dilemma is this: You are the engineer of a trolley and the trolley has gotten almost out of control. You cannot stop your trolley. You are approaching Lincoln Junction. On the right track is a school bus filled with children. On the left track is a homeless person whose poorly fitting shoes have caught in the track. As the engineer, you have the choice of moving your lethal train from the right track to the left. This is your only choice. What do you do? Is there an ethical justification for your choice?

Manhattan Project. He knows that though the proximate guise of the project is to extend basic research in physics, the ultimate goal is the creation of a weapon of mass destruction. Mr. X believes that this is an immoral ultimate goal. But he also realizes that if he checks out of the project, there are many others who are anxious for admittance. These others may be morally blind to what they are doing. They may be so wrapped up in the proximate ends of advancing fundamental knowledge in physics (the Principle of Plenitude) that they do not contemplate the implications of what they are ultimately doing (viz., creating a weapon of mass destruction). Because of this moral blindness, such scientists may allow the worst possible scenarios to occur. If the team contains at least a few people of good faith (i.e., ethical scientists who are sensitive to how their research is being put to use), then it is possible that—even if bad politicians try to misuse the atomic bomb—the scientists of good faith (members of the fifth column) might be there to sabotage the process.

The fifth column approach has been occasionally used in the political sphere. In one prominent case, Dietrich Bonhoeffer (a Protestant Christian theologian) pretended to be a Nazi in order to join in a plot to kill Adolf Hitler. Unfortunately for Bonhoeffer, the plot failed and Bonhoeffer was executed.[18]

The problem with the fifth column approach is that (at least in the short run) a person participates and supports a system that has an immoral end. Therefore, the saboteur is in the position of having to defend that which is really evil. He works and helps bring about evil. And if he, like Bonhoeffer, is unsuccessful in his act of sabotage, then the net effect of his action is actually to have promoted evil.

This can be particularly troubling when a significant resistance movement has taken as its mission to work *outside* the system in order to bring about the system's demise. If the resistance movements are almost effective, but need just a few more committed individuals, then the fifth column advocates deny the resistance fighters their point of inertia. In the Manhattan Project, J. Robert Oppenheimer might be called a fence-sitting fifth column advocate. Oppenheimer forever felt some conflict about his role as a scientist and as a man of conscience.[19]

We would say that there may be situations in which the strategy of the fifth column may seem to be the only way to overturn the immoral system (or research program). But it is a highly risky tactic that has many inherent drawbacks.

---

[18]See Eberhard Bethge and Victoria J. Barnett, eds., *Dietrich Bonhoeffer: A Biography* (Philadelphia: Fortress Press, 2000) and Dietrich Bonhoeffer, *Letters and Papers from Prison* ed. Eberhard Bethge (New York: Macmillan, 1997).

[19]Some of Oppenheimer's thoughts about science's obligation to society can be found in J. Robert Oppenheimer, *Atom and Void: Essays on Science and Community* (Princeton, NJ: Princeton University Press, 1989).

In conclusion, though the Principle of Plenitude is very alluring because it appeals to the mind's eternal quest for knowledge, it is not conclusive. There are moral constraints upon the quest for scientific knowledge: (a) instances in which the means of obtaining the scientific ends are immoral and (b) instances in which the ends themselves may clearly be seen to be involved in a larger action that is, itself, immoral. Both of these situations dictate that scientists should take the advice of Odysseus who ordered his men to stop their ears with beeswax and to bind him to the mast of the ship as they passed the region of the Sirens. Odysseus knew that knowledge had its limits, and though he was compelled to listen to the melody, he took precautions against his ability to act.[20] Odysseus knew that there are limits to the Principle of Plenitude. Modern scientists must also learn this lesson.

---

[20]Of course there are some that believe that the sin of Odysseus was his thirst for knowledge. Alfred, Lord Tennyson frames his poem "Ulysses" upon the thesis that the lack of self-control toward the acquisition of new knowledge was the cause of Ulysses' long journey home.

chapter eight

Genetic Testing and Screening

The next four chapters examine key areas of genetic engineering in a schematic fashion: Genetic Testing and Screening (Chapter Eight), Somatic Gene Therapy (Chapter Nine), Cloning (Chapter Ten), and Germ-Line Therapy (Chapter Eleven). Chapter Twelve discusses the relationship between science and business. In many ways, these are the core interdisciplinary areas of the book. In each case, we begin by defining the subject matter at hand, then move through a summary of how it is presently being performed, and end with an evaluation highlighting advantages and problems with this sort of practice.

The concepts set out in Parts One and Two (as well as in the previous chapter) are used to drive our evaluations.

I. What Is Genetic Testing and Screening?

Causative genes have already been identified for approximately 1,000 hereditary diseases, and as the Human Genome Project proceeds, this number will inevitably increase. Many of these diseases are monogenic, with mutations in a single gene leading to disease. However, even with genetic disease that is caused by mutations in a single gene, the type of alterations can vary tremendously. In some diseases, such as sickle cell anemia, the mutation is generally at the same position in all affected individuals, so that assays can be relatively easily developed to test for the specific mutation. In other diseases, there may be "hot-spots" in the gene where mutations are more likely to be found; in yet other diseases, the mutations appear to be almost random through the whole coding sequence. Other types of mutations leading to genetic disease include mutations in the promoter sequence rather than the coding region itself, exon deletions, and gene or chromosomal translocations.[1] To add to the difficulties, changes in a single base pair may be difficult to interpret unless the mutation leads to an obvious difference, such as premature amino-acid chain termination and hence a truncated protein. Many genes (and proteins) are polymorphic (the specific change occurs in more than 1 percent of the population), and yet there is no discernible alteration in function.

For correction of genetic diseases by gene therapy, the nature of the genetic mutation has to be identified, generally through genetic testing—the testing of individuals for a specific genetic disease because they are at increased risk, usually due to their family history or other medical signs or symptoms. In contrast, genetic screening is the testing of a population that has no specific risk factors. It may be performed for other reasons than to identify specific medical diseases, including forensic studies, paternity testing, and biomedical research.

II. How Is Genetic Testing and Screening Presently Being Performed?

As a result of the variety of different types of mutations that may occur and the different reasons for performing genetic screening, a variety of different methods are used. In addition, depending on the reason for doing the assay, a variety of different material may be tested, from blood samples, buccal swabs, and placental tissue for diagnostic testing to blood stains, body fluids, or saliva in forensic tests.

A. Chromosome Analysis or Karyotyping.

Some diseases, such as Down's syndrome, are caused by incorrect segregation of the chromosomes during division, leading to trisomy (trisomy 21 in Down's syndrome) or monosomy. In others, incomplete separation of the chromatids during division leads to translocations of DNA from one chromosome to another. One of the earliest methods for identifying these mutations was gross analysis of the chromosome structure. During metaphase (see Chapter

---

[1]For a more complete listing of the variety of types of genetic mutation and difficulties in interpretation, see Hai Yan, Kenneth W. Kinzler, and Bert Vogelstein, "Genetic Testing—Present and Future," *Science* 289 (2000):1890–92.

Four), the chromosomes are condensed and are easy to visualize. After treating with trypsin and staining, a characteristic banding pattern on the chromosomes is obtained, and this pattern, showing the size of the chromosome and the position of the centromere, enables accurate identification of each chromosome. An individual's chromosomal composition is known as the **karyotype.**

Additional information can be obtained from the karyotype with different staining methods. Increasingly, standard staining is combined with fluorescence *in situ* hybridization or **FISH analysis.** Fluorescently labeled DNA probes to known chromosomal regions, or even specific genes, are hybridized with the cells and then examined under the microscope. Using different colored fluorescent probes, several different genes or regions can be analyzed at the same time and used to confirm genetic abnormalities not readily visualized by standard staining.

B. DNA Sequence Analysis.

Due to the caveats outlined earlier, detection of genetic mutations at the DNA level can be fraught with difficulties, and for many genes, even when the complete coding and noncoding sequence is known, it may not be straightforward.

For genetic testing, if the specific genetic mutation is known from other affected family members, then testing can be relatively simple. DNA can be extracted, and the DNA region of interest amplified by the polymerase chain reaction (PCR). Formal sequencing of the DNA can then be performed. Alternatively, if the mutation leads to the loss or gain of a restriction enzyme site, the PCR product can be tested for presence of this site, or PCR primers can be designed that will specifically amplify the mutated DNA sequence only. Individuals can then be told whether they do or do not have the specific mutation. Such testing will say nothing about mutations in other parts of either that gene or the whole genome.

Similar assays can be designed for testing individuals or populations for specific known mutations, such as that seen in sickle cell anemia. Again, such testing does not exclude other mutations in other parts of the gene. If the mutations can be in a variety of positions, then the whole gene may need to be sequenced, on a variety of different PCRs performed (often known as multiplex PCR when multiple PCR reactions are preformed in the same tube), or specific probes designed that will pick up all possible mutations.

C. DNA Mutation Screening.

Although not specifically identifying the mutation at the molecular level, a number of alternative techniques have been developed to identify point mutations in a sequence of DNA compared to the control sequence. Denaturing gradient gel electrophoresis, also known as **DGGE,** works on the principle that double-stranded DNA, even if only mismatched at a single nucleotide, will have an altered mobility in denaturing gels compared to completely matched DNA. PCR-amplified DNA from the subject is mixed and hybridized with a labeled single-strand DNA probe, with the resultant labeled double-stranded DNA then run on a denaturing gel. DNA with a different mobility compared with the control DNA sequence can then be further analyzed by conventional sequencing to determine the nature of the mutation. Alternatively, chemicals or enzymes that cut mismatched DNA at the mismatch site can be used to cleave the mutated DNA.

Single-stranded conformational polymorphism analysis, **SSCP,** uses the principle that single-stranded DNA will form complex structures depending on its size and sequence, with even a single base change leading to major structural changes. Single-stranded DNA, between 200 and 300 nucleotides in length and obtained by PCR, are run on a nondenaturing gel, and again the gels are examined for sequences with a different mobility to the control sequences. Although all of these methods can be used for determining the presence of mutations, they are not readily applicable for large-scale genetic screening of populations but are generally performed for genetic testing purposes. And, as many genes have polymorphisms, it is not sufficient to identify a mutation; often further studies are required to determine if the mutation contributes to disease.

D. DNA Profiling.

Approximately 30 percent of the human genome appears to have no function in gene regulation or expression and is comprised of repetitive DNA sequences. There are two major types of repetitive DNA sequences. Satellite DNAs are DNA sequences between two nucleotides—short tandem repeats, or **STRs,** in microsatellites—to several hundred nucleotides (macrosatellites) in length that are head-to-tail tandem repeats. The whole satellite sequence can vary from less than a kilobase (microsatellites) to many kilobases, with the sequence repeated many thousands of times. In some cases, the same satellite sequences are found repeated throughout the genome and are known as multilocus satellites, as opposed to single locus satellite sequences that are only found at one position in the genome. The other type of repetitive DNAs is known as interspersed repeats and does not show the same tandem repeats as in the DNA satellite sequences. These interspersed repeats are also scattered throughout the whole genome.

The number of repeats in the different microsatellites varies markedly in different individuals, and hence these sequences, also known as variable number of tandem repeats, or **VNTRs,** can be used to generate a genetic profile of an individual. DNA can be obtained and cut with either one or a combination of restriction enzymes. After separating the fragments on a gel, Southern blotting can be performed using a labeled probe to either a multilocus or single-locus VNTR. By using different restriction enzymes and different probes, it is possible to get profiles that are polymorphic and potentially as unique to an individual as a fingerprint.

Similar profiles can be obtained using the STR (short tandem repeat) sequences. The conserved DNA sequence on either side of the STR is used to design primers and the intervening, variable length DNA amplified by PCR. This method markedly reduces the amount of DNA that is needed for the analysis, and by combining the number of different STRs that are screened, a genetic profile can be determined.

E. Gene Discovery.

Even though a genetic component is known for many diseases, the affected gene has not been discovered. One approach to try to identify the gene responsible is to analyze DNA from affected and nonaffected individuals. Because of the great genetic diversity in the human genome, until recently[2] this identification attempt has been done within family pedigrees, where DNA is available from closely related relatives, some of whom do and others of whom do not appear to carry the susceptible gene. Using techniques similar to those used in genetic profiling, DNA from affected or nonaffected individuals can be tested to determine which genetic markers or STRs best link to the disease. By using markers that are progressively closer together on the genome, and provided there are sufficient numbers of individuals being analyzed, it is possible to build a linkage map and identify the gene location. The gene can then be identified by conventional sequencing.

III. THE ADVANTAGES OF GENETIC SCREENING.

A. Diagnosis and Prognosis.

As we look into our crystal ball at the future of medicine, what might we see? Well, one vision is of genetic testing being carried out by medical technicians, then, as a result of this analysis, patients will be given a diagnosis of

---

[2]The population in Iceland is more genetically homogenous than most countries, and has both well-documented geneology going back to the eleventh century and an excellent national health care system. Recently, a company, DeCODE Genetics, has been founded to use this information to study the genetics of multifactoral disease in a way that would not be possible with smaller family groups. See J. Gulcher and K. Stefansson, "Population Genomics: Laying the Groundwork for Genetic Disease Modeling and Targeting," *Clinical Chemistry and Laboratory Medicine* 36.8 (1998): 523–27. As we will argue toward the end of this chapter, individual informed consent is extremely important in cases of genetic testing and in the creation of genetic data bases. Innocent parties may not be coerced into providing such information. In the precedent of fingerprinting, to which we refer in the end of the chapter, there is no blanket screening and recording of data. To do so will violate the Basic Good of being immune to unwarranted bodily harm. Furthermore, to take the body/genetic map of another for the sake of a research project is to exploit another as a means only and is prohibited under the terms of Chapter Seven.

what is wrong with them. Next, they will be given a list of courses of action based upon the tests. (Again, this list could be obtained by a technician who merely transfers the test results to the accepted database.) Once the list is presented to the patient, she will choose her treatment (with the help, perhaps, of some online tutorials). Then a clinician will inoculate her or otherwise administer the genetic therapy. The entire process might go forward without the intervention of a physician!

Another scenario might proceed with the physician intervening at the stage of genetic counseling so that the patient might become more aware of the full implications of the various options that confront her. In this view of the future, the physician might become an expert counselor who advises the patient on the background of the choices that she will have to make. In some ways, this harkens back to the origins of medicine in which the physician was a counselor who talked to patients at length about their disease and the options that confronted them.

In the nearer term, we do not need a crystal ball to see that genetic testing is already making diagnosis of some hereditary diseases more accurate, and that individuals at risk of diseases such as Huntington disease can be tested and told before symptoms commence whether they are at risk of developing the disease.

Genetic testing is not only confined to testing for susceptibility to hereditary disease. In the field of tissue and organ transplantation, one of the major reasons for failure is tissue incompatibility between the patient and the transplant. Today, genetic methods of tissue typing have virtually eliminated the less accurate serological and tissue-matching techniques. However, tissue mismatch still occurs, necessitating the use of immunosuppressive drugs to avoid rejection. However, the hope is that as we learn more about the minor antigens that are involved, genetic tests will be developed and better tissue matching will be reflected in less rejection and the need for immunosuppression will be reduced.

B. Genetic Tests for Prospective Parents.

The second group who might find genetic screening advantageous are prospective parents. The reasons that genetic screening might be used by prospective parents are as different as the situations these parents face. One circumstance occurs when people employ genetic screening to determine whether they want to risk having children. There may be conditions in which genetic screening can highlight probabilities that an offspring might have severe defects and/or genetically transmitted diseases for which there are no cures. In these situations, it is possible that a couple might opt not to have children as the results of the genetic tests.

Prospective parents might also employ genetic screening after the woman is pregnant for the same reasons (deformities and/or genetic diseases for which there is no cure). In this case, the purpose of the tests is to present these facts to the couple, who might need to decide whether or not to abort the fetus.

A third situation for genetic testing for prospective parents concerns enhancement: parents (either before implantation or during pregnancy) want to determine whether the healthy baby is "good enough" for them. On the basis of these tests, the parents may decide to abort or to undergo genetic therapy to improve the child (at this point this scenario is still science fiction). This scenario concerns secondary good enhancement (see later discussion). Some parents might like to choose the gender of their child and abort a child that is of the opposite sex. This particular scenario is not science fiction. Already in the world (especially in Asia) abortion due to gender is not uncommon. Genetic testing allows determination of the sex of a fetus much earlier in pregnancy, and thus aids those parents to whom this is an all-important factor.

Along the same lines, a genetic test that will positively indicate sexual orientation may be possible. If such a test becomes accurate and easy to administer, then we could also imagine that some parents might choose to abort a child because of sexual orientation.

C. Employers.

The third group that might profit from accurate genetic screening might be employers. Currently, the main restrictions upon corporate efficiency and profitability are illness and occupational accidents. Now genetic screening might be useful in both instances. For example, if there were an accurate genetic test for the propensity to develop cancer and if the test could also give us some idea *when* this cancer might occur, then an employer might be able to avoid hiring a job applicant who might not fully "earn out" the company's investment in training, benefits, and so forth. Companies might also be able to tell which typists might be more subject to carpal tunnel syndrome (one of the most common workplace injuries). If the company could avoid hiring such people, then they might avoid costly worker's compensation settlements and lost productivity hours. In both areas (sickness and accident), companies might be able to increase efficiency and profitability if they were permitted to perform preemployment genetic screening upon applicants.

D. Insurance Companies.

Widespread genetic testing could prove to be a boon to insurance companies. Insurance companies are really all about calculated betting or risk assessment. Health insurance, worker's compensation, or life insurance carriers could be able to test potential policyholders in order to have more complete information on which to make their decision to insure. This information could also be beneficial in setting premium rates. The more an insurance company knows, the more precise it can be about its "calculated risk."

E. Forensic Population Research.

Another possible advantage to genetic testing might be population research for the purpose of criminal law enforcement. This has already started in a small way in several high-profile cases, such as the O.J. Simpson case and a number of court cases in the United States in which inmates on death row were found innocent of the crimes they committed.

These examples give credence to the proposition that widespread genetic testing of the population at large should be done to provide physical evidence in a criminal case that might be compared to a centralized database and analyzed so that the culprit might be apprehended.

IV. A CRITICAL EVALUATION OF GENETIC SCREENING.

A. Diagnosis and Prognosis.

In the crystal ball scenario suggested in the previous section on the advantages of genetic screening, diagnosis, and prognosis, one account indicated that the physician might be virtually replaced by genetic tests along with preprogrammed responses. We believe that such a model is essentially flawed in that it fails to recognize the role that physicians should play in health care. Physicians are trained in the art and science of healing. Now, it is true that there is some controversy about what constitutes health,[3] but regardless of this, the physician essentially is the one who can provide both the fact and the reasoned fact.[4] This distinction refers to an individual who understands the raw data present in some event versus one who both recognizes the data *and* can assign a cause to it. Only when a person has both sorts of knowledge can we say that he has scientific knowledge.

Technicians can be trained to recognize "the fact." They can prepare and execute the genetic test. They can also plug the results into a computer for the "authoritative choices of action." But what technicians cannot do is provide the understanding that comes only from knowledge of the reasoned fact. This

---

[3]For example, see Arthur Caplan, H. Tristram Engelhardt Jr., and James J. McCartney, eds., *Concepts of Health and Disease: Interdisciplinary Perspectives* (Reading, MA: Addison-Wesley, 1981) and H. Tristram Engelhardt Jr. and Kevin William Wildes, "Health and Disease IV: Philosophical Perspectives" in Warren T. Reich, ed., *Encyclopedia of Bioethics* (rev. ed., New York: Simon and Schuster Macmillan, 1995), vol 2, pp. 1101–6.

[4]Cf. Aristotle, *A.Po.* II.1.

Hypervariable "Minisatellite" Regions in Human DNA.

Alec J. Jeffreys, Victoria Wilson, and Swee Lay Thein

Nature 314 (1985): 67–73.

The authors had previously shown that an intron in the human myoglobin gene contained a sequence of four tandem repeats of 33 nucleotides. They used this sequence to probe human genomic DNA cut with one of two restriction enzymes. In each case, the probe detected multiple DNA fragments. A human genomic library was also screened using the 33 nucleotide tandem probe, and ~40 positive clones were identified. Of these, 8 were further purified and sequenced. The results showed that all 8 contained minisatellite sequences with tandem repeat sequences inserted into different regions of the genome. In addition, the repeat sequences ranged in length from 16–62 nucleotides and were repeated between 3 and 40 times. In common to all the repeat sequences was an almost invariant core sequence of 10 nucleotides, preceded in most but not all by a common 5 nucleotide sequence.

When a probe comprising 29 repeats of the smaller 16 nucleotide sequence was hybridized with restriction enzyme digested genomic DNA, an even more complex profile of DNA fragments was identified, including most, if not all, the fragments previously identified. Similar complex patterns or DNA "fingerprints" were identified on unrelated individuals, indicating the polymorphism in the human genome. However, testing of a large Asian Indian pedigree showed that the polymorphic fragments segregated in a mendelian fashion, and that on average 50 percent of the bands were transmitted from each parent to the offspring, so that all bands in an offspring could be traced back to one or other parent. Despite this, the DNA profiles were sufficiently distinct to distinguish between first cousins.

The authors suggest that these DNA "fingerprints" will be generally useful for human "segregation" analysis, in particular detection of bands associated or linked with disease loci, and a powerful tool in paternity/maternity testing and forensic applications. In follow up papers (all within the same year), the authors show that these fingerprints are "individual-specific"[1] and demonstrate the use of this technique for confirming maternity in an immigration case,[2] and the potential forensic application.[3]

[1]*Nature* 316 (1985): 76–79.
[2]*Nature* 317 (1985): 818–19.
[3]*Nature* 318 (1985): 577–79.

understanding of causes is especially important in examining both the diagnosis (because even with precise tests there may be many "close calls") and the prognosis (because subtle variations in the facts of the test along with the individuality of the patient may require expert interpretation in order to determine what will happen). Genetically based multifactoral disease will give an individual an increased risk for the expression of that gene, but the full expression will depend on the environment. For example, a gene for obesity will make you fat only if you overeat. Similarly, genes for hypercholesterolemia will kick in especially if you have a high-fat diet. These situations require the intervention of a physician before any therapy should be undertaken.

In the second scenario the physician is a counselor. This is an appropriate role for the physician, but a physician is more than a counselor. Under the role of the physician as counselor only, the physician becomes a "fact giver," who can answer questions posed by the patient, who, in turn, makes her health decision. This model of extended patient autonomy is too simplistic, and it carries us to the autonomy-paternalism debate.[5] How much control should each of us have over our own health care choices? On the face of it, most of us would reply, "As much as possible." Who would turn over control of his or her life to another? Doesn't autonomy go hand in hand with the freedom and self-determination that are upheld by most moral theories?

The problem with this view is twofold. First, in order to be autonomous (literally a self-lawmaker), one must have adequate knowledge through which all the options are explored and examined. This specialized knowledge is beyond the ken of most patients, so that they must rely upon others to fill in the gap (often in a simplified version). It is also the case that the professional's judgment is generally superior to that of even an enlightened layperson. Thus, the factual understanding along with the judgment of experience generally puts the physician into a paternalistic posture from the outset. (*Paternalism* as used here refers to acting in the best interests of the patient. It is especially troublesome when the patient does not understand what is in his or her best interests, so that the physician is put in the position of ignoring the patient's wishes and acting as the physician, rather than as the patient, sees fit.) When the physician is seen only as a counselor, then it implies that the patient is

---

[5]For an introduction to some of the most important questions in paternalism and autonomy, see George J. Annas, "The Emerging Stowaway: Patient's Rights in the 1980's" in Bart Gruzalski and Carl Nelson, eds., *Value Conflict in Health Care Delivery* (Cambridge, MA: Ballinger, 1982, pp. 89–100); H.A. Bassford, "The Justification of Medical Paternalism," *Social Science and Medicine* 16.6 (1982), pp. 731–39; Thomas L. Beauchamp, "The Promise of the Beneficence Model for Medical Ethics," *Journal of Contemporary Health Law and Policy* 6 (spring 1990), pp. 145–55; James F. Childress, *Who Should Decide? Paternalism in Health Care* (Oxford: Oxford University Press, 1982); James F. Childress and Mark Siegler, "Metaphors and Models of Doctor-Patient Relationships: Their Implications for Autonomy," *Theoretical Medicine* 5 (1984), pp. 17–30; Lee Coleman, *The Reign of Error* (Boston: Beacon Press, 1984); Gerald Dworkin, *The Theory and Practice of Autonomy* (Cambridge: Cambridge University Press, 1988); T. Hope, D. Springings, and R. Crisp, "Not Clinically Indicated: Patients' Interests or Resource Allocations," *British Medical Journal* 306 (1993), pp. 379–81; Florencia Luna, "Paternalism and the Argument from Illiteracy," *Bioethics* 9.3/4 (July 1995), pp. 283–90; Mary B. Mahowald, "Against Paternalism: A Developmental View," *Philosophical Research Archives* 6.1386 (1980); Rosa Pinkus, "The Evolution of Moral Reasoning," *Medical Humanities Review* 10 (fall 1996), pp. 20–44; Daniel Sulmasy, "Managed Care and the New Paternalism," *Journal of Clinical Ethics* 6.4 (winter 1995), pp. 324–26; Mark R. Wicclair, "Patient Decision-Making Capacity and Risk," *Bioethics* 5 (April 1991), pp. 91–104; Henrik Wulff, "The Inherent Paternalism in Clinical Practice," *Journal of Medicine and Philosophy* 20.3 (1995), pp. 299–311.

competent to make informed judgments about his choice of treatments. But the overwhelming majority of patients do not possess the specialized knowledge requisite to make critical, independent judgments about what the physician puts forth in her depiction of the various alternatives.

In the practice of medicine, patients can (and should) be brought *into* the process, but they are rarely able to become full collaborators. Thus, knowledge and judgment are one pair of limiting factors upon patient autonomy.

Second, the patient is often in an impaired state (of one sort) that makes fully deliberative decision making rather difficult at best. Either the patient is in pain, emotionally traumatized, or in some way not up to his full disinterested, rational capacity. To burden a patient with the full weight of being an autonomous partner in the health care decision-making process may be unfair to the patient.

Still, there is much to be said for including the patient in the process as much as circumstances permit (often time constraints involved in split-second life and death situations act as an exterior constraint). By including the patient in the process, the physician is recognizing and affirming the dignity of the patient. Too often physicians have included only their more intelligent patients in the decision-making process. Also, paternalism can cloak racist or sexist predilections on the part of the physician. Thus, some form of autonomy seems absolutely necessary.

If both autonomy (in some form) and paternalism (in some form) are inevitable, then how should they be balanced? We believe that a strategy that engages a patient at the level that he or she is able to comprehend the choices offered and then enters into a semi-Socratic dialogue with the patient on this level is the best way to proceed, because it optimizes autonomy while not recklessly allowing the patient to make an uninformed and clearly medically harmful choice (informed consent). Genetic testing will clearly change the practice of internal medicine, but it will not eliminate or diminish the role of the physician.

B. Prospective Parents.

Genetic screening and genetic counseling with respect to prospective parents involves two sorts of issues. The first concerns those prospective parents who are not already pregnant. These individuals are considering whether it would be prudent to become pregnant. On the face of it, this seems like a very responsible position to take. These prospective parents want to know the probability of having children with deformities or fatal diseases. With this knowledge, they will decide whether or not to have children.

One difficulty with this position is the status of probability. Probability is often interpreted in several key ways: actual frequency of events, subjectively interpreted frequency of events, hypothetical relative frequency of events, and the propensity interpretation of probability.[6] These various positions base probability upon some interplay between theory and observation. For example, if theory predicts that a normal coin tossed in a uniform, nondiscriminatory fashion will turn up 50 percent heads and 50 percent tails, then any actual results that are different from this are likely to be discounted in some fashion. When people slavishly abide by the data in a relatively small sample space, then the "actual frequency" could very well be wrong. For example, we may throw up the coin in 50 trials and get 35 heads and 15 tails. Does this mean that this is the correct manner in which we should view the probability of this event?

In another case, we may think that the probability must turn out a certain way and so we discount the data because it *has to turn out* according to our hypothesis (subjective interpretation of data). This also has its problems, because in its extreme case it turns science into an *a priori* exercise.

A third approach is hypothetical relative frequency of events. Under this approach, one introduces the Law of Large Numbers. In this case, the probability of heads (h) equaling 50 percent increases as the error (e) decreases. If we toss the coin n times, then as n approaches infinity, e approaches 0 and h approaches 50 percent. Although this may sound like an improvement over subjective interpretation of data, is it really? One still solves the problem by a mathematical assertion that it must work that way through a thought experiment that no one can ever really carry out.[7] Thus, though it is a dogma in statistics that each event is independent, this does not address the issue of how we come up with a reasonable method for determining the basis of statistical probability to begin with. It is not necessarily a mechanical process based upon actual data but is instead a dialectical interaction between expected outcomes and the underlying accepted physical dynamics that would explain this sort of outcome.

The final gambit of probability that we are examining is the propensity tack. Under this approach, one is forced to insert a physical mechanism into a logical conditional that will supposedly solve the problem. For example, one might say, x is soluble if and only if x would dissolve if x were immersed under normal conditions.[8] This would seem to solve some problems via physical projectibility (à la Nelson Goodman)[9] if it didn't beg the question of what

---

[6]For a discussion of these various ways to understand probability in the context of biology, see Elliott Sober, *Philosophy of Biology*, 2nd ed. (Boulder, Co.: Westview Press, 2000), chapter 3; S. Mills and J. Beatty, "The Propensity Interpretation of Fitness," *Philosophy of Science* 46 (1979): 263–88; J. Beatty and S. Finsen, "Rethinking the Propensity Interpretation: A Peak Inside Pandora's Box" in Michael Ruse, ed., *What the Philosophy of Biology Is* (Dordrecht: Reidel, 1989):17–30.

[7]This is also the problem with so-called exhaustive induction in which one is theoretically forced to examine each and every possible case (when this is clearly impractical).

[8]This example comes from Elliott Sober, *Philosophy of Biology*, 2nd ed. (Boulder, CO: Westview, 2000), p. 63.

[9]Nelson Goodman, *Fact, Fiction, and Forecast* (Cambridge, MA: Harvard University Press, 1955), Ch. 3–4.

is a "normal condition." Unfortunately, this problem leaves the propensity approach in a similar condition as the subjective interpretation approach.

What, then, should our disposition be concerning statistical confirmation? This is a difficult question and deserves a book of its own. It is not our point here to enter into a lengthy discussion on how probability in biology ought to be interpreted. But the reader should be aware that this is by no means an exact mechanical measure in biology. It is even possible that it is not the same for each science.[10] Instead, it is the intent here to suggest that probability is not an adequately fixed concept through which absolute informed consent can be achieved. Since the foundation of the experimental principle itself is based upon relatively low numbers (such as 200–300 patients in some experimental control group), the best one can achieve is a propensity-style understanding of the possibilities of success. But at worst, this may be merely a subjectively interpreted frequency of events. Such nuances are difficult enough for the philosophers of biology who have studied statistics, but they are probably opaque for the average person. Thus, the couple contemplating whether or not to have children based upon genetic screening must take the results of their tests (under the present state of knowledge) as leaning in a particular direction but not factually conclusive.

The second group of potential parents includes those who are already pregnant and must evaluate the tests and then decide whether or not to proceed with the pregnancy.[11] This is a more complicated scenario than the last one because there is another entity involved: the potential person/embryo within the mother. Unlike the first example in which the couple is contemplating whether or not to *try to conceive*, in this case, the couple has already conceived. The issue of genetic testing in this case revolves around the issue of probability (involved in all experimental tests) and the issue of abortion (one of the possible reactions to the test).

This situation creates an ethical problem for the medical community. How should they advise (counsel) their patients? There are many issues here. For example, at the beginning, what should count as an adequate reason for an abortion? Boylan holds that there must be a significant threat to the worldview of the mother. But what counts as significant? Might it be the case that this is rather subjective? Not if we return to the Table of Embeddedness. The goods that the parents will lose must be weighed against the depiction of the fetus and the development of the pregnancy (with a fetus past the first

---

[10]What we are thinking of here is the Uncertainty Principle. In the Uncertainty Principle (the philosophy of physics), only actual frequencies seen in the context of the Law of Large Numbers will do. This would not be a fruitful interpretation of statistics from the point of view of biology.

[11]With respect to abortion, Boylan's position is set out in his article, "The Abortion Debate in the 21st Century" in Michael Boylan, ed., *Medical Ethics* (Upper Saddle River, NJ: Prentice Hall, 2000). Brown accepts many of the tenets of this article, but is rather more reluctant than Boylan to find justifications for abortion.

trimester demanding significantly more respect because of its developing powers of rational consciousness).

There is also the distinction of "being disabled" (e.g., Downs syndrome or other physical or mental disability) versus "having an incurable disease." To be disabled means that one has either an abnormal body and/or an abnormal mind. The agent is not at risk to die or to be in intense, incurable pain. To have an incurable disease means that the agent will (according to the best understanding of modern science) die or be in intense, incurable pain. In the first case, some argue that potentiality disabled people have no right to live. The foundation of this argument lies in two propositions:

a.   To have a disabled child is to incur a great deal of discomfort that will negatively affect a parent's ability to actualize her own life plan (a.k.a., a life-enhancing Secondary Good of Agency)

b.   To have a disabled child is to sentence another human being to a life of misery.

The first proposition (a) acknowledges that a disabled child will be a burden and will change the parent's lifestyle. But is this a significant level of threat? It may seem so, depending upon the agent.

The second (b) makes the paternalistic assertion that unless one is "normal," life is not worth living. This proposition is patently wrong. There are countless examples of severely disabled individuals who have enriched families, communities, and society.[12]

Thus, if parents wish to abort because of disability, they should recognize that it is their own convenience that is at issue (a self-oriented consideration) and not that of the child (an action of compassion on behalf of another).

When one's child has an incurable disease or a condition that will incline it to unremitting pain, then (b) is an authentic alternative.

These judgments become more acute as the pregnancy advances. But these issues essentially reduce the existence of any grounds that might legitimate the termination of a pregnancy.

It is also the case that "testing for some genetic predisposition" automatically stigmatizes that trait and inclines prospective parents to believe that the phenotypic trait is a defect that should be "treated" (either by genetic therapy or by abortion). What counts as the normal variation between people and what counts as an abnormality? We believe that there is a strong tendency to treat all differences that are socially inconvenient or competitively disadvantageous as "deformities." (For a continued discussion of this issue, see Chapter Nine, "Secondary Good Enhancement.")

Since abortion is such a controversial issue, physicians and others involved in genetic counseling (the consequence of genetic screening) incur a

---

[12]The examples are almost endless, but just to name a few, Helen Keller, Franklin D. Roosevelt, Stephen W. Hawking, Lawrence Becker, and many more.

tremendous responsibility.[13] As in any medical situation in which something happens contrary to one's worldview expectations, individuals are extremely stressed, creating the possibility of exploitation (paternalism in the bad sense). Some genetic counselor with his or her own agenda to promote can push a patient one way or the other. Informed consent becomes difficult.

Both of the authors of this book are strongly against the genetic testing of prospective parents for the sake of secondary good enhancement. This creates the sort of enhancement/eugenics that is totally unacceptable because it makes one's basic goods of potential agency dependent upon whether or not the fetus *seems to be* a trophy child. The Table of Embeddedness is not based upon merit and prowess, and this is an unacceptable reason for abortion/enhancement therapy.

We are also against abortion for the sake of gender or sexual orientation. These facts about a child do not pose the sort of threat to the mother that may justify an abortion. The argument that a culture may so devalue women that it is rational to abort female fetuses is wrong. It is likewise wrong to abort a fetus just because of sexual orientation. The argument to support this is similar to that given about disabilities in that it gives too much sway to a parent's idiosyncratic preference. In order for an abortion to be legitimate (according to Boylan), the threat against the mother must be so significant that it outweighs the developing intrinsic consideration that should be attributed to the embryo. We must be careful not to give too much weight to idiosyncratic preferences that are divorced from the foundations of action.

C. Employers.

Before we begin, it is important to understand that not all businesses are based upon the principle of exploitation. In a moral world, an employer will seek to provide goods and services that meet basic human needs at a profit margin not too far away from the standard manufacturing formula of

---

[13]This question (particularly in the context of the rights of the disabled) has been discussed by Ruth Chadwick, et al., "Genetic Screening and Ethics: European Perspectives," *Journal of Medicine and Philosophy* 23.8 (1998): 255–73; Wolfram Henn, "Predictive Diagnosis and Genetic Screening: Manipulation of Fate?" *Perspectives in Biology and Medicine* 41.2 (winter 1998): 282–89; and "Genetic Screening with the DNA Chip: A New Pandora's Box?" *Journal of Medical Ethics* 25 (1999): 200–203. Then there is the issue of consistent rules for counseling patients. This is enormously complicated. For some of these issues, see Bernadette Modell, et al., "Informed Choice in Genetic Screening for Thalassaemia During Pregnancy: Audit from a National Confidential Inquiry," *British Medical Journal* 320.5 (February, 2000): 337–42; Robin L. Bennett, et al., "Inconsistencies in Genetic Counseling and Screening for Consanguineous Couples and Their Offspring: The Need for Practice Guidelines," *Genetics in Medicine* 1.6 (1999): 286–92. The relationship of these decisions to individual autonomy is explored by Colin Gavaghan, "Deregulating the Genetic Supermarket: Preimplantation, Screening, Future People, and the Harm Principle," *Cambridge Quarterly of Healthcare Ethics* 9 (2000): 242–80.

materials + labor × 4 = retail cost of the finished product.[14] Some employers sincerely desire to make their workplace a safe and congenial place and seek to share the profits of a successful business with the employees.

However, in the real world, it is probably more often the case that those individuals drawn into careers in business are driven by the desire to make more money. In the case of business owners, this takes the form of trying to find ways in which to cut costs or to increase productivity. Both of these can involve exploitation—especially when employees are seen as mere extensions of their computers. One doesn't buy a computer without examining the hardware in order to ascertain whether or not it fully meets one's needs. Similarly, one might wish to know as much as possible about a worker before he is hired. If you know that he has a tendency toward alcoholism, then you might not hire him (even if he doesn't drink). One can imagine sophisticated tests of the future that might predict levels of hormones that might be secreted upon negative sign stimuli (e.g., anger). No one wants a hostile employee; therefore, the economically prudent thing to do would be to avoid hiring such a worker.[15]

In addition to preemployment tests, it is possible that present employees, too, might be subjected to these tests so that the organization might streamline its workforce toward more efficiency and greater profits.

What is wrong with these approaches is that they inherently dehumanize the agent because they view the transaction only from the employer's point of view. Certainly, it might be more efficient for the employer to test all employees for their tendencies toward sickness and accident. It might also be more efficient if the employer could put people in the houses of his choice and control the employees' lives as much as possible (as many employers did in the late nineteenth century and early twentieth century with factory towns). But this ignores the other half of the transaction: the worker. In order to exercise her basic human rights (a level two Basic Good), she must feel free from assault from her employer (a level one Basic Good). Thus, on this line of argument, mandatory genetic screening for purposes of employment is unethical. Forcing an employee to undergo genetic tests as a precondition of employment (as hitherto described) or as a precondition for continued employment is an instance of unwarranted bodily harm and is thus prohibited by the Table of Embeddedness.

It is also an instance of exploitation in several respects. First, it makes a person accountable for that which she has no control: her genetic makeup.

---

[14]For an exposition of some of these principles, see Michael Boylan, "The Principle of Fair Competition" in Michael Boylan, ed., *Business Ethics* (Upper Saddle River, NJ: Prentice Hall, 2001).

[15]Another twist upon this scenario is the activities of insurance companies. Insurance companies long to obtain further information upon their statistical sample space so that they might more precisely actuarially rate the proposed risk. Though this may be the most "efficient" way to operate, it is certainly not the best. Insurance companies need to be restrained from their desire for efficiency just in case their proposed action will make them act immorally. For a discussion of a few of these issues, see Ami S. Jaeger and William F. Mulholland, "Impact of Genetic Privacy Legislation on Insurer Behavior," *Genetic Testing* 4.1 (2000): 31–42.

Penalizing anyone for her genetic composition is contrary to the notion of fair deserts. We should be rewarded or penalized only for what we have done. In this way, deserts theory is always *retrodictive*. It looks to what you have done and says that as a result of these actions, A, B, and C, you deserve φ. Genetic tests are, by design, *predictive* so that they will look ahead to what *might be*. The outcome is not certain. The reason for believing that the outcome might occur lies in factors beyond the agent's control. We deserve only what is in our control and is the result of past actions. Therefore, there is no ethically justified reason for either requiring a preemployment genetic test or for penalizing someone for the results of the same. To do so violates the terms of deserts theory. To fail to respect deserts theory is to be exploitative. Freedom from exploitation is a level two Basic Good. Thus, on this line of argument, genetic screening for employment is unethical.

Second, it is exploitative because the good that the employer wishes to achieve, "the ability to utilize one's real and portable property in the manner she chooses," is a useful Secondary Good. At the very least, being forced to undergo genetic testing as a precondition of employment (or to retain one's job) is to pit a medium to low medium good of agency against one of the Basic Goods of Agency (e.g., basic human rights). To force supervenience of a lower good of agency (because it benefits the agent) over a higher good of agency for another is to be exploitative. Thus, this behavior, too, is unethical and should be avoided.

Therefore, because genetic testing is exploitative, represents unwarranted bodily harm, and otherwise denies agents of Basic Goods of Agency, it should be sanctioned.

If this argument is sound, then various subsidiary applications also apply. For example, it would be immoral to supply employers with information that they have no legitimate need to know. Let's consider an employee's medical records. It is important to keep confidential medical records private for similar reasons. Employers have no moral right to this information, and they should not be allowed to use economic leverage in order to extract it from those who wish to work for them. Likewise, in countries in which governments work very closely with big business, it would be unethical for those governments to supply businesses with data on citizens that it might have because of its sovereign status in order to control and exploit citizens. There are many such extensions of this sort of case through which some agent works to obtain the information that is, in turn, used by businesses unethically in order that they might make higher profits and obtain stability that is bought at the cost of basic human liberties.

D. Insurance Companies.

Insurance companies have not garnered the best reputation when it comes to balancing social conscience with their almost insatiable desire to obtain data upon those they intend to insure. The insurance companies wish to minimize their risk. After all, they are in the gambling business—they make their money by transferring risk from an individual or company to themselves for a price. In order to make the transfer economically feasible, the insurance companies require two things: (a) as much relevant information as possible and (b) a large pool of applicants so that the Law of Large Numbers works in their favor. Factor (b) is a function of the sales department. Factor (a) is what is at issue here. If a health or life insurer had unlimited information on all its applicants/policyholders, then it might be able to more accurately tailor premiums so that they exceeded expenses by as much as possible. The insurers claim that it is their right as a business to be able to garner as much money as possible (the espoused goal of most businesses). But this argument is hard to sustain when one considers the history of insurance. Insurance companies began as cooperatives of shareholders who shared profits and losses through increased and decreased premiums. In this way, they were a social institution not aimed at greed, since the policyholders, themselves, all shared in the ups and downs of the companies. The mission of insurance in these circumstances is for people to group together collectively in order to protect individuals from the "slings and arrows of outrageous fortune." These insurance companies are called mutual insurance companies. It is this mission of insurance that we endorse.

However, beginning in the 1970s, a trend began (and still continues) to make insurance companies stock-owned companies. In these companies, the stockholders instead of the policyholders are the owners of the company. In this new environment, insurance companies tend even more toward the single goal of profit maximization. They seek to acquire information on policyholders and potential policyholders with the purpose of surcharging or eliminating individuals who might pose a greater risk to the corporate bottom line. This is certainly different from the mission of mutual insurance companies.

Because of this change in the insurance environment, various excesses that insurance companies practiced in the past are even more accentuated.[16] These include (on the life insurance side) creating differential rates for African Americans and Caucasians. Such behaviors are unethical because (even if they are borne out by statistical correlation), they do not portray the *reasons* why this is the case. For example, let us hypothetically suppose that life insurers in 1970 were calculating rate tables based upon the previous 40 years of data

---

[16]For a discussion of the context of genetic testing and insurance practices, see W. F. Anderson, "Human Gene Therapy," *Nature* 392 (1998): 25–30; L. O. Gostin, "Genetic Discrimination: The Use of Genetically Based Diagnostic and Prognostic Tests by Employers and Insurers," *American Journal of Legal Medicine* 17 (1991): 109; P. Haim, "Insurers, Consumers, and Testing: The AIDS Experience," *Law, Medicine, and Health Care* 15 (1987): 212–22; K. L. Hudson, et al., "Genetic Discrimination and Health Insurance: An Urgent Need for Reform," *Science* 270 (1995): 391–93; A. Jaeger, "An Insurance View on Genetic Testing," *Forum for Applied Research and Public Policy* 8 (1993): 23–25; R. J. Pokorski, "Insurance Underwriting in the Genetic Era," *American Journal of Human Genetics* 60 (1997): 205–16; I. M. Verma, "Gene Therapy—Promises, Problems, and Prospects," *Nature* 389 (1997): 239–42; and S. T. Warren and D. I. Nelson, "Advances in Molecular Analysis of Fragile X Syndrome," *Journal of the American Medical Association* 271 (1994): 536–42.

(1930–1970). Let us also suppose that African Americans had a much higher mortality rate due to being greatly overrepresented in the ranks of the poor.[17] Let us also suppose that African Americans were so overrepresented because they were the victims of Jim Crow laws and other vestiges of slavery, and that lynching also affected the mortality rate of African Americans. Let us also suppose that lynching is an unjustified and immoral action. Given these facts, it is entirely possible that African Americans *did* have a higher mortality rate than Americans of European descent. Does this mean that they should be singled out for higher rates? Absolutely not! People should not be penalized by social institutions for that which is not their fault. Deserts theory suggests that x deserves ϕ just in case ϕ is the logical consequence of some prior action. This is equally true whether ϕ is something good or something bad. In the case at hand, African Americans were penalized with higher insurance premiums (ϕ) even though there was no action-oriented reason for ascribing ϕ to x. In fact, it is likely that the ascription of ϕ to x is not due to x's actions but to the actions of other agents, y (i.e., those perpetrating racism upon x). To penalize x (African Americans) for the actions of y (the racist majority society) is to punish x for being victimized.

Mere statistical correlation of health or mortality to insurance costs ignores the actual social dynamics of *why* the correlation exists in the first place and whether or not it is deserved. (In fact, it is generally held to be the case that in medicine one should accept patients as they are without passing judgment on how they got that way.[18]) At the very least, insurers should not be allowed to take genetic factors into account when setting premiums or offering coverage. To act otherwise would be to create a genetic underclass that would go against the grain of deserts theory, which lies at the heart of most theories of distributive justice.

E. Forensic Population Research.

A genetic file on every person in a society would provide physical evidence that might be an effective means of matching a criminal to a deed, as do fingerprint files. One difference is that the only people in fingerprint files are those who have been put in the database because they have committed a crime or for other reasons (such as job clearance) have volunteered to have their fingerprints put into the central files.

---

[17]Being among the ranks of the poor, per se, will not increase the mortality rate (though lack of nutrition and health care are certainly disadvantages). However, when one considers what it is like to be poor and to be a part of a persecuted minority group, then there are many possible physical disorders that may occur. The fact that hypertension (though the etiology of this disorder is not completely understood) is so high in African Americans leads one to believe that it may be environmentally caused and much of this cause may be attributable directly or indirectly to discrimination.

[18]For a discussion of this position, see Rosamond Rhodes, "A Review of Ethical Issues in Transplantation," *The Mount Sinai Journal of Medicine* 61.1 (1994): 77–82.

However, there are some other critical differences between fingerprint files and DNA files. The most important is that DNA files are more than mere identifiers; they give a significant amount of information about an individual, which can be used against the person. For example, if the DNA files showed that a person had the gene for alcoholism and that person was a prominent member of society, then this piece of information might be used as leverage (i.e., blackmail) in order to get special preferment, providing a great potential for corruption. In order to get to the root of this grave potential for evil, we must consider what the likely consequences are of such a program. The widespread creation of genetic databases for the purposes of forensic files poses a danger regarding privacy and human dignity as well as informed consent. These two areas are linked, but let us examine each in order.

We hold that the right to privacy is not absolute but is contingent upon other moral claims. This is not a position of Utilitarianism, but a recognition that there are times in which a person must give up privacy when others in his community face a pressing loss of Basic Goods. For example, if there were a fire or other natural disaster that occurred in town A, then people in town B ethically should help the people from town A find food, clothing, and shelter until the process of reconstructing their homes begins. It doesn't matter that some of the people in town B would rather not be bothered because they wish to maintain their privacy and isolation. The loss of Basic Goods by the people in town A and the correlative nature of rights claims and duties compel the people of town B to help.

However, the prospect of helping police create genetic databases is different from the scenario of natural disaster. The creation of this database is only remotely (and not proximately) related to helping specific people and because the danger of personal harm is much greater. For example, it is often unclear who might obtain access to the genetic records of John Doe. If governments, insurance companies, or local employers have any access, the potential exists for all the problems outlined earlier.[19]

Also, it is a mark of autonomy and dignity to have control of your body (as much as possible). To be pressured or forced into participating in a widespread genetic mapping of a population is to fail to respect the dignity of the citizens. It is to treat them as means only in order that they might give blood for the genetic file. "Mary Lane" is seen only as a provider of genetic materials necessary for the grand conceptual scheme to be completed.

Obviously, this now runs into informed consent difficulties. If Mary's dignity is to be considered (a level two Basic Good), then she must be allowed to say no. The very principle of informed consent in research situations involves

---

[19]For a further discussion of some of these issues concerning the abuse of genetic data, see J. McEwen, "Forensic DNA Data Banking by State Crime Laboratories," *American Journal of Human Genetics* 56 (1995): 1487–92 and W. F. Mulholland and A. S. Jaeger, "Genetic Privacy and Discrimination: A Comprehensive Analysis of State Legislation," *Jurimetrics* 39 (1999): 317–26.

the unforced choice of subjects to engage in the project or to decline to engage in the project.

The very dynamics of a comprehensive genetic testing program of a population creates the situation in which a conflict of interests exists. On the one hand, the police need a very large sample and so there is incentive to do whatever is necessary to bring this about. On the other hand is the citizen's right to make his own choice through a careful process of informed consent (that may significantly lower the sample and may, in fact, invalidate it).

In addition to this is the unfortunate history of police departments' actions in the past. There are some (perhaps many?) who are attracted to police work because it offers them the legal opportunity to exert their dominant presence among others. In this situation, it may be inevitable that coercion and *not* implied consent is the order of the day.[20]

If the police research team needs to cross the line and violate the rules of implied consent or otherwise to fail to respect the privacy and dignity of the potential research subject, then that police research team is acting unethically in its "means" and has crossed the boundaries of the limits of science into forbidden territory.

In order to address these concerns, we believe that the same protocols that have been observed in the creation of fingerprint files (i.e., only charged criminals—who if found innocent will have their files deleted from the database—and those volunteering to be profiled will be put into the base) should be followed. There should be no widespread genetic databases because of the interference with the issues of autonomy and informed consent.

Genetic testing and genetic counseling are complicated issues because so much is merely an extension of existing practice. What makes it different when we add the term "genetic"? The principal answer (excluding the germ-line risk) is that the process of implementation is far more powerful and the precision of it far too imprecise. Thus, even when one would seek to support genetic testing as supplanting traditional methods in medicine, it should always proceed at a prudent pace. This prudence is dictated by the nature of the powerful tool. Of course, there are other instances in which genetic testing, because of its greater precision, presents ethical challenges that a responsible society must heed.

---

[20]The conjecture that some police are overly violent by nature is impossible to prove. However, some support for this notion can be found in Lee Sigelman, "Police Brutality and Public Perceptions of Racial Discrimination: A Tale of Two Beatings," *Political Research Quarterly* 50.4 (1997): 777–93; Alexa P. Freeman, "Unscheduled Departures," *Hastings Law Journal* 47.3 (1996): 677–779; and Errol P. Mendes, ed., *Democratic Policing and Accountability: Global Perspectives* (Aldershot, UK: Ashgate, 1999).

chapter nine

Somatic Gene Therapy

I. WHAT IS SOMATIC GENE THERAPY?

Somatic gene therapy is, for the purposes of this book, gene therapy to correct the nonfunctioning or malfunctioning of a single gene in either a monogenic disease or a multifactoral disorder; and therapy that will affect the patient only. (This means that there is no interference with or crossover into the germ line.) We also consider *enhancement* that will affect the patient only.

A. Monogenic Disorders.

Let us begin by setting out what monogenic therapy comprises. Many congenital disorders, such as cystic fibrosis and sickle cell disease, are due to nonfunctioning or malfunctioning proteins caused by a mutation in a single gene. Although drugs may control the symptomatology, somatic gene therapy aims to "cure" the disease by the introduction of a fully functional and expressible gene into tissues or the affected organs within an organism, resulting in permanent correction of the genetic defect.

B. Multifactoral Disorders.

In contrast to monogenic disease, many diseases are not due to mutations in a single gene but are the consequence of mutations in interacting multiple genes often combined with environmental factors, and in some cases exposure to infectious agents. In these cases, correcting or mutating a single gene will not lead to a "cure" directly, but the somatic gene therapy may improve the body's natural ability to defend, heal, or alter itself. Somatic gene therapy in multifactoral cases is therefore extremely broad, theoretically covering gene therapy of malignancy, treatment or control of infections such as HIV infection and inflammatory disorders, to genetic treatments to increase one's height, decrease one's waist, and/or improve one's intelligence. The methods used for multifactoral therapy are no different from other forms of somatic gene therapy. However, concerns for long-term expression of the gene product or generation of an immune response to a vector may or may not be relevant.

We also consider somatic gene therapy in the context of improving a healthy person. These are also multifactor cases; hence, their inclusion in this chapter. "Healthy" is a rather difficult concept that is under some review.[1] In the case of infectious diseases, the definition of healthy is easier. When one brings somatic malformations into the picture, however, it becomes more complicated. What is a malformation? Some might say that homosexuality is a malformation. Others might say lack of stature is a malformation. Still others might bring eugenics and racism into the equation. (Remember that Aristotle defined a woman as a deformed man.[2]) This second category is dealt with more extensively in the next section of this chapter.

C. Secondary Good Enhancement.

By "enhancement" we mean secondary good enhancement—the good in question is not basic to agency. In other words, it is not *essential* to those goods described in the Table of Embeddedness as Basic Goods (see Chapter One). Others have discussed enhancement as a rather intuitive concept [e.g., growth therapy for a child below the third percentile (justified therapy) versus growth therapy so that a child might be able to play center instead of power forward on the basketball team (unjustified enhancement)]. The advantage of grounding everything in a theory of action is that the proposed good now has a much clearer demarcation of what is enhancement and *why*. Thus, we

---

[1]The two poles here are viewing "healthy" within the context of one's given soma type as opposed to an ideal soma type.

[2]*Generation of Animals* 728 a 18; c.f. 737a 28.

will stipulate that genetic enhancement in the context of somatic therapy will concern itself with secondary goods that have no germ-line interaction.

II. HOW IS SOMATIC GENE THERAPY PRESENTLY BEING PERFORMED?

A. Monogenic Disorders.

Although theoretically the disease mutation could be repaired *in situ* using either ribozymes or oligonucleotides, to date all human somatic gene therapy for monogenic diseases has been performed by the addition of functional genes using either modified viral vectors or DNA/lipid complexes. Currently, approximately 10 percent of the more than 300 clinical protocols approved or under review throughout the world are for monogenic disorders, with the most treated disease being cystic fibrosis. It is too early to talk about patients being "cured" by gene therapy, but recent results from two children treated with retroviral vectors for severe combined immunodeficiency-X1 disease are very promising.[3] They had improved cellular and clinical responses and have been able to live normal lives without additional therapy for more than ten months after treatment. In addition, initial results of treating three patients with hemophilia using AAV-based vectors also look encouraging. (See box.)

Currently, gene therapy protocols have been initiated or are pending on sixteen different monogenic diseases (Table 9.1). As can be seen, a wide variety of vectors and organs are being targeted, depending on the disease presentation.

To date, all protocols have been for treatment of infants, children, or adults, but with the promise of "cure" by gene therapy beginning to be realized, *in utero* gene therapy has been proposed.[4] Prenatal gene therapy would have the advantage of treating severe and life-threatening disease before birth, thus repairing the gene defect before the production of most of the disease complications become manifest. In addition, animal studies and culture experiments show that gene therapy of fetal cells appears to be both more efficient and less likely to induce an immune response than postnatal gene therapy. However, prenatal gene therapy has potential risks for both the mother and fetus, and a much greater potential for inadvertent insertion into or mutation of the germ line. Further studies, especially in animal models, are required before clinical studies of prenatal gene therapy are likely to be approved.[5]

---

[3]Marina Cavazzana-Calvo et al. "Gene Therapy of Human Severe Combined Immunodeficiency (SCID)-X1 Disease," *Science* 288 (2000): 669–75.

[4]Of course, many prenatal procedures may violate our fire wall provision against interaction with the germ line.

[5]Recombinant DNA advisory committee. "Regulatory Issues. Prenatal Gene Transfer: Scientific, Medical and Ethical Issues," *Human Gene Therapy* 11 (2000): 1211–29.

Evidence for Gene Transfer and Expression of Factor IX in Hemophilia B Patients Treated with an AAV Vector

Mark A. Kay et al.
Nature Genetics 24.3 (2000): 257–61.

Hemophilia B or Christmas disease (named for the first patient described with this distinct form of hemophilia) is a rare type of bleeding disorder due to mutations in one of the clotting factors, factor IX. Patients with hemophilia B cannot make effective fibrin clots and, depending on the level of factor IX activity, suffer from spontaneous bleeding into their joints, brain, and other organs with not only severely disabling but life-threatening consequences. The only treatment is with factor IX administration at the time of bleeding or in severe cases prophylactically. However, it is known that raising the factor IX activity to only greater than 1 percent of normal can modify the disease from severe to moderate and prevent most of the joint damage and life-threatening complications. With such a low level of expression required for therapeutic response, hemophilia B is an appropriate disease for genetic therapy trials.

Although adeno-associated vectors (see Chapter Six) can encapsidate only relatively short lengths of DNA, it has been possible to produce AAV-based vectors that express factor IX in tissue culture and in mice. In addition, vectors expressing the canine factor IX have been used to successfully treat hemophilic dogs, with the dogs remaining stable for more than 2½ years after a single treatment.

As part of a dose escalation study of the safety of AAV vectors encoding human factor XI, this paper describes three men with factor IX activity of < 1 percent who were treated with the lowest dose (2×10^{11} copies/kg). There was no evidence of toxicity or significant side effects following intramuscular injection of the vector. Biopsy of the site six weeks later demonstrated local expression of factor IX. Two of the patients showed a significant decrease in requirement of factor IX in the 100 days following treatment (the third case rarely required factor IX administration), and in one of the patients the levels of factor IX following treatment were recorded above 1 percent. Thus this treatment holds real promise of being able to convert severe hemophilia B to a less severe or even mild form.

B. Multifactoral Disorders.

In contrast to the original predictions that monogenic diseases would be the primary target of gene therapy, multifactoral genetic therapy is the most widely practiced form of genetic therapy today, with the vast majority of currently approved protocols being for the treatment of malignant disease. This is partly due to the difficulties in getting efficient and long-term expression of gene products that are critical for monogenic gene therapy, but also because there are only a limited number of individuals with monogenic disorders,

TABLE 9.1 Monogenic Diseases Treated by Gene Therapy (Active or Proposed Gene Therapy Protocols)

DISEASE	GENE	VECTORS	TARGET
Severe combined immune deficiency syndrome	Adenosine deaminase (ADA)	Retrovirus (2)[a]	Lymphocytes or blood stem cells
Familial hypercholesterolemia	Low density lipoprotein receptor	Retrovirus	Liver
Cystic fibrosis	Cystic fibrosis transmembrane conductance regulator	Adenovirus (10) Liposomes (2) AAV (4)	Respiratory tract
Gaucher's disease	Glucocerebrosidase	Retrovirus (3)	Blood stem cells
Alpha-1 antitrypsin disease	Alpha-1 antitrypsin	Liposome (2)	Respiratory tract
Hunter syndrome	Iduronate-2-sulfatase	Retrovirus (1)	Lymphocytes
Chronic granulomatous disease	gp47 phox/gp91 phox	Retrovirus (3)	Blood stem cells
Purine nucleoside phosphorylase deficiency	Purine nucleoside phosphorylase	Retrovirus (1)	Lymphocytes
Ornithine transcarbamylase deficiency	Ornithine transcarbamylase	Adenovirus (1)	Liver
Canavan disease	Aspartoacylase	Liposome (1) Adenovirus (2) AAV (1)	Brain
Hemophilia A	Factor VIII	Plasmid DNA (1) Retrovirus (1) Adenovirus (1)	Fibroblasts
Hemophilia B	Factor IX	AAV (2)	Muscle, liver
Fanconi's anemia	Fanc A, Fanc C gene	Retrovirus (2)	Blood stem cells
Gyrate atrophy	Ornithine delta aminotransferase	Not known (1)	Skin cells
Limb girdle muscular dystrophy	Sarcolan gene	AAV (1)	Muscle
Fabry disease	Alpha-galactosidase	Retrovirus (1)	Mesenchymal stem cells
Amyotropic lateral sclerosis	EAAT 2 gene	AAV (1)	Brain

[a]Number of different protocols with this type of vector.

therefore limiting the potential market for such therapies.[6] In contrast, treatment of malignant disease and other common diseases by gene therapy involves a huge market and creates great interest in the pharmaceutical industry. Hence, gene therapy is one of the fastest growing areas of experimental medicine in the United States.

Multifactoral genetic therapy for malignant disease can take a number of approaches, usually by enlisting the body's immune system to target and kill the cancerous cells. In many protocols, treatment is by the addition of genes (tumor necrosis factor, interleukin-2, interleukin-12) to enhance the immune response against the cancer cells, or suicide genes may be targeted to the cells themselves or to kill cells in the immediate area of a tumor (i.e., with HSV-tk, or p53) and also to stimulate a specific immune response. Alternatively, the malignant cells may be made more immunogenic (by the addition of B7 antigens) or specific antitumor antigens may be administered to initiate an antitumor cell response. In addition, gene therapy can be used as an adjuvant with conventional chemotherapy, with the addition of genes such as the multiple drug resistance (MDR) gene to bone marrow cells to protect them from the chemotherapy toxicity.

Inducing an immune response by gene therapy is not confined to antitumor responses, and genetic immunization is becoming a popular tool for developing novel vaccination strategies against infectious diseases. Not surprisingly, there is a great deal of interest in using a gene therapy approach to develop both protective vaccines and treatment strategies for HIV infection. Similar strategies are being pursued to develop DNA vaccines for malaria, hepatitis, and Ebola and even influenza viruses.

The identification of factors (proteins) that are involved in new blood vessel development has opened up the way for the development of gene therapy protocols for the treatment of a variety of cardiovascular disorders, including angina and heart disease, and limb ischemia (see box). Similarly, protocols are being developed for tissue regeneration, treatment of neurological disorders, prevention of tissue rejection following transplantation, and even treatment of allergies.[7]

---

[6]This is a real problem because it concerns the role that private companies play in the research marketplace. In this arena, the professional dictum of enhancing the well-being of the sick is not of principal concern. Rather, it is helping those sick people who can make the company a profit (because there are enough of them who will be paying customers). This creates a conflict of interest and can skew medicine away from its own professional standards.

[7]Gaetano Romano et al., "Latest Developments in Gene Transfer Technology: Acheivements, Perspectives and Controversies over Therapeutic Applications," *Stem Cells* 18 (2000): 19–39.

Left Ventricular Eletromechanical Mapping to Assess Efficacy of ph VEGF(165) Gene Transfer for Therapeutic Angiogenesis in Chronic Myocardial Ischemia

Peter R. Vale et al.
Circulation 102.9 (2000): 965–74

Vascular endothelial growth factor (VEGF) is a potent stimulator of neovascularization, and animal studies have suggested that local release or production of VEGF may be of benefit for ischemic disease of both myocardial and skeletal muscle. This paper describes the results of treating 13 patients with chronic stable angina who had failed conventional treatment, including drugs and cardiac surgery, with gene therapy using DNA expressing VEGF.

The approach used by the authors is unusual for gene therapy; it uses plasmid DNA directly as the vector for delivery of the 165 amino-acid isoform of VEGF, thus reducing the problems inherent in using some of the other viral-based vectors for gene therapy. However, in the current protocol, the plasmid is directly injected into the myocardial muscle following mini-thoracotomy, thus obviously limiting the feasibility of using this approach on a larger number of patients. Following gene therapy, increased levels of VEGF could be detected in the plasma, and there was evidence of symptomic improvement with a significant decrease both in the frequency of angina and in nitroglycerin consumption. In addition, there was objective evidence of improved myocardial function and myocardial perfusion scores.

Although the numbers are limited, the requirement for surgery to administer the plasmid means that there are no control or placebo patients, the positive results of this study offer the posibility of gene therapy as a treatment in diseases not generally thought of as being amenable to gene therapy. As the accompanying editorial emphasizes,[a] similar results have been obtained in studies using VEGF to treat skeletal muscle ischemia, and by other groups using viral vector-based gene therapy. However, as is also pointed out, there is no evidence so far that this approach will prevent heart attacks, and there is a long way to go before this kind of treatment is standard for treating heart attacks.

[a]Cam Patterson and Marschall S. Runge, "Therapeutic myocardial angiogenesis via vascular endothelial growth factor gene therapy. Moving on down the road."

C. Secondary Good Enhancement

Although in some cases medical treatments and plastic surgery are performed for secondary good enhancement, at present the practice of gene therapy for secondary good enhancement is not being performed.

III. The Advantages of Somatic Gene Therapy.

A. Monogenic Disorders.

To determine the advantages of somatic gene therapy, we must refer back to both the mission of medicine and to the ethical principle of "the duty to rescue." The dual poles of the physician's duty are the promise contained in the Hippocratic Oath to "concern myself with the well-being of the sick" and "do no harm" (see Chapter Two).

Thus, if somatic gene therapy is a more promising treatment than anything else available, then it would be justified by the professional dictum to be concerned with the well-being of the sick. If another therapy were equally efficacious and well established as being safe, then that course would most fully satisfy this claim.

In this way, somatic gene therapy falls under any other experimental therapy guidelines. If one were proposing a new drug to treat a specific illness, it would have to be tested, and few would complain that offering a new substance into the body constituted grounds for complaint. Somatic gene therapy is no different relative to the provision in the Oath to concern oneself with the well-being of the sick. When a new, uniquely beneficial treatment exists, then barring other considerations, it should be offered as a therapy option.

But what might these "other considerations" be? Obviously, they would fall under the category of doing no harm. What are the types of harm that could be caused? These can be classified as harm to the patient, harm to the environment, and harm to future generations. The foundation for these harms has been discussed in Chapter Two. If it were the case that the proposed therapy violated any of these harms, then the proposed end must be judged as wrong because doing harm to the patient, environment, and/or future generations is itself immoral. As we have seen from Chapter Seven, science may not pursue immoral ends—even if it extends the boundaries of knowledge or wins the physician a Nobel Prize.

This does not appear to be the case with somatic gene therapy, however. The way we have narrowed our definition to single-gene disorders with no germ-line interaction precludes the sort of concerns outlined earlier. Thus, upon grounds of professional practice and negative moral duties (prohibitions), there is no reason not to proceed with somatic gene therapy. Further, as we discussed at the end of Chapter One, there is an ethical duty to rescue another person whose Basic Goods of Agency are at risk. Clearly, someone who is severely ill or handicapped by a physical disorder has her Basic Goods of Agency at risk. If a treatment that has some reasonable chance of succeeding exists, then clearly it ought to be employed.

Many diseases or physical disorders have no effective therapy available. Gene therapy, if we know the gene and tissues/site of expression, could offer a real hope for a cure. Many times this hope may be a long shot, but baring the possibility of "doing harm," somatic gene therapy may be the patient's only chance for a cure.

B. Multifactoral Disorders.

It is assumed that at this level we are talking about treating diseases/abnormalities that have to do with the Basic Goods of Agency (see Chapter One). One prominent candidate in this category is cancer treatment, with its limited number of options. Traditional treatments are effective in certain clearly defined instances. For the balance, genetic therapy may be an option. A number of different strategies can be tried. The patients have a life-threatening disorder, which means that they are a good experimental risk because the "doing harm" option is less pronounced. When the patient has a lethal disorder that has no other cure, almost any other option will be an improvement—even when the possibilities of success are low.

Most cancer patients are older; therefore, there is less worry about adverse reproductive outcomes. This satisfies the sanction about harming the environment and future generations. Gene therapy among cancer patients often uses very experimental protocols that realistically will provide very limited benefit to the individual. Is it right to offer a patient a treatment that has next to no demonstrated chance of working—even in cases in which there are no proven cures? Often this is justified in the name of science or progress. The physician/researcher justifies the experimental therapy that has no proven efficacy because even if it does not work for this patient, it might advance the cause of science and bring us one step closer to a cure. Such reasoning, of course, runs the ethical risk of using another person as a means only (see Chapter One). One is morally prohibited from using either himself or another as a means only. This relates to the fact that the recognition of human dignity both in one's self and in others is a Basic Good of Agency. And Basic Goods of Agency are those to which we have the strongest moral claim (see Chapter One).

Many people are willing to try experimental protocols if they have terminal disease, either because they believe they have nothing to lose or to help the progress of science. Such cases are often relegated to ethics committees and institutional review boards (IRBs) in order to create a buffer against unethical actions against patients/experimental subjects. These unethical actions are generally centered on patient/experimental subject exploitation. In theory, such groups can safeguard our research establishment, but these ethical committees and institutional review boards also have vested interests. If research at a hospital or university is overly restricted by its IRB, new members will be added to the board to loosen the restrictions. There is a tremendous pressure to treat problems as always "modifiable." That is, an institutional review board has a definite "can do" mentality. There is *not* a lot of support for stopping some project or forbidding a procedure. Some further implications of this problem are discussed in Chapter Twelve.

The strongest case for the advantages of multifactoral gene therapy comes when we consider the Basic Goods of Human Agency. Though there may be many potential problems in implementation and possible exploitation of the patients for the researcher's own benefit and reputation, the possibility of saving lives and relieving other acute conditions justifies our continued research and experimental therapy in this area of genetic engineering.

C. Secondary Good Enhancement.

Secondary Good Enhancement is supported by its proponents as a way to improve peoples' bodies and capacities. This could take the form of individual initiatives or of societal dictates. From the point of view of society, some might contend that a concentrated program of genetic enhancement of secondary goods might enable the citizens of the society to become more uniform and possess desirable traits—such as good looks, cheerful dispositions, propensity toward hard work, and intellectual acuity.[8] Such a program might put a country front and center on the world stage as an economic and political power.[9]

From the individual's point of view, secondary good enhancement might provide the means to achieve the perfect figure, good looks, youthful vigor, and mental enhancement. All of these might contribute to increased happiness and pleasure, so secondary good enhancement could provide an easy path toward becoming the sort of person one always wanted to be. (We further discuss this form of genetic enhancement in the next section.)

IV. A CRITICAL EVALUATION OF SOMATIC GENE THERAPY.

A. Monogenic Disorders.

Given what has been said in the last section, the principal problems with somatic gene therapy are practical ones rather than moral ones. Limited by current technology, there are difficulties in getting efficient transduction of

---

[8]Of course, everyone's list here is somewhat different. For a different take on what might be considered here, see LeRoy Walters and Julie Gage Palmer, *The Ethics of Human Gene Therapy* (New York: Oxford University Press, 1997), pp. 101ff.

[9]The inclination toward societal improvement of its population has been very popular in the past among nations. For a discussion of some of these issues, see Diane B. Paul, *Controlling Heredity:1865 to the Present* (New York: Humanity Books, 1995) and Goetz Aly, Peter Chroust, and Christian Pross, *Cleansing the Fatherland: Nazi Medicine and Racial Hygiene* (Baltimore, MD: Johns Hopkins University Press, 1994).

suitable cells—especially of stem cells that may not be rapidly dividing. Currently, most vectors that are being used are retroviruses that transduce only dividing cells. Especially for hematopoietic applications, AAV vectors do not efficiently transduce hematopoietic stem cells. With any of the vectors that are used, however, getting long-term expression of genes of interest is difficult, even if there initially appears to be a high percentage of cells that have been transduced. In part, this may be due to clearance of transduced cells by the immune system, resulting from immune intolerance to the "new" protein. In addition, we are currently not inserting any promoter or controlling sequences, so that there is a limited ability, if any, to control the amount of gene product produced in cells. To date, overexpression of products has not been a problem but may be one if our ability to transduce cells becomes more efficient.

Second, the gene therapy may not be delivered or expressed in all the tissues or organs affected by the mutation: for some diseases to be treated effectively by gene therapy, the vector may need to be delivered to every cell in the body. Some tissues or organs are obviously more amenable to gene therapy, especially bone marrow stem cells that can be relatively easily harvested, manipulated in the laboratory, and then redelivered back to the body. However, many tissues or organs can be targeted only by direct injection of the vector, with only those cells in the immediate vicinity receiving the vector. To date, we are unable to administer the vector in the bloodstream and target it specifically to organs of interest (other than as directed by the blood flow itself).

A third problem concerns the vectors themselves. Most of the vectors are derived from viruses that naturally infect humans. Although a great deal of effort is taken to mutate the vectors so that they are not "replication-competent" and there is minimal homology with "wild-type virus" to limit the potential for recombination, a remote risk remains for the development of infectious or replication-competent virus, by recombination with endogenous viral sequences in the human genome or within the environment. Arguably this risk is greatest with retroviral vectors—especially with the known endogenous retroviruses that we all carry in our genome. Thus, there is the potential, however remote, for them to infect or affect other people, contacts, and so forth. This would violate the environmental sanction against doing no harm.

Fourth, the insertion of an extra (albeit corrected) gene may induce mutagenesis if inserted into another critical gene. None of the vectors currently in use allow targeted genetic insertion, and the insertion appears to be completely random. Studies are in progress to learn more about the sites of insertion of retroviral- and AAV-vectors,[10] but insertion does take place within coding sequences. In the context of treating a life-threatening disease, this may be an acceptable risk, but we need to learn more about how great the

---

[10]See for example: H. J. Kim et al. "Many multipotential gene-marked progenitor or stem cell clones contribute to hematopoiesis in nonhuman primates" *Blood* 96 (2000): 1–8.

potential for insertional mutagenesis is for both the different tissues targeted and the different vectors used. In addition, there may be long-term problems that we are not aware of due to random insertion or viral sequences. This means that (at the very least) we should advance very slowly, using all known safeguards that have been established for clinical trials.

Finally, not all monogenic diseases are equal. Should we be treating monogenic diseases because we can? (See Chapter Seven, The Limits of Science.) Who decides on the risk/rewards benefit? Prenatal treatment may be advantageous for many congenital diseases, but there are the potential problems of inadvertent germ-line gene therapy. If there is a need to detect these monogenic diseases early, should we be screening everyone? Obviously the answer to this question will have widespread implications for medical care, health insurance, and privacy.

Let us be perfectly clear about *why* we are engaged in monogenic gene therapy. It is not for the sake of profits for biotech firms or to establish a strategic position in the international marketplace. Our sole imperatives arise from the professional duty to concern ourselves with the well-being of the sick (subject to the constraint to do no harm) and our moral duty to rescue (subject to the constraints outlined in the limits of science). With these cautions before us, we can proceed at a deliberate pace.

B. Multifactoral Disorders.

In contrast to gene therapy for monogenic disease, for which the strategy is to replace a nonfunctioning gene with the corrected version, in treatment of multifactoral disease, the aim is often to modify the disease process, not necessarily to cure the patient directly. This leads us to another important practical problem. When physicians concern themselves with the well-being of the patient (as per the Hippocratic Oath), are they committed to *curing the patient* or merely to *modifying the underlying disease?* These are certainly two different missions and can have an important impact concerning which scientific research strategies to fund.

Obviously, curing the disease is the best-case scenario, but it is also the most difficult to achieve. In the long run, however, it will present the most complete solution to the problem. On the other hand, modifying the underlying disease may be easier to achieve on the short run, but inevitable side effects may make it unsuitable for a long-term approach. Thus, it would seem that both strategies must work in tandem. Working in tandem means that both approaches will be somewhat handicapped. Often the cost-benefit solution most sought after is to overfund the short-term approach until reasonable modification treatments are available and then shift research funding to the long-term solution of finding a cure.

As with other forms of somatic therapy, assorted practical problems are associated with multifactoral therapy. These include (but are not limited to)

1. *The way to deliver treatment.* If the treatment methods can be simplified—say in the form of vaccination, then some of our worry about immunization will disappear. It is also the case that enhanced immune response is
sometimes therapeutic. But perhaps we need not overworry about the common side effects of immunization. The use of the adenovirus or vaccinia expression vectors that were not designed for monogenic disease could also fit
in here as a potential vehicle for therapy.

2. *Use of multifactoral genetic therapy that treats symptoms but does not modify the disease nor constitute a cure.* For example, erythropoietin is beneficial for
patients with renal failure, and it is possible to design a gene therapy protocol to increase expression of erythropoietin in such patients. This will not
modify the underlying disease progression but will treat the symptoms of the
disease. The effect can be palliative, but is this really where we should be ex-
pending our financial and intellectual resources?

In this case, part of the practical answer may lie in the difference between using treatments "found by serendipity" to be useful versus seeking out
treatments that will merely treat the symptoms of the disease. There is a practical allocation problem as well as the ethical issue of providing false hope to
the patient who "feels better" but may *really* not be any better (because the disease is progressing more slowly).

C. Secondary Good Enhancement.

When we consider the category of enhancement (improving the body
or soma type even though there is no life-threatening illness), the level of advantage is relative to the sort of good that has been provided (see Chapter
One on the Goods of Agency). In this case, the sort of good in question is a secondary good. The secondary goods are categorized as follows:

Life-Enhancing: Medium to High Medium in Their Secondary Relation to
Action
- Basic societal respect
- Equal opportunity to compete for the Prudential Goods of Society
- Ability to pursue a life plan according to the Personal Worldview Imperative
- Ability to participate equally as an agent in the Shared Community World-
  view Imperative

Useful: Medium in Their Secondary Relation to Action
- Ability to utilize one's real and portable property in the manner she chooses
- Ability to gain from and exploit the consequences of one's labor regardless
  of starting point
- Ability to pursue goods that are generally owned by most citizens (e.g., in
  the United States today a telephone, television, and automobile would fit
  into this class)

Luxurious: Low in Their Secondary Relation to Action

- Ability to pursue goods that are pleasant even though they are far removed from action and from the expectations of most citizens within a given country (e.g., in the United States today a European vacation would fit into this class)
- Ability to exert one's will so that he might extract a disproportionate share of society's resources for his own use.

The designation of various sorts of gene therapies for secondary goods requires a clear sense of how enhancement relates to action. For example, if someone wanted enhancement in order to become "smarter," what level would this fulfill? Certainly several categories of life-enhancing seem to fit here. But even if we classified it at the very highest, would it be good to try to enhance intelligence? For one thing, such a project would require a definition of exactly what intelligence is. Some standardization of meaning here is a precondition for being able to improve something since "improve" indicates background standards against which we can judge whether improvement has occurred. Psychologists and philosophers have not agreed about what intelligence is or whether there can ever be a paradigm of intelligence.[11]

---

[11]Intelligence and testing is a tortured issue. The ability of aptitude tests to predict how intelligent people are (i.e., to "predict" success in school or employment) is a very controversial issue. One of the fundamental underlying questions is whether intelligence tests measure something that is, in fact, invariant. If it does not, it is not an aptitude test. (Achievement tests are rather different and are not at issue here.) The primary candidate for such an invariant factor is some sort of innate intelligence or heritability. It is here where the discussion usually has been engaged. Traditional advocates of the accuracy of such tests include R. M. Yerkes, "Testing the Human Mind," *The Atlantic Monthly* 131 (1923): 358–70; C.C. Bringham, *A Study of American Intelligence* (Princeton, NJ: Princeton University Press, 1923); and L. M. Terman, *The Measurement of Intelligence* (Boston: Houghton Mifflin, 1916). One of the most prominent detractors of the accuracy of such tests during this time period is Horace Mann Bond. For a discussion of his work, see Michael Fultz, "A Quintessential American: Horace Mann Bond, 1924–1929," *Harvard Educational Review* 55 (November, 1985): 416–42 and Wayne J. Urban, "The Black Scholar and Intelligence Testing: The Case of Horace Mann Bond," *Journal of the History of the Behavioral Sciences* 21 (October, 1989): 323–33.

Contemporary opinion leans in the opposite direction. Writers who support the link between heritability and intelligence include C. Burt, "The Inheritance of Mental Ability" in D. Wolfe, ed. *The Discovery of Talent* (Cambridge, MA: Harvard University Press, 1969); A. R. Jensen, "How Much Can We Boost IQ and Scholastic Achievement," *Harvard Educational Review* 39 (1969): 1–123; and Richard J. Herrnstein, who most recently with Charles Murray wrote *The Bell Curve: Intelligence and Class Structure in American Life* (New York: Free Press, 1994). On the other side sit N.J. Block and G. Dworkin, "IQ, Heritability, and Inequality" in Block and Dworkin, eds. *The IQ Controversy* (New York: Pantheon, 1976), S. J. Gould, *The Mismeasure of Man* (New York: Norton, 1981), M. W. Feldman, James Crouse et al. *The Case Against the SAT* (Berkeley, CA: University of California Press, 1988), and R. C. Lewontin, "The Heritability Hang-up," *Science* 190 (1975): 1163–68. Various environmental variables that might skew results are documented by T. B. Brazelton et al. "The Behavior of Nutritionally Deprived Guatemalan Infants," *Developmental Medicine and Child Neurology* 19 (1977): 364–72 and J. Brozek, ed. *Behavioral Effects of Energy and Protein Deficits.* NIH Publication No. 79-1906 (Washington, DC: National Institutes of Health, 1979). For some evidence of the most recent scholarship, see Daniel Seligman, *A Question of Intelligence: The IQ Debate in America* (New York: Carol Publishing Group, 1992) and especially Audrey Shuey, *The Testing of Negro Intelligence*, 2nd ed. (New York: Social Science Press, 1996)— excellent discussions of the issues.

But even if one could get a group of people to agree, would it be good to move toward genetic and somatic uniformity here? On evolutionary grounds diversity is a Good; it enhances fitness over various environmental pressures (see Chapter Four). Now, in this case, we are still talking about somatic therapy of a multifactoral problem, so we can assume no interference with the germ line. (This may be overly optimistic.) However, even if we could ensure that the germ line was safe, there would be a resulting loss of *social* diversity if this sort of genetic engineering were carried on over time in a large population. It is possible that those masses who have been treated would turn society into something out of George Orwell's novel *1984*, namely, uniform to the point that human freedom itself becomes jeopardized.[12] Certainly that would be a high price for "enhanced" intelligence. Social diversity may also be a per se good. Its advantages mirror those of evolutionary diversity. Thus, to engage in enhancement on any large scale would greatly lessen diversity and work against the per se good.

On moral grounds, enhancing mental capacities via genetic engineering seems to be very dangerous because of two categories of reason: (a) the choice of a general paradigm is inherently fraught with errors and (b) the implementation of any general genetically engineered paradigm is fraught with ethical problems. Let's examine these in order. First is the difficulty of choosing a general paradigm of mental functions. This difficulty amounts to saying that X,Y, and Z are asserted to be the mental structures of the optimal person.[13] We might choose cheerful (excise depression and sadness), energetic (excise sloth), and ready to do the job assigned to us (excise deliberate and obstinate character traits). Let us encourage everyone to be X-, Y-, and Z-like. We have chosen these qualities because this is the paradigm that the wealthiest and most powerful industrialists and money brokers in the United States and Western Europe have decided is best for all *other* people. Since these scions are the success stories in our society, they are obviously the best to choose since they've "won" in the game of life. The other people (the rest of us) will be altered to be obedient, good workers, smart enough to make them money, and . . . did we say—*obedient?*

This example shows how much is at stake when we tinker with intelligence, personality, and behavior. These heterogeneous traits are what mark us off as people, *Homo sapiens*. Each of us is comprised of a unique mix of intellectual capacities that constitutes our personal worldview. In a real way, our personal worldview is who we are, and if we alter it, we are altering our personal identity. This is ethically repugnant because it violates that which fundamentally defines who the agent is. Each agent possesses dignity. That

---

[12]There is also the logical possibility that some may desire to be "enhanced" to a state that the society at large judges to be a disability in order to garner compensation from society.

[13]Enthusiasts might choose various moral virtues such as Courage, Justice, Wisdom, and Self-Control—or they might go the other way and view classes of people as being tamed for social exploitation. In either case we will argue that such attempts are unethical and should not be pursued.

dignity is grounded in the structure of the worldview itself and its unique capacity to express itself. This freedom of expression anchors the agent's claim for basic goods in order to act.[14] The very ground of the Personal Worldview Imperative would be undermined if the personal worldview, itself, were modifiable. Thus, modification of the functioning of the cognitive functions of the brain from which our sense of self emerges would be ethically forbidden.

Further, the very act of choosing any single standard of perfection would relegate all other possibilities to the category of defect or deformity. If we extend this to its possible (probable) conclusion, entire races, ethnic groups, and religions might be termed "defective" by the standard makers and thus be targeted for discrimination until they were willing to come around and undergo genetic mental enhancement.

It is the consideration of what is implicit in the formation of a general paradigm that leads us into these practical implementation issues. One might imagine that the standard makers might try to avoid these charges by creating a statistical standard. They might say that "whatever 90 percent or more of the population exhibit is normal, and whatever 10 percent or less of the population exhibit is abnormal and defective—look to the bell curve." Statistical standards such as these have traditionally been popular with operationalists—especially those involved in creating intelligence tests. But even the statistical standards people get us into trouble. They would have us define as defective homosexuals and short people (among many other groups we could mention). Such a standard (category a) would have the effect of diminishing the Basic Goods of Agency to many groups of innocent people (category b). Diminishing the Basic Goods of Agency without cause is immoral. Thus, genetic enhancement based on a bell curve of statistical anomalies is unethical.

Since there are so many difficulties with genetic engineering for enhancing secondary goods, it should not be attempted on any large scale. It could affect social diversity, and there are intractable problems in setting a general standard and implementing the standard.

From this it seems clear that the alteration of the mind or physical features (for nontherapeutic reasons and merely for secondary good enhancement) is impermissible if it affects the human dignity of the individual by altering permanently his or her personal worldview. This is the irreducible unit from which all imperatives of morality are derived.

Another possibility is that these genetic enhancements to nontherapeutic conditions (therefore associated with Secondary Goods of Agency) might be pursued not in a *general* way, but rather individually. This is how much of cosmetic plastic surgery is practiced today, individually by those who have the

---

[14]Obviously, much of this discussion has a Kantian flavor. For an argument that links a Kantian-styled argument for freedom with the claim for basic goods, see Deryck Beyleveld, "Gewirth and Kant on Justifying the Supreme Principle of Morality" in Michael Boylan, ed. *Gewirth: Critical Essays on Action, Rationality, and Community* (Lanham, MD, New York, London: Rowman and Littlefield, 1999), pp. 97–118.

money to pay to have those double chins tightened up and those extra pounds liposuctioned away. All the gain without the pain!

This issue surrounds the limits of human action when we are dealing with the body. Some, like Kant, have suggested that we may not mutilate our body if it alters natural function. Others have suggested that our bodies are our own to do with as we please.[15] This question is too complex to deal with here. Let it suffice that since the general use of genetic therapy for enhancement is too fraught with moral difficulties to be recommended, any policymaker ought to be wary of making such enhancements available at all. If they are exercised only as plastic surgery is today for the rich and vain, then it probably does no harm for these people to indulge themselves as they like (so long as the germ line is not involved). This might be accomplished by disallowing such procedures under normal medical insurance. Since few could pay out-of-pocket, the problem is generally solved except for the privileged few who might pay for treatments. But even this solution is problematic if it becomes too popular, since prices might be driven down and soon the "individual solution of the few" collapses into the general paradigm for the many (with the unfortunate consequences listed for this path).

The possibility also exists of a developing genetic underclass that is left out of the calculation altogether. With the upper class and the upper middle class enhancing themselves at ever increasing rates, it is entirely possible that there might emerge an underclass that cannot compete in a game controlled by large discretionary income. Thus, the gap between rich and poor increases and distributive justice becomes an increasingly irrelevant concept. We believe this would not be a good path for society to follow. The constraints of social justice must always be foremost in the minds of policymakers.

It would also be wrong for governments to adopt the general paradigm. But it might also be too intrusive into individual liberty to disallow those who can pay to experiment with secondary good enhancing treatments. These difficulties necessitate that this path be trod with caution. In the end, enhancement therapy for therapeutic cause is justified under the imperatives of professional practice (both medical and medical research) and the ethical duty to rescue. Nontherapeutic enhancement is immoral if it permanently alters the abiding sense of self that is captured in the personal worldview. In cases in which the personal worldview is not in jeopardy, then treatment can proceed under much of the same guidelines that govern cosmetic plastic surgery today, with the caveat that society must guard against the possible emergence of a genetic underclass.

---

[15]This cleavage cuts between those who support individual autonomy over the body at all costs, as per the Stoics—for a balanced discussion of these underlying issues, see Lawrence C. Becker, *A New Stoicism* (Princeton, NJ: Princeton University Press, 1998) and those who would hold that our body is not ours, but the property of God, who created it. Philosophical support for this position can be found in Alvin Plantinga, *Warrant and Proper Function* (Oxford, UK: Oxford University Press, 1993).

chapter ten

Cloning

I. What Is Cloning?

Cloning is the production, as a result of asexual reproduction, of a population of bacteria, cells, or organisms that is genetically identical. Cloning is a common technique in molecular biology for the production of large amounts of bacteria containing a specific plasmid for DNA analysis purposes. In higher organisms, genetically identical offspring can be obtained by either spontaneous or deliberate division of the fertilized egg prior to blastocyst formation, but more often cloning refers to the formation of a genetically identical organism (or suborganism, i.e., tissue or organs) by nuclear transfer or transplantation. Thus, cloning at the nuclear transfer level is for the creation of entire animals (or, still in the future, humans) and/or the creation of cells and tissue (and perhaps in the future custom-made organs). However, cloning can also be used to describe the asexual reproduction of cells, and perhaps tissues and organs, from stem cells.

We concentrate here on cloning due to nuclear transfer, with only limited reference to the production of stem cells. Cloning that would proximately affect the germ line is discussed in Chapter Eleven.

II. How Is Cloning Presently Being Performed?

A. Nuclear Transfer.

Although it was only in early 1997, with the announcement of the cloning of Dolly the sheep, that the idea of human cloning began to be seriously discussed in public,[1] the groundbreaking experiments were done back in 1952 when Briggs and King reported their results of transferring frog nuclei from very early embryos (blastula cells) into nonfertilized eggs.[2] In these frog experiments, the nucleus was removed from an unfertilized egg with a glass needle, and an intact nucleus from a diploid cell was injected into the enucleated egg. In more than 50 percent of cases, the cell began to divide normally, with a significant number going on to develop into normal-looking tadpoles. Similar experiments were subsequently performed with nuclei from more mature cells, including gut epithelial cells, and also injected into other species of amphibia. Similar experiments in mammals were unsuccessful. It was, therefore, the reporting of the cloning of a mammal from the nucleus of an adult cell that really took the world by storm and opened the possibility of making human clones.

Dolly was not the first lamb cloned from differentiated cells. In 1996, Keith Campbell and colleagues described the production of five lambs from a **differentiated embryonic cell line**.[3] Two of these lambs, Megan and Morag, survived to become healthy, fertile adults. In contrast to early experiments, the cultured cells were deliberately cultured in serum-free media to induce a state of quiescence before being fused with the enucleated metaphase-arrested oocyte by electrical stimulation. The stimuli also induced cell division and embryonic development. A similar approach was used for the production of Dolly, although in this case the nucleus was from an adult cultured mammary gland cell line that had been stored frozen in liquid nitrogen.[4]

Since the birth of Dolly, cows, mice, and pigs have all been cloned from adult cells, and goats and cats are not far behind.[5] The technique is similar in all cases: the oocytes are obtained and the nucleus removed; donor cells are cultured with nutrient deprivation to induce quiescence and then fused with

---

[1]For a discussion of some of these popular notions see Dorothy Nelson and M. Susan Lindee, "Cloning and the Popular Imagination," *Cambridge Quarterly of Healthcare Ethics* 17.2 (spring 1998):145–49.

[2]Robert Briggs and Thomas J. King, "Transplantation of Living Nuclei from Blastula Cells into Enucleated Frogs' Eggs," *Proceedings of the National Academy of Sciences U.S.A.* 38 (1952): 455–63.

[3]Keith H. S. Campbell et al., "Sheep Cloned by Nuclear Transfer From a Cultured Cell Line, " *Nature* 380 (1996): 64–66.

[4]Ian Wilmut et al., "Viable Offspring Derived from Fetal and Adult Mammalian Cells," *Nature* 385 (1997): 810–13.

[5]For a review of the current species that have been cloned, see Elizabeth Pennisi and Gretchen Vogel, "Clones: A Hard Act to Follow," *Science* 288 (2000): 1722–27.

the enucleated oocyte. In the case of mice and pigs, the donor nucleus is removed from the cultured cells and microinjected into the oocyte. Cell division is induced by electric stimuli; and once embryogenesis has begun, the embryos are placed in surrogate mothers and allowed to develop normally. At present, the efficiency of this process is extremely low, with only about 2 percent of attempts to clone an animal resulting in a live birth, and some of those that survive have serious developmental abnormalities.

Apart from the general wish to learn more about embryonic and fetal development, a lot of the impetus to clone animals is to use them to produce therapeutic proteins or tissues and organs for transplantation purposes. For this to be realistic, cloning needs to be combined with genetic modification, either to introduce genes of interest or to knock out genes such as the α-1, 3-galatosyl transferase gene, the enzyme that adds galactose to the carbohydrate chains on porcine cells, which is the principal cause of tissue rejection of pig organs in humans. Until recently, targeted gene therapy had only been possible in mice, but now gene-targeted transfer has been combined with cloning to produce sheep with human α1-antitrypsin excreted in the milk[6] (see Chapter Eleven).

B. Pluripotential Stem Cells.

Stem cells are undifferentiated cells with both the potential for self-renewal and the ability to give rise to differentiated progeny. Such cells are described as unipotential if they give rise to one cell type, or pluripotential if they give rise to more than one cell type. There are multiple types of stem cells in the body, including epidermal stem cells whose daughter cells are the differentiated cells lining the gut or outer surface (skin) of an organism, and hematopoietic stem cells in the bone marrow that produce blood cells. Cells obtained from fetuses have a greater potential for both renewal and differentiation and have been used as a valuable source of cells for experimental tissue transplantation.[7]

These stem cells generally give rise only to cells of a defined tissue type (but see the next paragraph). In the early stages of embryonic development, embryonic stem (ES) cells from the blastocyst, so-called totipotential stem cells, are self-renewing and have the potential to produce all the cell types in an organism. Although mouse ES cells have been used for many years to study embryogenesis and as a way of producing genetically modified mouse models (see Chapter Eleven), it was not possible to grow similar human ES cell

---

[6]K. J. McCreath et al., "Production of Gene-Targeted Sheep by Nuclear Transfer from Cultured Somatic Cells," *Nature* 405 (2000): 1066–69.

[7]See, for example, a commentary on the use of fetal tissue for Parkinson's disease in Marcia Barinaga, "Fetal Neuron Grafts Pave the Way for Stem Cell Therapies," *Science* 287:5457 (2000): 1421–22.

Hematopoietic Potential of Stem Cells Isolated from Murine Skeletal Muscle.

Kathyjo A. Jackson et al.
Proceedings of the National Academy of Sciences 96.25 (1999):14482–86.

Using a mouse model, the authors were able to show that hematopoietic cells could be generated from adult mouse muscle. Muscle tissue was removed from 6-week-old mice, all other tissue was carefully removed, the muscle was minced and treated with enzymes to separate the individual cells, and the muscle cells were grown in culture for 5 days. These cells were then tested as a source of bone marrow hematopoietic stem cells in a bone marrow repopulating assay. In this test, the muscle cells were mixed with bone marrow cells from a second strain of mice, chosen so that the cells could be genetically distinguished from progeny from the muscle cells, and the mixture inoculated into a mouse that had previously been lethally irradiated to destroy its natural bone marrow cells.

Six weeks after the marrow transplantation the peripheral blood was examined. Despite more than 10 times more bone marrow cells than muscle-derived cells having been used in the repopulating assay, more than 50 percent of the lymphocytes (B and T cells) and myeloid cells (granulocytes and macrophages) were derived from the muscle cells, suggesting that muscle was a better source of hematopoietic stem cells than bone marrow itself! In addition, if this bone marrow was itself used as a source of hematopoietic cells in a further lethally irradiated mouse, the muscle-derived progeny again contributed to more than 50 percent of the bone marrow cells of the new recipient.

These results clearly showed that muscle stem cells, probably the muscle satellite cells, could not only contribute to hematopoiesis, but could themselves be transplanted, a marker of a "true" hematopoietic stem cell. In similar studies, alluded to at the end of the paper, others have shown that hematopoietic stem cells can also develop into skeletal muscle, suggesting that stem cells can develop into different cell types depending on their environment, and opening up the possibility of using either hematopoietic stem cells or even muscle biopsies to generate different types of cells or tissues.

lines. In 1998, James Thomson and colleagues reported that they had developed ES cells from human blastocysts donated by patients undergoing infertility treatment,[8] and later the same year James Gearhart and colleagues described the production of totipotent human embryonic germ (EG) cell lines derived from the germ cell ridge of aborted human fetal material.[9] Not only

---

[8]James A. Thomson et al., "Embryonic Stem Cell Lines Derived from Human Blastocyts," *Science* 282.5391 (1998): 1145–47.

[9]M. J. Shamblott et al., "Derivation of Pluripotent Stem Cells from Cultured Human Primordial Germ Cells," *Proceedings of the National Academy of Sciences U.S.A.* 95.23 (1998): 13726–31.

are these cells a valuable self-renewing source of cells to theoretically produce any type of cell, and perhaps tissues and organs, in the body, but combined with nuclear transfer they could be "made to order" with the recipient's own genetic makeup.

Until recently, it was thought that stem cells could give rise only to progeny cells of a defined tissue type. Recently, it has been shown that there is much more plasticity in the stem cells than was originally thought. In mice models, neuronal stem cells from the brains of adult mice have been shown to behave like hematopoietic stem cells and produce a variety of different blood lineages;[10] hematopoietic stem cells have contributed to cells found in the liver, muscle, brain, and bone; and adult mouse muscle has produced bone marrow blood cells (see box on page 128).[11] It remains to be seen if these stem cells are truly totipotential and could be used to produce any cell type. Using stem cells from adult humans to produce different cell types would open up the potential for producing new tissues or even organs from readily harvestable cells such as bone marrow or muscle biopsy.

III. Advantages and Disadvantages of Cloning.

Cloning of plants has been occurring for centuries, and technically, cloning could be used to improve both animals and humans. As in other chapters of this book, our main concern here is with human usage. (Some of the nonhuman applications are also discussed in Chapters Eleven and Twelve.) At the present time, cloning is inefficient, time-consuming, and expensive. It is unlikely that it would be profitable to engage in cloning in animals in which there was no germ-line interaction.

Thus, our principal topic is cloning of humans. Cloning theoretically could occur at several different levels:

A. Cloning of a whole person. This is currently being done in animals, and is theoretically feasible in humans.

B. Cell and tissue cloning.

C. Cloning to produce whole organs. This now seems to be one of the science fiction applications of cloning. Such cloning is interesting from an ethical point of view because it involves a great number of potential problems. Remember, the science fiction of today *may* become the standard practice of tomorrow.

---

[10]Christopher R. R. Bjornson et al., "Turning Brain into Blood: A Hematopoietic Fate Adopted by Adult Neural Stem Cells in Vivo," *Science* 283.5401 (1999): 534–37.

[11]See for example the special issue of *Science* with several articles on the use of stem cells, including Gretchen Vogel, "Can Old Cells Learn New Tricks?" *Science* 287.5457 (2000): 1418–19.

A. Cloning of Whole People.

There are at least three scenarios in which the cloning of an entire human organism might be desired:

1. Cloning as an alternative to *in vitro* fertilization (IVF) therapy for infertile couples.
2. Cloning as a way to bring back a dead child or other loved one.
3. Cloning as a way to reproduce oneself.

All such cloning is still in the realm of science fiction. However, persistent rumors abound that some private laboratories are attempting human cloning of an entire organism—even now. Let's address these three scenarios in order.

Cloning as an Alternative to In Vitro *Fertilization (IVF) Therapy.*

This sort of cloning is unlikely as an alternative to current *in vitro* fertilization therapy because present IVF techniques are so far advanced, reproducible, and less expensive than cloning that it seems to be an unlikely direction for this field to take. Also, there is an inherent pleasure in having children that contain genetic material from both parents. Thus, the continuation of IVF practices for infertile couples is more likely than the alternative of cloning.[12] Be that as it may, we see that cloning may be developed as an alternate form of IVF therapy. As such, it is just as acceptable as IVF therapy itself—if the techniques can be perfected. The present success rates even in animals are too poor. We should not "experiment" on people when perfecting such therapies because we would be using people as mere tools for scientific progress.[13] This research

---

[12]Of course there are situations in which single women might want children without the intervention of another person. Such individuals may well create a demand for such treatments.

[13]Some would say that we should not experiment upon animals to perfect these treatments. This line of argumentation rests upon the admission that animals have some sort of status that deserves respect. The level of respect varies from full moral rights to some proportionate level of respect that corresponds to the rationality of the creature (since rationality and its application in purposive action are the basis of human rights.) For a discussion of some of these arguments, see David DeGrazia, *Taking Animals Seriously* (New York: Cambridge University Press, 1996); Eugene C. Hargrove, ed., *The Animals Rights/Environmental Ethics Debate: The Environmental Perspective* (Albany, NY: SUNY Press, 1993); Tom Regan and Peter Singer, eds., *Animal Rights and Human Obligations* (Upper Saddle River, NJ: Prentice Hall, 1989); Tom Regan, *The Case for Animal Rights* (Berkeley, CA: University of California Press, 1983); and Peter Singer, *Animal Liberation: A New Ethics for Our Treatment of Animals* (New York: Avon Books, 1992). Our position on this subject is that there must be a compelling and unique rationale for animal experimentation. We should always use plants before protists, and protists before animals, and animals with lower

strategy would be unethical because using people as means only is unethical. Science may not employ immoral means or seek an immoral end. Using people as means only is to employ immoral means (see Chapter Seven). Thus, it would be ethically prohibited.

On the practical side, the clientele for cloning in this group would be exceedingly small (if the previous assumptions are correct), so there would be no long-term harm to the gene pool by using cloning as a therapy for infertile couples. Even if we add single women who currently seek IVF therapy via donor sperm, or couples who for genetic reasons do not want to use their own gametes (eggs or sperm), we do not have a statistically significant number of children who would be "conceived" by this route, so that there is no real harm to the germ line via these asexual techniques that tend to diminish genetic diversity.[14]

A legitimate question at this point is whether there is a moral right to have children. And if so, what sort of good might it be, so that we might determine the strength of the claim. This, of course, is a difficult question. Obviously, it is not a Basic Good of Action. People can perform basic action with or without children. However, it would seem to be a secondary good relating to one's ability to actualize a personal life plan according to his or her worldview.

Thus, the answer to the question of whether one has a right to this sort of therapy is one that has to be answered in the context of other goods. Certainly the society has a responsibility to provide Basic Goods of Agency to all who are deprived of them *before* it provides others with secondary goods. Societal support can include funding for research, sponsorship of clinical trials (in one form or another), and finally legislation to make it a part of regular health insurance.

Certainly one must support this sort of effort above lower secondary goods such as luxury items (a yacht), but it is not as important as providing all people with food, shelter, clothing, education, and the other Basic Goods.

By this analysis, there is nothing ethically wrong with pursuing human cloning as a form of IVF therapy (when techniques have been perfected), as long as society's resources are not diverted from providing goods to more basic human needs of action.

---

levels of rationality before those with higher levels of rationality. Primates ought not be used except in the most extreme circumstances (e.g., to avert massive worldwide death due to some infectious disease).

[14]One might even go so far as to say that there might be genetic *advantages*. This issue has been raised recently in cases involving sperm donors who do not factually cite their family histories. Thus, women choosing this method of fertilization put themselves at risk for unreported diseases and genetic abnormalities. And since sperm donors are paid, there is financial incentive for them to represent their genetic profile as excellent.

Cloning as a Way to Bring Back a Dead Child or Other Loved One.[15]

It is possible that if human cloning techniques were developed at the level of re-creating an organism, some might want to try to bring back a dead child or other loved one. It is important here to understand what cloning can and cannot do. First, as was mentioned in Chapter Four, the concept of a gene is a rich one that involves a dynamic interaction between chemical and environmental conditions. Thus, if one tried to clone a child who had died, it is possible that the new person may not look exactly like the dead person. Further, even if they were similar in appearance, the social environment of development may well create different personalities (cf. the variety of personalities found in identical twins). Each person in the world interacts with his or her environment in a unique way such that he or she creates an individual worldview that is a mix of free choices and the unique perspective on the values that constituted those choices (the Personal Worldview Imperative) and the result as judged by those same values.

Thus, parents who seek to "revive" their dead child will probably be disappointed. We cannot re-create what was lost. Each person is unique—even when she is biologically identical to her sister. The impulse to hold on to a lost loved one is certainly understandable. The grief of death is beyond comparison. However, to try and make cloned Judy into dead sister Judy will end up exploiting the new child. One should not have to grow up in the shadow of another. This violates the prohibition against exploitation.[16] Thus, it would seem that cloning to revive a dead child or other loved one is fraught with difficulties and ought not to be pursued.

Cloning as a Way to Reproduce Oneself.

"Life is short, art is long." So says Hippocrates in *Aphorism* I. It has, since the dawn of time, been the deep desire of humankind to live after death. This desire for immortality is what may drive some to want to clone themselves.

---

[15]The implication in this subsection is a dead family member. However, "loved one" might be understood more broadly to include anyone that one admired and/or felt affection for. This is taken to a rather twisted extreme in the fictional venue of Ira Levin's *The Boys from Brazil* (New York: Random House, 1978). In this case the "loved one" is Adolf Hitler. If we assume the premise of the novel, then we must ask ourselves whether we want to make available such whole organism clones. Since Adolf Hitler was a person who committed great immoral atrocities, it would seem that allowing science to clone him (or any other such rogue) would be to have science commit to immoral ends (also prohibited by Chapter Seven).

[16]For a discussion of some of these issues, see Søren Holm, "A Life in the Shadow: One Reason Why We Should Not Clone Humans," *Cambridge Quarterly of Healthcare Ethics* 7 (1998): 160–62 and John Harris, "Cloning and Human Dignity," *Cambridge Quarterly of Healthcare Ethics* 7 (1988): 163–67.

There are unsubstantiated rumors that some wealthy individuals are already funding private efforts to do just this. However, as in the case of reviving a dead child, trying to reproduce oneself mistakes what cloning can and cannot do. We cannot create carbon copies of ourselves because expression of genes involves a complicated interaction with the environment and development is unique since each human individual is unique. (This is what underlies the deep sense of human identity and dignity.) The issues here are basically the same as with re-creating the dead child except that one is holding up himself as the model. This may be worse since internal reflection may yield more exacting standards for success. What a terrible burden to place upon a newborn person. Thus, cloning as a way to reproduce oneself ought not to be pursued.

B. Cloning of Cells and Tissues.

The potential for cell and tissue therapy is huge, and in the foreseeable future, human cloning may include cloning of tissue and cells. Theoretically, tissue transplantation could be used to treat a wide range of disorders, including neurodegenerative illnesses, diabetes (with pancreatic islet cells), spinal cord injuries, and even heart and muscle repair following myocardial infarction or muscle ischemia. There are many examples like this.

Generally the acquisition of acceptable cells and tissue has been painstaking. There are many more people who could profit from such therapy than there are available cells and tissues. Thus, if we could obtain a reliable source of cells and tissues for this therapy in a relatively inexpensive and plentiful procedure, we could go a long way in caring for the well-being of our patients (all things being equal). The prospect of human cloning of these cells and tissues could allow the physician to better fulfill his professional responsibility to care for the well-being of his patient and to do no harm. It would also satisfy the moral duty to rescue. These ought to be the cornerstones of the worldview of any practicing physician or medical researcher. There is little to no germ-line crossover in this form of cloning, so that negative duty to do no harm (in this case to future generations) does not become an issue. The key caveat here is the source of the cells.

There are potentially three ways to obtain stem cells: (1) from fetal tissue, (2) from ES or EG cells obtained either from "normal" blastocysts/germ cell ridges or following nuclear transfer, and (3) from pluripotential or totipotential stem cells from adult tissue.

The current source of human stem cells (for tissues other than blood and bone marrow) is aborted fetuses (postorganogenesis). Human embryonic germ cell lines are also produced from embryos during and after the time of organogenesis (weeks five to nine postfertilization). In addition, ES cells are obtained from embryos (preorganogenesis). Thus, if one is seeking these cells from human fetuses or embryos, then one is involved in questions concerning abortion.[17]

Stem Cells/Tissue and EG Cells from Aborted Fetuses.

Let us begin with cells from aborted fetuses. There are many problems with this source of stem cells. When the research community—especially the *for-profit* research community—decides that it is in its interests to obtain fetuses from abortions, a market in aborted fetuses will arise. This may encourage women to have abortions because they will be able to sell their aborted fetuses to the companies for thousands of dollars. Some women might even consider this a profitable side source of income. If a woman could sell an aborted fetus for $10,000, and do it twice a year, then she would have a considerable supplement to her income.

But such a practice would be unethical. It would violate the doctrine of not exploiting yourself or others as a means only. People who get pregnant merely for the purpose of making money also exploit the person with whom

---

[17]For the purposes of this book, our position on abortion will be that of Michael Boylan, "The Abortion Debate in the Twenty-First Century," in *Medical Ethics*, pp. 289–305. Boylan's view suggests criteria to set the limits of the permissibility and impermissibility of abortion. This variation is due to the differences in personal worldviews. Instead of focusing on the definition of personhood or on the expression of autonomy, Boylan suggests that it is more productive to focus on maternal threats versus fetal respect. This approach implies that various levels exist that should be considered when evaluating how much respect anyone deserves: (a) full personhood (at some time in the first few years of development); (b) possible personhood (protected by precautionary reason from some base level to full personhood—Boylan would put this moment at the end of the first trimester of pregnancy); and (c) potential possible personhood (from the moment of conception to possible personhood).

Full moral rights obtain necessarily to those enjoying full personhood (since they are actual deliberating agents). Something proportionally approaching full moral rights may be claimed for the possible agent. And some proportionally lesser level of respect (with its associated rights) should be granted to those on the lowest level.

Contra the traditional anti-abortionists who generally argue for full moral rights for the fetus from conception, this theory creates three levels of respect that move well past birth in order to be complete. Contra the traditional pro-abortionists, who generally argue for the right of abortion at will, this theory denies abortions at will. What is requisite is demonstrating a level of maternal threat that is greater than the level of respect we ought to give the developing (though not yet actual) person. The levels that one sets for threats versus respect will follow from one's complex web of values that Boylan calls the worldview. Through a dialectical interaction between the question at hand and these values emerges personal ownership of a universal theory dealing with "if, when, and under what conditions" an embryo may be separated from its biological mother.

It should also be noted that Brown believes abortion to be morally wrong—especially after implantation and organogenesis. However, Brown does believe in Boylan's principle of frugality that sanctions wastefulness. Thus, since abortion is legal in the United States, Brown believes that aborted fetuses should be put to productive use in medical research instead of merely being wastefully discarded and thus benefiting no one. But it is Brown's desire (as it is Boylan's) that the best source for stem cells will be pluripotential stem cells from adult tissue. This would sidestep a number of professional and ethical difficulties.

they conceive the child and the potential life itself. Though Boylan has written supporting a woman's right to choose abortion, he still makes it clear that abortion is not without consequences.[18] Having an abortion is different from having a mole removed from your arm. Creating a market for fetuses in anything like the presented scenario would degrade all of humanity because it would institutionalize and encourage a paid supply of fetuses.

Some might say that there would never be a commercial market for fetuses. If women are having abortions already, why shouldn't the tissue go to some use instead of being simply discarded?[19] There is power to this argument so long as there are no payments made nor pressure exerted on the donor woman. If abortion is legal and morally permissible in certain circumstances, then the donation of the fetus for the benefit of research that may help others must be seen in the light of a person who acts for others even when she does not have to. The action is not completely altruistic since a woman's principal purpose in having an abortion is to alleviate a threat to herself. She could have the embryo discarded or, instead, have the embryo used for some positive purpose. Under this description, a woman undergoing the abortion would fall under the frugality doctrine of not wasting what might profitably be used. For a woman to insist that the embryo be disposed of (when it could help others) is extravagant wastefulness and prohibited on environmental grounds.

But some would say that the research companies make money from the results of their research, so why shouldn't the woman donor share in this?[20] The answer is that it involves self-exploitation by treating one's reproductive apparatus as a means only. However, it is also true that the general public should not be subsidizing the profits of biomedical companies without some sort of recompense. What we would suggest is that the donation of the fetus by the woman (or other sources of stem cells such as eggs that might become blastocysts or adult tissue that may be converted into stem cells) should be viewed as a public act. Thus, when a company receives the consequences of a public act, it should compensate the public. In this way there is a sort of payment or transfer of goods or services that occurs. The company receives a valuable commodity and instead of compensating the donor directly, the

---

[18]Just what the consequences of abortion are is a disputed question. For a selected list of sources, see footnote 29. As stated earlier, this book will adopt the position of Michael Boylan, "The Abortion Debate in the Twenty-first Century." The point to be made is that in cases in which an abortion is morally permitted, a person is in a different position about donating the resultant dead fetus than in cases in which abortion is not morally permitted—such as abortion solely because of a gender preference (i.e., someone wants a boy child, but the fetus is female, therefore; the woman aborts so that she can try again to get a boy).

[19]It is obvious that fetuses from spontaneous abortions (miscarriages) would be useless since those cells have already been demonstrated to be defective (otherwise the body would not have aborted them).

[20]There are other possible entities that may profit from this such as hospitals and doctors. Since these institutions and individuals are bound first by morality and their professional ethics, the input of profit can create a conflict of interest that might compromise these primary obligations.

company compensates the society. This compensation might take the form of subsidized treatments for low-income people or some other public project that serves to balance the preferment that the company has been given.

Though we believe that this is a strategy that is permissible to adopt in the short-term, it can never be a long-term solution. In the long term, in which certain procedures are adopted for creating cells, tissue, and (possibly) organs, the reliance upon aborted fetuses (even if the woman is not compensated) will create a conflict of interest of sorts. And though the stem cell bank, once established, will cease to be dependent on new inputs (except for improvement of the existing bank of cells), there is still the necessity that the cells procured have not been acquired by immoral means. Acting according to immoral means is beyond the limits of science as per the criteria outlined in Chapter Seven.

ES Cells as a Source of Stem Cells.

An alternative source of stem cells, and potentially more useful than fetal tissue, is ES cells. Many of the arguments applying to the use of fetal tissue also apply to embryonic stem cells. However, these cells are available prior to organogenesis and prior to implantation. The human ES cell lines that have currently been described have been produced from frozen blastocysts produced after IVF treatment and are no longer needed by the "parents."

The second (and perhaps more preferable over the first) source of stem cells might come from the cloning techniques that were described at the beginning of this chapter (i.e., through nuclear transfer). It could be possible to take a muscle cell from the one needing the transplant and to insert the nucleus into a donated egg that has had its nucleus removed. This act seems to promote initial cell division, and the zygote could be cultured *in vitro* to the blastocyst stage and the ES cells harvested.

Pluripotential Stem Cells from Adult Tissue.

Finally, if it is possible to obtain pluripotential stem cells from adult tissues, then the so-called procurement problem has been solved. In this case, no moral difficulty concerning the source of the cells exists. The only difficulties might concern whether the criterion of not violating the irreducible sense of self that we represent as the personal worldview might be violated. Although it appears that a number of different sources of stem cells appear to have the pluripotential, if it turns out, for example, that only neuronal stem cells can be used in human tissue as a stem cell source, then there might be a new difficulty in the source of stem cells. (Currently this does not appear to be the case in mice, but this might not be true in other species.) Since it has been established that the genetic alteration of the basic sense of self is immoral, and if brain cells as a source of stem cells proves to be a viable option, then one is engaged in immoral means in the pursuit of science and, by the criteria set out in Chapter Seven, it ought not to be pursued.

C. Cloning to Produce Organs.

In the twenty-five years since the advent of effective surgical transplant techniques, a growing shortage of organs and tissue available for transplant has developed. These organs (such as hearts, livers, and lungs) constitute Basic Goods of Action. Without them the agent will die. (What could be more basic to action?) Thus, it would seem that society has a moral duty to support research, all things being equal, that would provide enough organs for those whose lives are at risk due to disease or malfunction.[21]

It is, in the present state of research, impossible to even consider growing organs for transplantation. However, it is useful to consider the implications of what it would entail given current understandings of what is scientifically possible (even in the very long range). If one were to employ the nuclear transfer strategy, one could imagine this process operating in two ways.

1. *An embryo in which the organs have begun to develop.* In the first way, the blastocyst would be allowed to grow into an embryo in which the organs have begun to develop. At that point, all the organs would be "harvested" and grown in some artificial environment until they are suitable for transplantation. The problem with this approach is that it allows the development of an embryo past the point of undifferentiated or semidifferentiated cells to the point in which a potential human was present. This technique for growing organs is fraught with the problem of human exploitation. Based on the Principle of Precautionary Reason,[22] this strategy for growing replacement organs should be rejected.

2. *Creation of organs through some artificial growth mechanisms.* This approach has many practical problems. For example, organs in normal development are produced in an environment that contains nerves, muscles, and

---

[21]There are some who would contend that one's right to an organ is conditioned by the lifestyle of the claimant. For example (under this argument), a smoker would have a diminished right to a lung transplant compared to a nonsmoker. For the purposes of this book, we will avoid this problem. Readers interested in pursuing the issue should see Brian Smart, "Fault and the Allocation of Spare Organs," *Journal of Medical Ethics* 20 (1994): 26–30.

[22]This principle dictates that based on the philosophical problem of other minds, we should refrain from acting against potential human agents when they have all the necessary organs (brain, heart, etc.) and machinery (i.e., nervous system) to constitute a human being. Under this principle it would be impermissible to grow an embryo to the sixth month just to harvest its organs. See Deryck Beyleveld and Shaun Pattinson, "Precautionary Reason as a Link to Moral Action," in *Medical Ethics*, ed. Michael Boylan, pp. 39–52.

blood. Any organs that are created would have to have a suitable environment in which to grow. Further, we would have to discover the optimum developmental time for transplantation. These are, of course, practical problems, but they are real obstacles (even though we are still in the realm of science fiction).

There are two great practical advantages in growing tissues and organs through *cloning* over conventional techniques. First, present transplant procedures must deal with the problems of human rejection that will always be present when foreign organs and tissue are introduced into the body. The same mechanism that protects us from disease also attacks transplanted organs and tissue. This would not be the case (we believe) with cloned tissue and organs because the organs would be compatible with the host.

Eliminating the drug therapy presently necessary for transplant patients would mean a great change in their ability to act (a Basic Good). This possibility makes cloning for the sake of organs an attractive research strategy and one that society (all other things being equal) should support.

In addition, cloning may possibly provide an almost unlimited supply of organs that can be used to save lives. The onerous waiting lists that now hang over transplant patients would be lifted. (Perhaps everyone who wanted an organ could get one!) Since having working organs is a Basic Good, this also would be a moral reason to support this sort of research (all things being equal).

IV. A CRITICAL EVALUATION OF CLONING.

One phrase that was repeated in the last section was "all things being equal." This is a caveat that has many expressions as one approaches the question of cloning. For our purposes, let us group the criticisms into *practical problems* and *moral issues*.

A. Practical Problems.

As we have mentioned, the first question concerns supply. According to our criteria, there are two modes of cloning: (1) nuclear transfer to a donor egg and (2) asexual reproduction of stem cells. The source problem is a real question for both methods. In the first case, nuclear transfer cloning requires the existence of an egg, which has to be extracted from a donor. Will there be enough donors? Should the donors be paid? Answers to these questions can create the dilemma that was discussed in the last section. In the same way, it would seem that the biomedical companies should not be given something of value to them without giving something in return. However, we cannot allow people to sell their eggs. The alternative is to compensate the public. Biomedical companies would be forced to pay a price for the eggs they obtain, but that price would go to society at large and not to the donor.

In addition, the donor eggs do not just have a passive role in the ultimate development of the embryo and fetus. There is the role of the mitochondrial DNA and the impact of the cytoplasm from the egg donor. This can be a problem because the rosy model outlined earlier suggested that the female egg would merely be a host for the patient's own personal blueprints (nucleic DNA). Such attitudes about the egg may be false.[23] An increasing number of diseases are known to be transmitted through mutations in the mitochondrial DNA (see Chapter Four) and thus may have a role in the transference of disease to the newly cloned cells or tissues.

The second scenario involves concerns with the source of the stem cells. As we have seen, the stem cells can come from a variety of sources: fetal cells, embryonic ES or EG cells, or adult cells. Stem cells from aborted fetuses may present a moral problem. Even though Boylan asserts a woman's right to choose abortion under many conditions, it is never without consequence. As was mentioned earlier, there are inherent problems in relying on aborted fetuses as a source of stem cells, because the state does not ever want to be in the position (perceived or otherwise) of *promoting* abortion.

It is our suggestion that research should proceed very guardedly in this domain. It is far better to wait until we can develop an alternate source of stem cells before we crank up our research program with stem cells. The risks of viewing fetal tissue as merely another input in the relentless process toward knowledge are too great. Science must never employ immoral means nor pursue immoral ends. This would seem to require public and private restrictions (though not prohibitions) on the use of fetal tissue as a source of stem cells.

ES and EG cells may overcome this problem to some extent. These cells themselves could be obtained either from fusion of eggs and sperm or from nuclear transfer as described earlier. The advantage is that they should be self-renewing, therefore markedly reducing the amount of original source material that would be required.

However, if the source of stem cells is adult cells, then the source problem vanishes. When we have a technique that will allow individual adult donors to give a renewable biological resource—such as bone marrow—as a source of stem cells, there would be no problem. So long as normal procedures for informed consent are followed, the researcher is merely modifying adult tissue for the purpose of creating alternate cells or tissue.

---

[23]Compare with Aristotle's notion that the male provided the final, formal, and efficient causes to conception while the female only provided the material cause. See *De generatione animalium* 730b, 8–11, 19–23.

Second, there is much that we do not understand about both nuclear transfer and the production of tissues and organs from stem cells.[24] Nuclear transfer techniques are extremely inefficient, with less than 2 percent of transfers leading to viable infants even in the most experienced hands. Although telomere length correlates with the ability to self-renew, and in stem cells there is generally high telomerase activity, after nuclear transfer both longer and shorter telomeres have been observed in different experimental species. The significance of this is still unknown. In addition, during normal zygote development, there is an epigenetic mechanism whereby genes derived from the maternal or paternal genome are differentially switched on or off, a process known as imprinting. It has been suggested that the high percentage of non-viable embryos following nuclear transfer is due to a failure of correct imprinting,[25] but how to amend this faulty imprinting is unknown.

B. Moral Issues.

As with the practical issues myriad moral issues need to be examined. In our brief study we can only review the most important of these.

Animal Research.

Animal research is an issue that is not merely associated with cloning but has to do with the more general issue of the way we treat animals in biomedical research. From the time of Aristotle onward, philosophers have asserted that there is a sharp difference in the *scala naturae* between humans and animals. This may be the case. But at the very least, given almost every theory of human evolution, we should not view all animals alike. There are some bioegalitarians who assert that all animals (including humans) are on a par.[26] However, even anthropocentric thinkers such as the authors of this book hold that there is a differential respect that ought to be afforded to those animals that are asserted to be phylogenetically closer to *Homo sapiens* than would be afforded to other animals. For example, for a researcher, exposing an insect to

---

[24]See Anne McLaren, "Cloning: Pathways to a Pluripotent Future," *Science* 288.5472 (2000): 1775–80, for an historical review of cloning and a summary of the current difficulties.

[25]See, for example, Tomohiro Kono, "Influence of Epigenetic Changes During Oocyte Growth on Nuclear Reprogramming after Nuclear Transfer," *Reproduction, Fertility and Development* 10 (1998): 593–98.

[26]Andres Brennan, *Thinking About Nature* (Athens, GA: University of Georgia Press, 1988). Robert Elliot, and Arran Gare, eds., *Environmental Philosophy* (University Park, PA: University of Pennsylvania Press, 1983). Tom Regan, *All that Dwell Therein* (Berkeley, CA: University of California Press, 1982.). Holmes Rolston III, *Environmental Ethics* (Philadelphia: Temple University Press, 1988). Judith N. Scoville, "Value Theory and Ecology in Environmental Ethics: A Comparison of Rolston and Neibuhr," *Environmental Ethics* 17.2 (1995): 115–34. Christopher Stone, *Earth and Other Ethics* (New York: Harper & Row, 1987).

a lethal spray would be a different moral act than exposing a monkey to a lethal spray. This is because monkeys are closer to performing purposive action (even on operational terms) than insects are.[27] Though many scientists accept this hierarchy, in the end they have viewed all animals as instruments of their research needs and have performed whatever experiments they wanted because (after all) their subjects are only *animals!*

But if the basis of moral respect lies in action, then even if monkeys and other primates do not possess rationality such that they can fully commit purposive action, they do approach this standard and should be afforded proportional respect as such. Further, if we accept the Principle of Precautionary Reason, then those species that are evolutionarily very close to us should be afforded something approximating the respect we show for humans. Certainly, inflicting gratuitous harm on chimpanzees, would not be acceptable. Humans should recognize this on a principle analogous to the one by which they ascribe moral rights to humans.

Thus, it is one thing to perform all sorts of tests upon bacteria and drosophila, but it is another thing altogether to subject evolutionary higher animals to all sorts of cloning experiments that may cause them pain and death. This is a moral issue since most cloning research is performed on mammals.

Is the End an Inherently Immoral End (as per Chapter Seven)?

This is also a tricky question because it depends on one's understanding of the fundamental character of morality and the mission of science.

Science sees as its mission to know everything that can be known. The emphasis (obviously) is on the natural world. Modern science is an empirical discipline. The sources of information are all sensory. Thus the conclusions will reflect their source. This does not, however, exhaust the possible sources of knowledge. Those who believe in God, for example, hold that there are other sources for knowledge aside from nature. These are characterized as *super*natural. The supernatural is beyond the natural. If such a realm exists, then there is a whole different realm that may or may not be attuned to the rules of the natural realm.

The Personal Worldview Imperative recognizes that religious values can be an important ingredient in the construction of our individual worldview.

---

[27]This, of course, is a tortured question. It is generally based upon the physiology of the animals involved. If we assume that (at the very least) a brain (with cerebral cortex) and central nervous system are necessary for purposive action, then the insect (without either) is in a different moral class than the monkey. Even if the monkey does not possess the sort of consciousness necessary for full moral agency, there is some sort of real principle of precautionary reason that should be operative here. For a discussion of some of the fundamental issues at stake here, see Deryck Beyleveld and Shaun Pattinson, "Precautionary Reason as a Link to Moral Action" in Michael Boylan, ed. *Medical Ethics*, pp. 39–52.

Some religious views of reality declare that tinkering with the essential elements of God's created order go beyond the mission of science. In the language of Chapter Seven, they commit the researcher to seeking immoral ends. When a research design seeks ends that are inherently unethical, then it should cease and desist.

But is cloning this sort of immoral end? To say yes, one would have to assert something like "any variance from God's created order is immoral." However, this, itself, is problematic because it begs the question of why we are able to be in the position to engage in such research in the first place. If God is the omnipotent creator of everything, then if he/she/it did not want us to delve into certain questions, it would certainly be within his/her/its power to remove it from our available questions to ask. He/she/it didn't do so; ergo, it seems peculiar to say we should not go forward.

However, another tack suggests that humans have the power of free will. They have the power to do evil. God allows us to do evil for whatever reason. Thus, it is possible that this design *is* evil. But on this line of argument there would have to be a conclusive violation of the realm of ethics or of a religious worldview. Since religious worldviews (however widely held) are not universal, this must remain as a secondary justification for sanctioning action in a pluralistic society.[28]

Cloning for the Sake of Producing Cells, Tissue, or (Perhaps) Organs.

This question was touched on in the previous section of this chapter. There are basically two strategies for creating organs through cloning. The first would be to clone entire individual humans and then kill them to harvest their organs. This first strategy is unacceptable because it requires creating an entire individual merely for the sake of providing key organs, such as the heart or kidney. After the heart is removed, the surrogate will die. This involves murder. Murder is defined as the killing of an innocent, at will. Murder is immoral, thus this strategy of cloning entire individuals merely for their organs is unacceptable.

Besides being unethical, the creating of an entire individual merely for the sake of providing key organs is not cost efficient. There are enormous costs involved in bringing an organism to life and for their organs to develop sufficiently to be suitable for transplant. Thus, the first strategy is a loser on both the ethical and the practical domains.

A second strategy would be to insert the donor's DNA into an egg and then let the cells divide until the blastocyst stage, which contains approximately

---

[28]For a discussion between ethical and religious tenets, see Michael Boylan, *Basic Ethics*, Chapter Six.

100 undifferentiated cells, including the embryonic stem (ES) cells. It is at this point that we may be able to steer the development of these cells to become specialized cells or tissues (and possibly an entire organ such as a lung or liver).

The ethical question that needs to be asked is whether steering the ES cells toward becoming pancreatic islet cells, bone marrow, brain cells, heart tissue, or even an entire organ is also in some way murder. Such an argument would be built on the doctrine that human life begins at conception. On this theory, any human intervention that interrupts this process would be to terminate that which (all things being equal) would become a human life. The fertilized (or, following nuclear transfer, diploid) egg is a potential human. To intervene against it (so that it dies) is to intervene against a potential human. To intervene against a potential human so that it dies is to kill that which is innocent. Killing that which is innocent, at will, is murder. *A fortiori*, cloning to obtain human ES cells is murder. Those who would make this argument might find a link to arguments against abortion.[29]

---

[29]The context of our argument here can profitably be seen against Michael Boylan's article, "The Abortion Debate in the Twenty-first Century" in *Medical Ethics*, pp. 289–72. For a review of some of the key arguments involved in the literature, see Judith Jarvis Thomson, "A Defense of Abortion," *Philosophy and Public Affairs* 1 (1971): 47–66. The responses to this article have been enormous. Some of the most interesting of these include Robert N. Wennberg, *Life in the Balance: Exploring the Abortion Controversy* (Grand Rapids, MI: Eerdmans, 1985); John T. Wilcox, "Nature as Demonic in Thomson's Defense of Abortion" in Robert M. Baird and Stuart E. Rosenbaum, eds., *The Ethics of Abortion: Pro-Life vs. Pro-Choice*, rev. ed. (Buffalo, NY: Prometheus, 1993): 212–25; Keith J. Pavlischek, "Abortion Logic and Paternal Responsibility: One More Look at Judith Thomson's 'A Defense of Abortion'," *Public Affairs Quarterly* 7 (1993): 341–61; David Boonin-Vail, "A Defense of 'A Defense of Abortion': On the Responsibility Objection to Thomson's Argument," *Ethics* 107 (January, 1997): 286–313; Martha Brandt Bolton, "Responsible Women and Abortion Decisions" in Onora O'Neill and William Ruddick, eds. *Having Children: Philosophical and Legal Reflections on Personhood* (New York: Oxford University Press, 1979), pp. 40–51; Baruch Brody, "On the Humanity of the Foetus" in Robert L. Perkins, ed. *Abortions: Pro and Con* (Cambridge, MA: Schenkman, 1974), pp. 69–90; Douglas J. Butler, *Abortion and Reproductive Rights: A Comprehensive Guide to Medicine, Ethics and the Law* (CD-Rom. Requirements 486 PC/20 MHz or greater, 8RAM, MSCDEX version 2.2 or greater. Westminster, MD: *http://www.qis.net/-butler*. 1996; Ronald Dworkin, *A Matter of Principle* (Cambridge, MA: Harvard University Press, 1985); Ronald Dworkin, *Life's Dominion: An Argument About Abortion, Euthanasia, and Individual Freedom.* (New York: Knopf, 1993); H. Tristram Englehardt Jr., "The Ontology of Abortion," *Ethics* 84 (April, 1974), pp. 217–34; Jane English, "Abortion and the Concept of a Person," *Canadian Journal of Philosophy* 5 (October, 1975), pp. 233–43; John M. Finnis, " 'Shameless Acts' in Colorado: Abuse of Scholarship in Constitutional Cases," *Academic Questions* 10 (fall 1994); Patricia King, "Should Mom be Constrained in the Best Interests of the Fetus?" *Nova Law Review* (spring 1989), pp. 393–404; Catherine A. MacKinnon, "Abortion, Precedent, and the Constitution: A Comment on *Planned Parenthood of Southeastern Pennsylvania v. Casey*" *Notre Dame Law Review* 68 (1992), pp. 11ff; John Noonan, ed. *The Morality of Abortion: Legal and Historical Perspectives* (Cambridge, MA: Harvard University Press, 1970); Louis P. Pojman and Francis J. Beckwith, *The Abortion Controversy: A Reader* (Boston: Jones and Bartlett, 1994); Michael Tooley, *Abortion and Infanticide* (New York: Oxford University Press, 1983); Mary Anne Warren, "On the Moral and Legal Status of Abortion," *The Monist* 57.1, with "Postscript on Infanticide" from Joel Feinburg, ed., *The Problem of Abortion*. 2nd ed. (Belmont, CA: Wadsworth, 1984).

Several replies can be made against this attack. First, the cloning procedure is not the same as human conception. It is true that all things being equal, a cloned egg that is properly implanted in a female uterus will develop into a fully developed organism (if all goes right—at present the success rate in other mammals is not very good). But strictly speaking, no instant of fertilization occurs. Instead, an artificial procedure replaces the nucleus of the egg with the diploid nucleus from one of the cells from the patient. Thus, all the terminology that accompanies normal fertilization and reproduction must be transposed to this new procedure.

Second, the blastocyst is a group of undifferentiated cells that are about five days in development. Five days is hardly very far along in human development. It is stretching things to say that there is any *actual* organism at all. All is potential. Thus, the actual status of those cells can be characterized as having no determinate character. This is what it means to be a blastocyst.

Third, there is no intended killing at all. Unlike abortion in which the fetus is removed from the mother with a very high probability of ensuing death, there is no intended killing of cells in this procedure. In fact, the entire purpose of cloning is to ensure that the stem cells develop into a healthy lung, heart, or liver. The cells are given every opportunity to continue existence. Soon all of the original cells will die and be replaced by *their* filial progeny, but that is the way with all the cells of the body: they die and are replaced. The same situation exists with any blastocyst that is formed through haploid meiotic reproduction. Some of the cells will become nerve cells; others will form the heart, and so forth. We do not think one cell to be slighted just because it is destined to become part of the colon instead of part of the brain. No, what matters is that scientists are trying to stimulate the formation of heart tissue for Jane Doe. If it is successful, then those cells and their progeny will continue to live and thrive. Though the procedure is artificial, the end goal is to stimulate an entirely natural process (that is admittedly out of normal epigenetic sequence). Thus, it would seem that the abortion analogy is not suitable here.

Fourth, some might say that since the blastocyst (even though it is only five days old and is actually only 100 or so undifferentiated cells) must be seen as a potential person; and even if it is not being killed, it is being exploited because we are using it as a means only—meaning that we are not letting it naturally develop into a human but steering its development merely to become heart tissue. This is an interesting and perhaps the most subtle and difficult of the attacks. For it *is* true that we are not allowing the blastocyst to become all that it can become, that is, a human person.[30] Instead, we are relegating it merely to becoming a group of cells or tissue. Now we ask you,

---

[30]Though to be fair here we should note that a good portion of the blastocyst will, under normal conditions, become the placenta and be discarded just after birth.

who would willingly say that he would rather be a group of cells or tissue than a whole integrated person? Neither of us would.

However, the sense of exploitation is certainly extenuated. Since the blastocyst is not an *actual* organism of any type, and since blastocysts (even in those formed through meiotic haploid reproduction) very often do not develop into surviving organisms (because of the immense problems connected with development that result in spontaneous abortion, which during the first month are practically undetectable), it is rather an overstatement to characterize any particular blastocyst as a potential person (realistically). There is, in reality, a rather difficult road ahead for all blastocysts.

But this does not answer the pure question of whether we are exploiting any given potential person via the blastocyst stage by steering its development into becoming heart tissue instead of becoming a whole, integrated person. As we have indicated earlier, practical issues incline a person into thinking that the strength of any individual claim (of blastocyst cells cum potential person) is rather weak because in nature there is such a high attrition rate at this stage.

Finally, the use of stem cells from aborted fetuses is (at best) a short-term solution. This is because no country wants to get in the business of preying on women in such unfortunate circumstances nor do we want to be in the business of acting as if we were encouraging abortions. This would amount to an infringement on a very changed private decision. Thus, though (in the short run) this source of cells for asexual reproduction of specialized cells or tissue may be used under tight guidelines, it must never be a part of a long-term permanent protocol.

In conclusion, the various fanciful science fiction scenarios that have been perpetrated since the first cloning of Dolly and its implications upon humans are largely impractical. *Jurassic Park* and other scenarios are not at the horizon of most research. What we have concentrated on in this chapter is first the cloning of tissue and single cells for use in existing medical treatments and on both the source of these cells (either through nuclear transfer to a human egg or asexual reproduction using either fetal tissue, ES and EG cells, or adult stem cells) and their application (either through the direct production of specialized cells and tissue or through the implantation in the uterus in order to grow new people or in order to grow something that will be used as a means only to supply new therapeutic material—such as an organ).

It seems clear that the best strategy for the source of cells is the cloning of adult diploid cells for the purpose of directly creating specialized cells or tissue. This method does not tread on the thorny path of human conception that is (and forever will be) a source of much controversy. The Shared Community Worldview Imperative enjoins communities to find policy solutions that conform to the core values of its members. This means that our long-term strategies in cloning must be away from controversial sources of stem cells (such as aborted fetuses or embryonic stem cells). Though these are ethically permitted on a short-term basis under tight controls, we must focus our research strategies in other directions.

The most problematic categories are the cloning of entire people and the implantation of eggs that have undergone nuclear transfer. These ends and means are (in practice) too fraught with moral dilemmas concerning exploitation, dignity, and violation of the Personal Worldview Imperative for them to be ethically acceptable. It may be possible (in principle) that technology might advance mammalian cloning so that the current 2 percent success rate might approach 100 percent. If science proceeds carefully and prudently according to its most stringent criteria, then perhaps the law of unforeseen consequences might be confronted in the spirit of due diligence. Under those circumstances, one might envision some cases in which whole organism-cloning (such as IVF therapy for infertile couples or couples with one parent who carries a lethal gene) might be ethically acceptable. But for the present, we should refrain from this research activity entirely. We should also be guarded in the sort of animal research we engage in.

Such ethical cautions may slow the progress of science, but as we have stated in Chapter Seven, science must never be allowed to proceed recklessly and unchecked. Immoral means and ends are prohibited. What can be known must be checked by the dictates of morality. This applies to both public and private research. Cloning offers a clear case of taking this precaution very seriously. At present cloning should proceed only under the comprehensive constraints outlined in this chapter.

chapter eleven

Germ-Line Therapy

I. WHAT IS GERM-LINE THERAPY?

Germ-line gene therapy is the introduction of a fully functional and express-ible gene into **germ-line cells** (cells that will eventually produce viable eggs or spermatozoa) resulting in a permanent correction of a specific genetic de-fect in not only the individual treated but potentially all future offspring. Al-though this is currently performed in animals (livestock) and in plants, it is not being done in humans. In fact, because of the potential implications of germ-line therapy, much effort is being expended determining the risk of exposure of germ-line tissue in somatic gene therapy protocols (see Chapter Eight).

II. HOW IS GERM-LINE THERAPY PRESENTLY BEING PERFORMED?

Germ-line gene therapy is currently performed only in animals and plants and is the basis of the science of transgenesis, whereby exogenous DNA, the transgene, is introduced into the genetic makeup of the resulting transgenic animal or plant. Most of the technology has been developed in mice, and transgenic mice are a common tool in many areas of medical research, but similar studies have been performed in cattle, pigs, and sheep.

Transgenic mice can be made by a variety of different procedures:

1. Standard gene therapy vectors, particularly retroviral vectors, can be used to transfect early embryos (usually at the 8-cell stage) prior to implantation with the gene of interest. The transfected cells are implanted into the foster mother, and after birth the pups can be tested for the presence of the transgene. However, retrovirus sequences may also be integrated into the genome, and for this reason, microinjection is the preferred method for producing transgenic mice.

2. In the microinjection method, donor females are induced to superovulate by the injection of hormones, mated, and then immediately sacrificed. The fertilized eggs are obtained at the stage when the female and male pronuclei are still distinct. The large male pronucleus is directly injected with the linear transgene DNA. After inoculation, approximately 25–40 transgenic eggs are implanted microsurgically in a mouse foster mother that has been made pseudopregnant by mating with a vasectomized male, the only known method of preparing the mouse uterus for implantation. Three weeks later the transgenic pups will be delivered, and tissues tested, often by polymerase chain reaction (PCR), to determine which pups have the transgene. Mating to another mouse can determine whether the transgene is in the germ line of the founder mouse.

3. Both retroviral transfer and microinjection of the transgene will lead to random integration of the DNA in the genome. To overcome this, targeted gene therapy of embryonic stem (ES) cells can be used to direct the transgene to specific positions in the genome. Similar techniques can also be used to introduce nonfunctioning genes, in so-called "knock-out" mice. Embryonic stem cells are cells taken from the inner cell mass of a mouse blastocyst. These cells can be grown in cell culture and retain the capability of differentiating into all cell types, including germ cells, when they are reinjected into recipient blastocysts (see also Chapter Eight). The gene-targeting technique relies on homologous recombination of sequences of similar DNA. The transgene is flanked by pieces of DNA that are identical to chromosomal DNA on either side of the target area. The method is very inefficient, and therefore often the transgene includes a selectable marker (often the neomycin resistance gene), with other similar markers outside the homologous region to aid in identification of cells that have undergone recombination. In addition, cells can be screened by PCR and cultured *in vitro* prior to inoculation into the recipient blastocyst and implantation into the pseudopregnant foster mother. The resulting pups are often chimeras and are screened by mating studies to determine which have the transgene in their germ line.

Although transgenic animals have been produced in other species, studies to develop ES cells from animals other than mice have been very difficult. In 1998, James Thomson and colleagues reported that they had developed ES cells from human blastocysts donated by patients undergoing infertility treatment.[1] There is a great deal of interest in using these and related pluripotent cell lines for producing tissue and organs for tranplantation medicine (see Chapter Ten), but these cells also have the potential for manipulation to produce corrected gene or "knock out" humans.

4. Finally, cloning by nuclear transfer, as described in Chapter Ten, can be used to produce transgenic animals. This process is very inefficient currently and not widely used to produce transgenic mice. However, the ability to target genes to specific sites in the chromosome, or specifically alter individual genes opens up the realistic possibility of "pharming"[2] for medical use (see box).

III. The Advantages of Germ-Line Therapy.

The principal advantages of germ-line therapy are that it potentially can permanently correct defects in genetic populations, and can enhance existing populations so that they might meet current standards more readily. Mechanically, this potential might be achieved by genetic therapy of germ-line stem cells/ES cells and the treatment of ES cells, themselves. Let's examine each of these issues in order.

First is the issue of permanently correcting a genetic population. What would this mean? In the case of humans, it would mean knocking out or eliminating genes that cause congenital disease—such as Tay-Sachs disorder, hemophilia, or sickle cell hemoglobin production. These genes create potentially lethal conditions for their hosts. If germ-line genetic therapy were carried out on a wide scale (much as vaccinations are), then there might be a reasonable expectation that the human species might rid itself once and for all of these lethal genes. This would seem like a tremendous improvement for those suffering from these abnormalities. It also appears to fulfill the professional role of the physician: "I will concern myself with the well-being of the sick," and "do no harm" (cf. Chapter Two).

It also appears to fulfill the basic ethical duty to rescue those whose Basic Goods of Agency are being threatened (cf. Chapter One). What could be more basic than one's life? What could fulfill this duty more completely

---

[1]James A. Thomson et al., "Embryonic Stem Cell Lines Derived from Human Blastocyts," *Science* 282.5391 (1998): 1145–47.

[2]Pharming is the production of modified domestic livestock for pharmaceutical use.

Production of Gene-Targeted Sheep by Nuclear Transfer from Cultured Somatic Cells

K. J. McCreath et al.
Nature 405 (2000):1066–69.

In this paper the same company that produced Dolly, the sheep, shows the production of lambs that have genes targeted to the α1 procollagen gene locus, using the technique of homologous recombination (see Chapter Four). Two separate constructs were made, one to introduce the neomycin resistance gene (as a marker study), and the second to introduce the neomycin resistance gene, plus human α1 antitrypsin gene under the control of the β-lactoglobulin promoter so that the antitrypsin protein would be produced in the sheep milk if the targeting was successful.

First the two targeting vectors were used to introduce the genes into sheep fetal fibroblast cells, and the cells were then grown in culture in the presence of a neomycin analogue. Cells with neomycin resistance, indicating that they had incorporated the new genes, were then tested by PCR to ensure that the gene had been correctly targeted to the procollagen gene locus. Four clones were chosen that had successful targeting, and apparently normal chromosome numbers and appearance at metaphase. Nuclei from these clones were then obtained and transferred to enucleated donor eggs by nuclear transfer, impanted into pregnant ewes, and allowed to go to term. Of the 417 "reconstructed" embryos, there were 14 live births, but 7 of these died within 30 hours of birth, illustrating the inefficiency of our current cloning methods. However, tissue from 15–16 lambs or fetuses showed evidence by Southern blotting of correctly targeted gene inserts.

Only one lamb with the antitrypsin construct survived more than 1 week after birth (of 5 live-born lambs). This lamb was hormonally induced to lactate, and antitrypsin protein could be detected in the milk by western blotting, demonstrating the feasibility of using this approach to use animals to produce humanized therapeutic proteins in their milk.

than rescuing the entire human species from various genetic diseases *forever?* The Personal Worldview Imperative enjoins us all to create a worldview that is good. What could be better than to rid humanity of these genetic scourges? This might be a much stronger version of the argument given for single and multiple enhancement therapy (that must be repeated on each individual patient).

In the plant and animal realms, there might be a huge market for making common foods pharmacologically beneficial to humans. If one were to create a cholesterol-reducing agent in apples, for example, then every time you crunched into a Golden Delicious or a Gala Special, you could be lowering your bad cholesterol. (There is already such a product as a butter/margarine substitute.)

Additionally, many strains of genetically altered tomatoes are resistant to insects and will stay ripe for a longer time. The list goes on and on.[3] Some plants have a limited "germ" life, since the companies that manufacture them want to resell the seeds to farmers over and over again (see Chapter Twelve). Thus, on the positive side, genetic engineering in plants promises to deliver plants that are resistant to pests (thus eliminating the need for polluting pesticides), bigger, juicier, tastier (more conforming to consumer tastes), and also more healthy (with compounds that will lower cholesterol, improve excretion of fatty materials, and make one more energetic). What could be better? Isn't this what creating a personal or shared community worldview that is *good* is all about?

A similar role exists in the animal kingdom. Animals can be bred so that when eaten they provide the same sort of benefits as plants. Additionally, certain animals, such a pigs, might be able to be bred such that their organs could be transplantable into humans with little to no immune rejection.

These are powerful arguments. Unless there are other issues at stake (as per the "all things being equal" clause), then it would seem that the practical, professional, and ethical issues are all on the same side. However, it is not so simple.

IV. A CRITICAL EVALUATION OF GERM-LINE THERAPY.

Germ-line genetic engineering is the most controversial of all the avenues of genetic engineering (from the viewpoint of science). We begin our discussion with plants and proceed to animals and then to humans. Some further issues will carry over to Chapter Twelve if their primary focus concerns the overlap of science and business.

A. Plants.

In the last section, many of the touted advantages of genetic engineering in plants were highlighted. These genetic alterations have been going on for years—particularly in the United States. But what disadvantages might such genetic engineering bring?

---

[3]The generation of hybrid plants has been around since the beginning of civilization. This has created a rather blazé attitude about how we treat plants. This complacency is changing. With the advent of genetically altered seeds new attention has been focused upon whether what we are doing has unforeseen deleterious consequences. For an overview of some of these concerns, see Jane Rissler and Margaret Mellon, *The Ecological Risks of Engineered Crops* (Cambridge, MA: MIT Press, 1996) and Roger Beachy, Thomas Eisner, Fred Gould, and Henry Way Kendall, *Bioengineering of Crops: Report of the World Bank Panel on Transgenetic Crops* (Washington, DC: The World Bank, 1997).

The most obvious practical issue is the so-called law of unforeseen consequences. According to this objection, there are many possible practical side effects that the genetic engineers cannot anticipate. For example, a real threat of allergies exists among humans who consume the genetically altered products. Some of these may be life threatening or life altering (at the level of Basic Goods levels one and two). Others may be inconvenient. Since the regulatory process in the United States is different (and more rigorous) for drugs and for plants that may act as drugs but are classified as food, the potential for practical problems such as severe allergies is great.

The most obvious ethical issue is the lowering of genetic diversity in the breeding population. As was mentioned in Chapter Four, evolution depends on a diverse breeding population because it is a given in most standard evolutionary theories that the environments will change. Each change alters the differential fitness for genotypes and pheonotypes. There is no such thing as a good genotype. There is only a good genotype for a particular environment. For example, sickle cell expression is fit in an environment that is full of malaria (call this environment-1). Those people lucky enough to have sickle cell expression in such an environment will be more successful reproducers than those who do not. However, in a second environment (environment-2) that has no malaria, sickle cell individuals will die in greater numbers and will have a lower fitness coefficient than those without it. Thus, is possessing the gene for sickle cell positive or negative? The answer is simply that it depends on the environment. In one it is good and in another it is bad.[4]

What is important is that a diversity exists. Thus, as environments change, the species will be able to survive despite the changes as differential fitness coefficients change.

From this we can see that diversity is a big deal. Anything that compromises diversity is bad for the species (if our current theories of evolution are correct). When we genetically engineer plants and crops so that they can compete more effectively than wild species, we diminish the diversity of the genetic population for that species. This harms the species. The harm will be realized in future times when the environment changes and the altered (now

---

[4]For a discussion on general concepts of fitness, see Alexander Rosenberg, *The Structure of Biological Science* (Cambridge, UK: Cambridge University Press, 1985). M. Williams, "The Logical Basis of Natural Selection and Other Evolutionary Controversies" in *The Methodological Unitity of Science*, ed. M. Bunge (Dordrecht: D. Reidel, 1973) discusses the tautology problem (what ever survives, survives) and suggests an axiomazation method grounded in a logical empiricist flavor. J. Beatty, "The Evolutionary Contingency Thesis" in G. Wolters and J. Lennox, eds. *Concepts, Theories, and Rationality in Biological Science* (Pittsburgh: University of Pittsburgh Press, 1995), 45–81, suggests that empirical foundations of evolutionary biology mean that there are no authentic biological laws (given the definition of a scientific law given to us by the logical empiricists).

more homogeneous) species is less able to cope with the changes. It is possible that many flora species (or at least subspecies) will become extinct.[5] This is intrinsically wrong to the biotic community and in anthropocentric terms it harms future generations of humans. It will be remembered from Chapter Two that there is a moral duty to future generations. Thus, on biocentric and on anthropocentric terms, the lowering of a species' genetic diversity is immoral.[6]

The value-duty relation (see Chapter Two) says that when we value something, we incur a duty to defend it. Virtually everyone, if they thought about it, will admit to valuing the world's flora. Thus, all of these people incur a duty to defend that flora. Genetic engineering in plants that involves the significant lowering of genetic diversity is unacceptable and should be sanctioned by appropriate international legislation.[7]

B. Animals.

The second category to examine is the realm of fauna. The animal kingdom has also been the object of genetic engineering that affects the germ line. It is an interesting characterization of popular attitudes that few evince shock at the report that germ-line genetic engineering occurs in plants or animals. We think that the basis of this blasé attitude is rooted in the classical *scala naturae*, which includes three levels. At the bottom are the plants. Aristotle said they had only nutritive souls. In the middle are the animals. They have nutritive souls and sensitive/locomotive souls. At the top is humankind, who have nutritive souls and sensitive/locomotive souls and rational souls. St. Augustine added that the rational souls come from God and are the link between humans and God.[8] In each case, humans are at the top and given

---

[5]Some may contend that this has been going on for centuries in the arena of flora. However, this is not to say that it should be that way. Just because immoral practices have been going on in the past is no reason for them to go on in the future.

[6]For an overview of this debate, see examples of the biocentric position from Holmes Rolston III, "The Intrinsic Value of Nature: Values in and Duties to the Natural World" in F. Herbert Bormann and Stephen R. Kellert, eds, *The Broken Circle: Ecology, Economics, and Ethics* (New Haven, CT: Yale University Press, 1991) and Paul W. Taylor, *Respect for Nature: A Theory of Environmental Ethics* (Princeton, NJ: Princeton University Press, 1986). For a view of the anthropocentric position, see: Onora O'Neill, "Environmental Values, Anthropocentrism and Speciesism," *Environmental Values* 6 (1997): 127–42. An attempt at reconciliation can be found in James P. Sterba, "Reconciling Anthropocentric and Nonanthropocentric Environmental Ethics," *Environmental Values* 3 (1994): 229–44.

[7]Generally, such decisions must be taken at the national level. At the writing of this book the only international body that is capable of such sanctions is the World Trade Organization. However, the mechanism for punishment is still largely a national decision.

[8]Augustine, *On the Free Choice of the Will*, tr. Anna S. Benjamin and L. H. Hackstaff (Indianapolis, IN: Bobbs Merrill, 1964), Bk II.5.43–44.

dominion over all.[9] From this, we believe, an attitude has arisen that humankind can do whatever it wants to with plants and animals. We believe two premises are at the basis of this argument:

A-1.   This little act that I am performing can't hurt plants and animals that much.

A-2.   Even if what I'm doing hurts plants and animals to (at least) a significant degree where I am living, I have to do it in order to survive.

Both A-1 and A-2 are important attitudes and need to be addressed. In the case of A-1, it is true that if only agent A (in the whole world) were doing such and such (like dumping one's raw sewage into the local river), the environment would be resilient enough to handle it.[10] But it is rarely the case that such instances happen in isolation. Generally one person acting to pollute (because it's easier to do so than the alternative), breeds copycats. And so the pyramid grows outward.

Thus the advocates of A-1 are seen to be undercut in their assertion that they are not doing too much harm. If we accept the principle of generalization in ethics, then my doing *x* must be seen in the context of *everyone* doing *x*. If it cannot be universalized, then it probably involves a logical contradiction and would be prohibited by the Personal Worldview Imperative as being inconsistent.[11]

In the case of A-2, one has a more tricky proposition. If I have to kill all the small animals around the area in which I live in order to feed myself and my family, then (assuming that there is no other way for us to get the calories needed for survival), I am permitted to do it under the principle of human survival.[12] However, this is a slippery slope because what is basic survival to some may be luxurious living to others. For example, some may be inclined to have fur coats made from the skins of 100 animals while others are content with cloth coats made only from plant materials.

To answer this difficulty, we would refer the reader to the Table of Embeddedness (Chapter Two) showing Basic and Secondary Goods in order to gauge in a semiobjective way whether, in fact, one's claim to be exempt from ecological duties is born from real human need (as judged against the conditions of action) or from desires to satisfy some level of pleasure fulfillment beyond even second-level Secondary Goods.

---

[9]*Genesis* 1:29.

[10]Of course there are also cases in which the environmental damage is so great that one person or company *can* cause irreparable harm—such as draining a key wetland or dumping toxic waste into an improper storage facility.

[11]Arguments for this sort of position are made by Immanuel Kant, *Groundwork of the Metaphysics of Morals*, tr. H. J. Paton (London: Hutchinson, 1948), 421/52 ff., and by Alan Gewirth, *Reason and Morality* (Chicago: University of Chicago Press, 1978), p. 135.

[12]See Michael Boylan, "Worldview and the Value-Duty Link to Environmental Ethics" in *Environmental Ethics*, ed. Michael Boylan (Upper Saddle River, NJ: Prentice Hall, 2001), pp. 180–96.

Thus, the scale of nature used to justify exploitation of lower-level members at will rests on premises that may have a narrow application (only in isolated cases) but generally are false.

We would agree with the argument that the basis of ethical consideration resides in the possession of reason and free will (à la Kant and Gewirth)[13] and the fundamental conditions of action (i.e., the Basic and Secondary Goods of Agency). But such an admission does not commit one to harming animals, plants, or the land, for that matter, in a permanent way because of the value-duty relation and because of the duty to future generations. This argument has both its anthropocentric and biocentric components and is morally binding.

The Personal Worldview Imperative enjoins all people to create a worldview that is comprehensive, internally coherent, and good. A well-grounded moral claim is all three. Thus, the moral requirement for protecting animals, plants, and the land ought to be a part of everyone's personal worldview and as such should find expression in any shared community worldview.

Let us examine further issues that relate directly to animals. First is the crossover issue about raising animals for the tastes of humans rather than for what is good for the animal. The classic example of this is the goose and pâté de foie gras, liver paste. If you are Farmer Jacques and someone asks you whether that goose over there is a good goose, you might reply, "Yes, he certainly is. Why that goose has a liver so large that he'll drop over dead any day now." This sense of "good" means "good for producing pâté de foie gras." This dish needs lots of liver and so if you can produce geese that have enormous livers, you can make lots of money. Thus the goose in question is a good goose. This is called extrinsic analysis. Something is judged to be good only as it fulfills the conditions of some other agenda external to that entity. In this case it is a human delicacy.

However, when we ask about what is a good goose from the goose's perspective, the story is different. Having a huge liver is unhealthy. A goose with an enormous liver will soon die. It is therefore intrinsically bad for the goose to have a large liver (i.e., it does not promote the agenda of that goose). Thus, there is an apparent contradiction that the goose is both good and bad. The contradiction vanishes when we consider "good for what?" Then it is clear that the goose in question is good extrinsically and is bad intrinsically.

So often when we are dealing with animals, we humans think only of the extrinsic good of animals relative to our own needs. The principle of human survival says that it is permissible to kill animals and plants for our basic and

---

[13]An exposition of this connection is made by Deryck Beyleveld, "Gewirth and Kant on Justifying the Supreme Principle of Morality" in *Gewirth: Critical Essays on Action, Rationality, and Community*, ed. Michael Boylan (Lanham, MD, New York, Oxford: Rowman and Littlefield, 1999), pp. 97–118.

moderate survival, but this does not extend to luxuries. But what about using animals for the sake of potential patient therapy that might save human lives? Is this not simply an extension of the principle of human survival?[14]

The answer is yes to the degree that the information gained by using animals *cannot* be gained from other sources. And certainly not all animals deserve the same respect. Bacteria and animals that have no central nervous system are sufficiently disconnected to the fundamental basis of respect, the ability to commit rational action, that one may have broad latitude for research. However, even with bacteria, this range is not unlimited. According to the value-duty relation outlined earlier, we should not attack other species—even protists—unless their existence is a direct threat to humankind (such as virulent bacteria). Even here we must be careful because the bacteria exist as interactive partners in a given biome and to alter the biome irreversibly (as creating extinction must do) would be to harm the biome and therefore violate the value-duty relation. It is one thing to protect ourselves against virulent bacteria via inoculation or genetic engineering. It is another thing to take lethal measures to alter the biosphere by eliminating species just because certain animals are problematic to us.[15]

Another difficulty that arises in relation to animals is the use of animals as organ donors. Researchers may genetically alter the organs of pigs, for example, so that they might be transplanted into humans. This case would entail the widespread use of animals for extrinsic purposes. Though we are not talking about luxurious food (as with the goose example), still it constitutes the widespread exploitation of mammals for extrinsic purposes. This is morally unacceptable under the doctrine of the value-duty relation. A person is not protecting the species when this is allowed. It is one thing to kill an animal in order to eat it. It is another thing to alter the germ line of a population within a species for the sole purpose of creating replacement organs. In this case, we would be manipulating a species for our own use without regard for what would be good for the pig. Though we do not believe that any particular pig has full moral status such as a human possesses, still it is unacceptable to alter a pig for our own purposes. This is not what it means to *defend* and

---

[14]The Principle of Human Survival says that humans may be obliged in their struggle for survival to kill animals, plants, and to alter the natural landscape. In this way, humans are acting just as other animals do in their own quest for survival. It is further assumed that humans are justified to continue in these practices past the point of basic, primitive survival to some level of moderate, comfortable living. See Michael Boylan, "Worldview and the Value-Duty Link to Environmental Ethics" in Boylan (2001) op.cit.

[15]Following the worldwide smallpox eradication campaign, the last case of smallpox was in 1978, and that was following exposure in a laboratory accident. Since this last case there have been numerous calls for the stocks of variola, the virus that causes smallpox, to be destroyed. One of the arguments for not destroying these stocks is the potential importance that any genome, even the variola genome, may have for us, in the future.

protect the environment. On the contrary, we have already argued that there is a *Duty not to Harm Nature:* "We should never act in such a way that we knowingly leave nature worse than when we first encountered it."

Instigating a wide-scale alteration in the germ line of pigs for the sake of humans only (extrinsic reasons) is thus prohibited.

Other genetic alterations in animals are, in a practical sense, harmful to humans. For example, reducing the genetic diversity through widespread germ-line genetic engineering might lower the resistance to new diseases, because one of the key defenses that any species has against disease is the diversity in its genetic population. If a genetic population is robustly diverse, then the invasion of a virulent strain of bacteria or a deadly virus may not kill off the entire species, since some subgroups within the population will be immune to the infecting agent. Thus, diversity within the plant and animal kingdoms is an essential element to some species' survival (i.e., its fitness over various environments).

C. Humans.

The last issue to discuss is germ-line therapy for humans.[16] In order to evaluate this properly, we need to review a few of the general principles that have been discussed so far. In the previous section of this chapter, the strongest argument for germ-line genetic therapy was given, namely, that it would knock out various genetic diseases such as Tay-Sachs. Wouldn't it be wonderful if we could eliminate this and other such single-gene disorders?[17] Certainly, so long as the "all things being equal" caveat was not violated. On the one hand, if we could knock out a genetic disease so that it would never occur anywhere in the world ever again, it would fulfill the professional duty of physicians that they will concern themselves with the well-being of the sick, both present and potential. But will it also satisfy the other side of the oath that they do no harm? This ambivalence perhaps is more indicative of the current state of the art than it is about the question per se. Because of the Principle of Precautionary Reason, the Duty Not to Harm Nature[18] (here understood as the genetic population), and the Duty to Future Generations, we must tread very gingerly here. This caution requires that we explore conventional therapies

---

[16]Cases of "enhancing" the germ line via eugenics are rejected on the same lines as have been enunciated in Chapter Ten.

[17]Germ-line gene therapy will not eradicate these diseases. Spontaneous mutations will mean that these cases will still arise in the human population.

[18]We should never act in such a way that we knowingly leave nature worse than when we first encountered it.

first and only when they are ineffective to move toward modest, well-defined goals.[19] There is *so much* potentiality for harm that caution is morally required. This source of potential harm is a direct function of our ignorance. Our methods for genetic therapy are really rather crude. Because of this, researchers (despite their sophisticated apparatus) are really operating on a model that is far less precise that one would like, especially if, as a patient, your life is at stake. Thus, a part of this criticism is really a criticism of our present knowledge. This sort of criticism, often called an "in practice" criticism, is often contrasted to an "in principle" criticism.

To be more precise, at the present state of the art, any change in the germ line involves too many possibilities for error. The results of these errors would be very severe and would affect many people. Because of this, the relevant moral principles mentioned earlier would sanction bold forays into this arena. However, working at the edges in a cautious way would not be prohibited because the mission of both medicine (the well-being of the sick) and ethics (the duty to rescue) dictates that we move forward—*cautiously.*

However, some may say that science never got anywhere exhibiting caution. Proscribing such restrictions might cripple the pace of progress. We would reply that despite the prudential good that might be performed if we moved more aggressively, the long-standing harm that could occur if we made a crucial mistake is decisive.

Chapter Seven argued that the mission for science that "whatever could be known should be known" is too broad. Rather, this imperative must be restrained by the limits of science that prohibit scientists from using immoral means or immoral ends in the achievement of their goals. Acting without complete knowledge is always a risk. On the other hand, complete knowledge never exists when one is involved in discovery.[20] Thus, one must create a threshold of risk that dictates caution. This threshold must take account of all relevant factors:

Practical

1. Can we reasonably do what we say we can?
2. Do the goods outweigh the harms?

---

[19]These genes can be eradicated from the population by "selective" breeding, either by preventing those who have the gene from having children, or by testing embryos, even at the preimplantation stage and not allowing implantation or aborting those that are carriers, thus reducing the chance of harm by direct intervention.

[20]This debate goes back a long ways. It is given excellent, accessible voice in the Clifford-James debate. See William Kingdom Clifford, "The Ethics of Belief" in *Lectures and Essays*, vol. 2 (London: Macmillan & Co, 1901), pp. 163–205 and William James, "The Sentiment of Rationality" in *The Will to Believe and Other Essays* (New York: Longmans, Green & Co., 1897), pp. 63–110.

Professional

1. Are we fulfilling the goals of the Hippocratic Oath, namely, to concern ourselves with the well-being of the patient and being cognizant that we do no harm?
2. Are we free from conflicts of interest (i.e., are we really after the well-being of the patient as opposed to any professional prize)?

Moral

1. Are we exploiting anyone as a means only?
2. Does this procedure or research strategy violate any maxims of the Personal Worldview Imperative?
3. Does this procedure or research strategy violate the dictum not to harm human nature?
4. Does this procedure or research strategy violate the principle of precautionary reason?
5. Does this procedure or research strategy violate the duty to future generations?
6. Have the priorities of the Table of Embeddedness been maintained?

This checklist creates a reasonable guideline for research that might impact the germ line. The moral imperatives for helping people dictate that we move, albeit very cautiously, in this direction.

chapter twelve

Where Business
and Science Intersect

I. What Is the Present Relationship
Between Science and Business?

The biomedical engineering field is one of the most active in science today because so much potential spin-off from this research into therapies can significantly alter our lives. Whenever there is a large practical, consumer crossover, one finds businesses itching to get into the action for the potential profits. So it is that bioengineering firms have been proliferating in this research atmosphere. In some cases private companies[1] conduct their own research cloaked in corporate secrecy—as opposed to the openness that characterizes the work that is funded by public money, such as that done by the National Institutes of Health (N.I.H, Bethesda, Maryland) or various university laboratories. Thus, in this first model a lacuna exists between what is being done in the public sphere (which is more open, e.g., the Human Genome

---

[1]The term "private" here is not meant to imply a closely held corporation. It may, in fact, be a publicly traded corporation. The intent is to contrast the interests of a business that are (because of pecuniary reasons) selfishly oriented as opposed to the avowed mission of labs funded with public money that ostensibly are operating in the interests of all humankind.

Project publishes its results in real time, and the results are available to everyone worldwide over the Internet) and that which is done in the private arena (in which work is done in private and everything imaginable is patented).

In the second model, research labs work in conjunction with private companies, and responsibilities and rewards are parsed proportionately. Oftentimes, the only reason that businesses will choose this second model is if they lack the laboratories, personnel, or expertise to effectively work alone.

II. HOW IS SCIENCE BEING CARRIED OUT IN THE PRESENT RELATIONSHIP?

In the first model, there are those interested in the public good versus those whose interest is in personal gain. However, the relationship is not that simple. In many cases, universities have allowed directors of research labs to create companies, or the universities, themselves, have created subsidiary corporations. Thus, from an outsider's view a university might appear to be operating for the public good, but in fact it may be motivated by the same imperatives that drive the corporations: creating goods that the general public is willing to buy in order to make money. Such situations muddy the two-model scenario outlined in the last section.

A further complication is that many of those in the public sphere who have created corporations have not done so for the sake of monetary gain alone, but rather to sidestep some of the myriad public regulations.[2] In this way they hope to be able to better control and expedite their research in order to put themselves forward as world-class scientists. These individuals are motivated by fame and international prizes.

This situation makes the first model appear to be identical to the second. In fact, many of the same characteristics are visible, namely, acting in secrecy and for the sake of the internal benefit of the quasi-public entity.

Businesses, themselves, are in the market of selling what they have as soon as possible so that they might show their investors some profits. Thus, nothing is shared or given away. Everything is proprietary. If anyone wants to know what the companies are doing, then he has to ante up and pay the price.

In the second model, business is generally financially supporting a laboratory that without its help would shut down. Thus on the "benefits" side, business usually has the possible outcomes heavily skewed its way. In business's defense, it should be said that it is putting money up front for potential results that *may not* materialize.

---

[2]For example, in fetal tissue research, or in the funding of Clonaid, a company that has been set up to produce the first human clone, an area of research that has been prohibited in many countries, and would not be possible using public funds. (*Science* 289 (2000): 2271 for more information)

III. The Advantages of the Status Quo.

A. Genetic Information.

It cannot be denied that if efficiency is the measure, the status quo is doing very well. For example, one prominent project has been the mapping of the human genome. The Human Genome Project (HGP) is an international collaboration to map and sequence the 3×10^9 nucleotides that make up the human genome.[3] Because it is critical to the usefulness of the sequence information, it was deemed that the sequence had to be accurate (> 99.99 percent), assembled (it is important to know exactly where and in what order on the chromosomes the sequences are arranged), and accessible to all. The approach has therefore been to accurately map and clone large pieces of DNA from each of the 23 pairs of chromosomes, and now that the whole genome has been mapped, to proceed to obtain the sequence of these different chromosome fragments by an approach known as shotgun sequencing.[4] Using this approach, two chromosomes have been "completely" sequenced (chromosomes 21 and 22), and more than 85 percent of the whole human genome has now been sequenced to an accuracy of 99.9 percent and is widely available in public databases.

In contrast to this, a private company, Celera, decided to take a different approach and do shotgun sequencing on the whole of the human genome, using a supercomputer to reassemble the sequence and building on and incorporating into its model the publicly available data.

This strategy characterizes much of the work in the private sector. After a publicly funded project has reached critical mass (i.e., has produced the critical maps of the whole human genome) and the data from the publicly funded project is put into the public domain (as part of its mission the data are released to the public within 24 hours), then a private company creates a computer algorithm based upon this publicly funded data in order to finish up the task before the publicly funded agency, which is working according to a slower protocol designed to ensure accuracy. The private company then claims to have finished first and claims patents on data based on its speed to market.[5]

---

[3]How many genes this represents is very unclear. Original estimates had suggested 100,000, but as the genome of other species is being elucidated, the number of human genes has become less clear, with different scientists ranging in their estimates from as low as 30,000 to more than 150,000. See Elizabeth Pennisi, "And the Gene Number Is . . .?" *Science* (2000) 288: 1146–7.

[4]In shotgun sequencing, restriction enzymes are used to cut the DNA into several hundreds of random bits that are then individually sequenced. Computers are then used to determine the sequence from all these overlapping sequence lengths.

[5]In the end the announcement of the sequencing of the human genome was made as a joint presentation, although as yet neither Celera nor the HGP have completed a final version of the genome. See Elizabeth Pennisi, "Finally, the Book of Life and Instructions for Navigating It," *Science* (2000) 288: 2304–7 for more information about the different strategies and the implications.

Is this fair? The private company could never have created its algorithm without the mass of data that are within the public domain. Yet the private company enters the game in the end stages and then has the gall to claim how clever it is to finish first and that it should be rewarded for doing so by being awarded patents on those last pieces of the puzzle. Those patents declare that the company *owns* those genes and can either limit the research on those genes or make large profits on any therapies based on them!

In the theory of deserts, we often try to decipher what percentage of an action is due to our own efforts as opposed to preferment given to us.[6] The notion here is that we are only entitled to be compensated for what we, ourselves, have done *without* outside assistance. In the case of a private company making use of public data to create an algorithm, one might justifiably say that the company has only an incremental desert. On the one hand, its whole methodology is based on others' research, for which it pays no compensation because the information is in the public domain. On the other hand, it also expects the more meticulous public research project to work to the end so that any errors the private company has made might be corrected while the private company still claims all the patent rights. This violates the ethical principles of desert. The interface between the private and the public spheres on the levels of basic research can be troublesome (see the next section).

Variation in the genetic sequence exists within the human genome, and it is these polymorphisms, or differences, in our genome that give rise to the wide range of human variability, including our susceptibility to human disease (see Chapter Four). Thus, the sequencing of a human genome is not the end of the project. Much of the variation is single base pair differences, known as single nucleotide polymorphisms (SNPs, pronounced "snips"), and both HGP and Celera have announced plans to create SNP databases that can be used to identify markers for different diseases and disease susceptibility.

In addition, other genome projects exist. The sequence of a bacterium (*Escherichia coli*), baker's yeast (*Saccharomyces cervisiae*), a round worm (*Caaenorhabditis elegans*), and the fruit fly (*Drosophila melanogaster*) have already been completed. Plans to sequence the mouse and make the data publicly available have been announced.[7] And there are already plans to sequence

---

[6]This book will accept the position of proportional deserts outlined by Boylan in his essay, "The Future of Affirmative Action," *Journal of Social Philosophy* (2001) forthcoming. This position suggests that we only deserve that portion of a final result that we, ourselves, are actually responsible for. Thus, if someone is by birth or fortune given nine-tenths of a result, the agent can only claim credit for one-tenth. For a general treatment of attitudes toward deserts theory, see Louis P. Pojman and Owen McLeod, eds., *What Do We Deserve?* (NY: Oxford University Press, 1999).

[7]Celera has already sequenced three strains of mouse, but the data is not available to researchers without a fee. The public/private consortium will make the mouse data available using the Human Genome Project as a model. See Eliot Marshall, *Science* (2000) 291: 243–44.

the rat, with pilot projects to sequence the zebra fish and probably the chimpanzee in the works.

All these projects are extrinsically oriented toward understanding human disease and the creation of new medicines for humans. Although some of these projects are being funded by public money, several companies are getting involved in genomic sequencing[8] with the aim of creating proprietary genetic property that can be marketed to other companies at a profit. These strategies range from selling subscriptions to annotated genome databases, making available and selling access to DNA clones, and developing personalized medical tests.

B. Bioinformatics and Data Mining.

The huge amount of raw data that are being generated by the genome projects needs to be translated into a form that other private pharmaceutical companies can readily use. These are the second-level players in the business market. These bioinfomation sources[9] seek to provide systems, databases, computer software, and services that make it easier for their clients to identify and characterize more precise drug targets for therapeutic intervention. The strategies of these companies range from providing enterprise-wide (often desktop available) bioinformatics, tools, and systems to providing drug discovery through software and hardware development. If there was ever a level in which private business could do a better job than the public to interface with those actually producing the genetically engineered drugs or therapies, it is at this second level. This is because not only are the private companies better able to tailor a mass of data in the public domain toward targeted private use, but with the dependence on Silicon Valley technologies, often only the private companies have the financial resources to attract the personnel with the required computer skills to this emerging area.

C. The Transcriptome and Proteomics.

Although every cell in the body contains all of the genomic DNA, only a small number of genes are active, or expressed, in any cell or tissue. A large area of current interest as we learn more about the human genome is

---

[8] At the writing of this book, the major companies involved in the genetic sequencing enterprise include Celera Genomics (Rockville, MD), Human Genome Sciences (Rockville, MD), Incyte Genomics (Palo Alto, CA), and Millennium Pharmaceuticals (Cambridge, MA).

[9] Some of these companies include Lion Bioscience (Heidelberg, Germany), Genetics Computer Group (Madison, WI), InforMax (Bethesda, MD), Oxford Molecular Group (Oxford, England), NetGenics (Cleveland, OH), DoubleTwist (Oakland, CA), Compugen (Tel Aviv, Israel), Silicon Genetics (San Carlos, CA).

understanding which genes are "turned on" and ultimately which proteins are active in a cell. The mRNA that is being actively transcribed (see Chapter Four) is known as the transcriptome and can now be analyzed by gene chips, glass, or silicon slides that have thousands of individual pieces of DNA on them. RNA can be extracted from a cell or tissue and hybridized with the chips, allowing identification of all the mRNA in a cell. Their strategies range from manufacturing DNA chips for mRNA identification and scanners for diagnostic use, to increasingly developing the software and bioinformatics systems to interpret all of the information.[10]

As we mentioned earlier (Chapter Four), proteins are the key components in cells, and it is the interaction of proteins in a cell, tissue, or organism that is crucial to its function. Until recently we have not had the tools to study proteins at the same level as DNA, but this is beginning to change. Similar technologies to gene chips are being developed to identify all the proteins in a cell or tissue (the proteome).[11] And increasingly, especially with computer modeling, the tertiary structures of proteins are being revealed and understood. This allows insight into how proteins interact so that they might be employed in a realistic, applied strategy.

All of these strategies promise new efficiencies that may work to improve the well-being of the patient.

IV. A CRITICAL EVALUATION OF THE CURRENT SYSTEM.

A number of ethical problems are contained within our current method of mixing business and science. Before we begin, we must acknowledge that because the health delivery system and the pharmaceutical industry in the United States are private and the system that creates, manufactures, and distributes biomedical devices is also private, and the research community is both private and public, a mixing of the public and the private is inevitable. This is a structural fact that we will have to deal with.

Let us address this reality by reviewing some of the ethical and professional imperatives that have been outlined earlier. Let us begin with the professional imperatives. A physician is supposed to concern herself with the well-being of the sick and to do no harm. When a physician owns a stake in

---

[10]One of the pioneering companies in this area was Affymetrix (Santa Clara, CA), with the development of silicon chips with thousands of different oligonucleotides on them. Glass slides with cDNA on them, or methodologies to "read" DNA chips are produced by a large number of companies, including Amersham Pharmacia Biotech (Uppsala, Sweden), Incyte Genomics (Palo Alto, CA), Molecular Dynamics (Sunnyvale, CA).

[11]Some of the companies involved in this arena include Ciphergen Biosystems (Palo Alto, CA), CuraGen (New Haven, CT), Oxford GlycoSciences (Oxford, England), Millenium (Cambridge, MA), Hybrigenics (Paris, France), Large Scale Biology (Rockville, MD).

a biomedical research company that also provides products useful to the physician in her practice, then she is involved in a conflict of interest. If the conflict reaches the threshold described in Chapter Two, she may very well be using products and devices from her own company just because they are from her own company. She may be doing so either out of a profit motive or because she wants to create a database sufficient to convince others of her brilliance. (Remember, one of the most tantalizing prizes to the very intelligent is lavish praise and recognition.) If she acts out of a motive of profit, she is short-changing her patients for her selfish monetary gain. This may be working against the patient's well-being and causing harm. If this is so, then such an action is prohibited on the grounds of *professional practice.* The action may also be prohibited on *ethical grounds* through (1) the existence or appearance of a conflict of interest and (2) the using of the patient as a "means only" for her own personal profit.

If the physician acts out of the motivation of convincing others of her brilliance, then she also commits the same infractions as well as acting contrary to the *professional duty of the researcher* that enjoins the researcher to declare, "I'm part of a community dedicated to help others; I don't care who gets credit so long as we help people. I'm part of a team dedicated to help others, and none of us cares who gets credit so long as we help people." This is the professional ideal of the researcher. In this case mentioned earlier, it is likely that this ideal is being compromised.

Thus, the professional roles of the physician and of the researcher can be compromised by physicians and researchers who are employed at universities or in private practice creating business links that have to do with their research and practice.

But what about those physicians/researchers who are employed by private companies and commit themselves to "work for hire"? This is also an important situation to consider. The physician/researcher generally submerges the self for the greater good of the company's research strategy. So long as that strategy is ultimately for the public good (even though it may also bring the company a profit), there is no professional problem. In fact, the submergence of self that is generally required in the work-for-hire atmosphere fulfills a primary tenet of the professional responsibility for researchers. This is professionally laudatory.

However, in this submission of the self in such situations, there is also the tendency of *absolving* the self from responsibility for the outcomes of the project because in the corporate setting, the goals and projects are dictated by the company. Certainly there is input from the research staff, but they are required to bend to the will of the corporation. Now since many scientists choose the business atmosphere largely because they want to increase their pay significantly, they are not inclined to rock the boat. Instead, the inclination is to be a team player and do whatever is required.

It is a good thing to be a team player in science. Chapter Two suggested that research science should transform itself from an individualistic cowboy mentality to one of cooperation and teamwork. However, even team members must have a conscience. Each researcher on the team must accept personal responsibility for the moral dimensions of the project on which he is engaged. This is dictated by the Personal Worldview Imperative. There is no escaping it. You cannot just put in your time and deposit your paycheck. You are responsible for what you do—even when it is at the dictates of your corporate superiors.

Thus, for the physician/researcher who works for a private company, the most important issue is following the Personal Worldview Imperative and making sure (as much as is reasonably possible) that one's work is truly in the patient's good. It is the patient's good and not the company's good that is paramount. Further, since the physician/researcher is engaged in a business enterprise, further *professional imperatives from the business vantage point,* such as the Principle of Fair Competition, exist.[12]

Second, let us examine some key ethical principles that are relevant in many of these problems. We proceed in this section rather apolitically by looking at selected emblematic examples from the realms of plants, animals, and then humans.

One difficult situation in agribusiness (in which germ-line genetic engineering has been going on for years) is the way that many multinational seed companies operate. In the case of wheat, for example, various countries allow seed companies to buy seeds (in some cases, when countries have not given their permission to buy seeds for genetic engineering, the companies have stolen these seeds) in order to "improve" them, that is, genetically alter them. Then after altering the seeds so that the wheat might produce another essential vitamin or be pest resistant, the seed company sells the seeds back to the same people who sold them the seeds (or from whom the seed companies stole the seeds). This may seem like a harmless exchange to some. But it violates the moral principle of exploitation. Since these seed companies rarely (if ever) pay royalties to the countries or individuals who sold them their seeds, they are exploiting a natural resource without recompense. This puts the seed companies in the position of using others as a means only for their own gains.

Now some might want to argue that the DNA found in wild strains of wheat that the seed companies covet does not belong to the farmers or the countries that provided the seeds. We tend to agree with this to the extent that

---

[12]Michael Boylan, "The Principle of Fair Competition" in *Business Ethics,* ed. Michael Boylan (Upper Saddle River, NJ: Prentice Hall, 2001).

no one can really own anything natural in a strong sense.[13] But the fact that the provider of the seeds does not really *own* the seed DNA does not permit the seed companies to merely pay a small fee and then patent their results for large proprietary profits.

It would seem that the seed companies should compensate both the farmers from whom they have taken their seed and who will be hurt when new strains of seed (and their resulting fruits) become the standard in the marketplace (instead of the old-fashioned wild strains) *and* the general human community. The former compensation rests on the principle that those who benefit you should share in the results of their benefit.[14]

The latter compensation rests on the principle that the emergence of a new strain of wheat may (probably will) have an impact on wild strains of wheat. This, in turn, affects all people and all living organisms. With respect to people, the duty to future generations comes into play, and with respect to the biotic community as such, the value-duty relation comes into play (see Chapter Two).

How does a company compensate the general biome for its actions? This is a very difficult question, but it contains the essential element that the wild strain of wheat that gave birth to the genetically engineered hybrids should not be artificially pushed out of existence (as seems now to be the case).[15] One possible way to compensate the biotic realm for this intrusion might be to buy land in the countries that provided the seed and to maintain wild prairie grasslands that can be a home to uncultivated wheat. In this way, the wild strains would not be subject to a double fitness pressure of the natural environment and artificial human intervention. This proposed solution is not meant to be

---

[13]The position of limited ownership of natural resources is argued for by many environmentalists. For a flavor of some of these arguments, see Murray Bookchin, "Recovering Evolution: A Reply to Eckersley and Fox," *Environmental Ethics* 12 (fall 1990): 253–73; Murray Bookchin, *The Philosophy of Social Ecology: Essays on Dialectical Naturalism* (Toronto: Black Rose Books, 1990); Murray Bookchin, *Remaking Society: Pathways to a Green Future* (Boston: South End Press, 1990); J. Baird Callicott, ed., *Companion to the Sand Country Almanac* (Madison, WI: University of Wisconsin Press, 1987); J. Baird Callicott, *In Defense of the Land Ethic* (Albany, NY: SUNY Press, 1989); Jim Cheney, "Naturalizing the Problem of Evil," *Environmental Ethics* 19.3 (1997); 299–314; John Clark, *The Anarchist Moment: Reflections on Culture, Nature and Power* (Toronto: Black Rose Books, 1984); Denis Collins and John Barkdull, "Capitalism, Environmentalism, and Mediating Structures," *Environmental Ethics* 17.3 (1985): 227–44; Bill Devall and George Sessions, *Deep Ecology: Living as if Nature Mattered* (Salt Lake City, UT: Peregrine Smith Books, 1985); Bill Devall, "Deep Ecology and Radical Environmentalism," *Society and Natural Resources* 4 (1991): 247–58; Michael Boylan in "Worldview and the Value-Duty Link to Environmental Ethics" in *Environmental Ethics* (Upper Saddle River, NJ: Prentice Hall, 2001).

[14]This is even the case when the providers of the benefit do not engage in risking their capital to develop the new strain of seed. The point is that the company would not be where it is without those hardy wild strains of wheat.

[15]The economics and some practical consequences of this situation are discussed in Roger Beachy, Thomas Eisner, Fred Gould, Henry Way Kendall, *Bioengineering of Crops: Report of the World Bank Panel on Transgenetic Crops* (Washington, DC: The World Bank, 1997).

conclusive, but merely suggestive of ways to create a generalized compensation (as was suggested, in a different context, for egg donors).

If seed companies would act in an ethically responsible way, they would seek to insert these ethical concerns into the way they intend to do business.

A second example concerns animals. Fish farming has been with us for some time. Presently in Maine, genetically engineered salmon have been bred so that they might more completely fulfill the consumer's ever expanding taste for fish. This includes size, color, and taste. As with the genetically engineered wheat, it also includes resistance to disease and increased "shelf life" (the amount of time that a fish may stay palatable after catch).

What would happen if these fish were to escape from their fish farms and interbreed with wild strains of salmon? The answer is that they would become a new "player" in the genetic environment. But what if the genetic engineers were not as clever as they would have liked to be and had created an unforeseen problem in the mix? The answer is that if the problem creates differential positive fitness, then the species will thrive. If it does not, then it will fail. Sounds simple, right? But might there be some rough edges along the way? Certainly. Since fishing techniques are becoming ever and ever more efficient (much to the detriment of our fish population), many of these unforeseen consequences may end up in your stomach or ours. What happens then? Perhaps a disease. Perhaps a new parasite. Perhaps a new virus. If the results are benign, then no problem. If not, then they may be epidemic.

What happens when a predator to the salmon eats one of these genetically altered hybrids? The same as just noted, except that each predator has its own predator and so the problem may progress as a geometric progression. Bad news.

In order to prevent such a scenario, some fish farms try to ensure that the genetically altered fish are sterile, so that if some escape, the negative scenario will not occur. But then there is the case of really ensuring that the salmon will, in fact, be sterile. This is an "in practice" problem. "In principle," if one could perform this sort of engineering carefully, the results might not occur.

However, even if the genetically altered fish are successfully rendered sterile, they are likely to escape from their fish farm boundaries (as is commonly the case). If and when this happens in significant numbers, these genetically altered salmon may very well outcompete wild species for food supplies and thus drive the wild species to extinction.

The big question concerning the interface of business and science here is how much incentive is there for companies concerned with the bottom line to go to proper lengths to create safeguards against these and other deleterious results? Generally there is little. Unless consumers demand some sort of accountability and recompense in this domain, it will not occur. Since businesses, like slime molds, generally move according to the laws of physics (i.e., least resistance), they will not for the most part fulfill their ethical responsibilities unless there is some help from the sidelines.

In the case of genetic engineering in plants and animals, there is always the grave problem that the public may not recognize their intrinsic value. So often plants and animals have only been seen for their extrinsic value—their value to us. Such an attitude will ultimately be self-defeating since if we destroy the environment, we also will be destroyed. But it is also wrong in the moral sense that if we consider nature as such, we will (necessarily) value it. To do otherwise is to be inattentive. And if we value it, we must protect and defend it.

Concerning humans and genetic engineering, there are too many cases to raise in this abbreviated venue. However, perhaps the most pressing issues (at the writing of this book) are the questions of patenting genes and tissue ownership.[16] These issues are so complicated that they could each encompass an entire volume. However, we can say this much: the practice of patenting genes is, in one sense, bizarre, because no one can really say he owns a natural object, in an absolute sense.[17] If *I* have a genetic disease and a company pays the hospital for a sample of *my* blood and if the company determines the gene defect that causes the problem, then how can they be said to *own* my gene? Even further, how can I say that it is even *my* gene? Perhaps a better locution would be *the* gene that is collectively owned by all those who possess it. This gene exists. This gene possesses a fitness coefficient within some given environment. All of this is true due to a mechanism that supersedes any single company. Thus, the most a genetic-oriented company can hope for is the permission to use a particular domain of research for its own so that it might get a return on its investment should a discovery of economic importance ensue.

What the company cannot do is to claim patent rights over a gene. If this were true in an absolute sense, then all the people in the world might be owned by a company or companies. The understanding of humans in this book is that they possess moral dignity, that is, they have no market value and cannot be the property of another. Thus, it is a giant hubris to assume that any company can *own* a gene. They can only have research territories for the sake of gaining a return on their investment (which is legitimate). But they do not own a gene because that would imply that super company ABC might be able to own the entire genome of *Homo sapiens*. This would amount to being the greatest slave trader in history.

---

[16]This is obviously a very tortured issue that sets the interests of the biomedical business community against those of publicly funded research projects and those of the general public. Some of these issues are discussed in Robert Weir's anthology, *Stored Tissue Samples: Ethical, Legal, and Public Policy Implications* (Ames, IA: University of Iowa Press, 1998).

[17]What we mean by "absolute" sense of ownership is that the owner of x is allowed to do *whatever* she wants with x, where x is the good that is absolutely owned.

Thus, we need to work at redefining the way we describe the rights of research so that they do not imply a master-slave relationship with the giants of biomedical research.

A second situation that should be considered is the ethical problem that may exist in the situations involving the difference between basic and applied research. Basic research in science is essential (so long as it meets the guidelines in Chapter Seven). But the general public has never been very enthusiastic about supporting science unless there is a technological payoff. In fact, it is our opinion that there is not a per se moral imperative to engage in scientific research at all.[18] However, if the society is engaged in applied science, then it should also be engaged in theoretical science, as well. This is a professional research obligation that follows from the medical professional's obligation to do no harm. Unless the basic research umbrella is broad enough to substantially cover the practical investigations, there is cause for concern because practical application of biomedical research must follow a long way behind basic research in order to provide the sort of safeguards that are necessary to satisfy the exploitation prohibition.

This is very similar to the principle in teaching that one must never teach a subject unless one is professionally trained several levels above what she is teaching. I suppose that this is also an extension of the Principle of Precautionary Reason, mentioned earlier.[19]

In the end, there are two sorts of constraints upon biomedical researchers and the commercial interests that support them. The first concerns basic constraints on the proper conduct of business in a moral fashion. This includes the principle of conflict of interest and the principle of fair competition.

The second sort of constraint concerns the professional and moral responsibilities of both the physician and the researcher. Both roles are present in the discovery process. Science moves according to the principle that whatever can be known should be known. Business moves according to the principle that revenues should exceed expenses. Both of these practical imperatives must be supervened by the moral and professional imperatives in cases of conflict. If we leave businesses unchecked, then they will do whatever they can to make a profit without regard for anything else. This means that they will

---

[18]Through the greatest part of human history, scientific research was seen to be merely the eccentric explorations of the "natural philosopher." This was because people thought that there was no money to be made of it. If the earth is flat or round, what does that have to do with the price of my wheat crop? Science was a domain for people who had time on their hands. When it was discovered that there was money to be made—i.e., in the sixteenth and seventeenth centuries with more accurate charts for navigating boats that would provide a 1000 times return on investment, then the general public (albeit from the impetus of the wealthy few) decided to take notice.

[19]Beyleveld, op. cit.

not naturally be inclined to think of the ethical duties owed to the patient or the professional duties of the physician and researcher. The only way that we can ensure that biomedical research companies will act responsibly is to make it more profitable for them to do so. If they know that violation of the standards set out in the shared community worldview will have grave consequences to their profitability, then they will instantly come in-line (provided we make it very difficult to cheat).

Obviously, in our global community tremendous opportunity for cheating on moral and professional restraints exists. All that we can say to this is that we all must be vigilant to prevent it. The consequences of acting otherwise are too unthinkable to entertain.

Glossary of Scientific and Ethical Terms

acquired immune deficiency syndrome: See AIDS.

adapters: A small piece of DNA used to link two pieces of double-stranded DNA together prior to ligation with DNA ligase.

adenine: One of four nitrogen bases in DNA and RNA; pairs with thymine in DNA, and with uracil in RNA.

adenovirus: A group of DNA viruses originally identified in human adenoid tissue, used as a vector for gene therapy.

AIDS: Acquired immune deficiency syndrome; a condition caused by a virus that attacks and kills cells of the immune system so that the system is unable to protect the organism against disease.

allele: One of two or more possible forms of a gene, each form affecting the hereditary trait somewhat differently.

amino acid: An organic compound composed of a central carbon atom to which are bonded a hydrogen atom, an amino group ($-NH_2$), an acid group ($-COOH$), and one of a variety of other atoms or group of atoms; the building block of polypeptides and proteins.

anaphase: The stage of mitosis and meiosis in which the chromosomes move toward the poles of the spindle.

anticodon: The three-nucleotide sequence at the end of a tRNA molecule that is complementary to, and base pairs with, a specific amino acid codon in mRNA.

β-galactosidase: An enzyme that hydrolyzes galactoside; often used as a marker gene in bacterial plasmids or gene therapy studies.

bacteriophage: A virus that infects bacteria.

blastocyst: The stage of very early embryo development with a layer of cells surrounding a central cavity or blastocoele, and a mass of cells at one pole, known as the inner cell mass, which contains the embryonic stem cells that go on to develop into the fetus.

capping: Modification of the 5' end of RNA to prevent degradation.

cell: The basic living unit.

cell body: The enlarged portion of a neuron that contains the nucleus.

cell cycle: An ordered sequence of events in the life of a dividing cell; composed of the M, G_1, S, and G_2 phases.

centromere: Region of the mitotic chromosome that holds the sister chromatids together and which joins to the mitotic spindle during metaphase.

chimera: An organ or organism with cells with different genetic makeup.

chromatid: One of the usual paired and parallel strands of a duplicated chromosome joined by a single centromere.

chromatography: A process in which a chemical mixture (liquid or gas) is separated into individual components as a result of differential flow over a stationary phase.

chromosome: A long, threadlike group of genes found in the nucleus of all eukaryotic cells and most visible during mitosis and meiosis; chromosomes consist of DNA and protein.

clone: A population of genetically identical plasmids, organisms, or individuals.

coding strand: The one DNA strand, during transcription, that directs the synthesis of RNA.

codon: The basic unit of the genetic code; a sequence of three adjacent nucleotides in DNA or mRNA.

competent (of bacteria): The ability of bacteria to take up DNA, usually in the form of plasmid DNA.

complementary DNA: cDNA; a DNA molecule made by reverse transcription of a mRNA molecule, and therefore lacking introns in genomic DNA.

cosmid: A large plasmid (~50 kb) vector that includes specific sequences enabling it to be also packaged as a bacteriophage.

cyclin-dependent protein kinases (Cdk): Proteins critical in the control of the cell cycle.

cyclins: Proteins with Cdk's that are critical in the control of the cell cycle.

cystic fibrosis: A common hereditary disease that appears usually in early childhood; involves functional disorder of the exocrine glands.

cytokinesis: The cytoplasmic changes accompanying mitosis.

cytoplasm: The entire contents of the cell, except the nucleus, bounded by the plasma membrane.

cytosine: one of the four nitrogen bases in DNA and RNA; pairs with guanine.

dATP: Deoxynucleotide adenosine triphosphate, one of the building blocks of DNA.

dCTP: Deoxynucleotide cytidine triphosphate, one of the building blocks of DNA.

degenerate: Indicating that different nucleotide triplets (or codons) code for the same amino acid.

deletion: The loss of a piece of a chromosome with the genes it carries.

denaturation: To modify or destroy the tertiary molecular structure of a molecule, often by heat, alkali or ultraviolet radiation.

Deontology: The ethical theory that emphasizes one's duty to do a particular action because the action itself is inherently right and not due to any calculation about the consequences of the action.

deoxynucleotide triphosphates: dATP, dCTP, dGTP, dTTP; the building blocks of DNA.

deoxyribonucleic acid: DNA; the hereditary material of most organisms; composed of nucleic acids containing deoxyribose, a phosphate group, and one of four nitrogen bases; DNA composes the genes.

DGGE: Denaturing gradient gel electrophoresis; a method for detecting mutations in a DNA sequence.

dGTP: Deoxynucleotide guanosine triphosphate, one of the building blocks of DNA.

dideoxynucleotide: ddNTP; a nucleoside triphosphate that lacks -OH groups on both the 2' and 3' carbons of the pentose sugar, so that chain extension cannot continue. Labeled dideoxynucleotides are used for sequencing.

diploid: Having the basic chromosome number doubled; a single cell, individual, or generation characterized by the diploid chromosome.

disease: An abnormal condition of an organism, as a consequence of infection, inherent weakness, or environmental stress, that impairs normal function.

DNA: See deoxyribonucleic acid.

DNA ligase: An enzyme that joins two pieces of double-stranded DNA together.

DNA polymerase: An enzyme that catalyzes the syntheses of a new DNA strand, using one of the original strands as a template.

dominant: The member of a pair of alleles that is expressed, even though both alleles are present.

dTTP: Deoxynucleotide thymidine triphosphate, one of the building blocks of DNA.

duplication: The presence of more than one copy of a particular chromosomal segment in a chromosome set.

EG cells: See embryonic germ cells.

electroporation: Electrical treatment of cells that allows DNA to be taken up into the cell.

embryonic germ cells: EG cells; cells having the potential to develop into any cell, tissue, or organ in a body, obtained from the gonadal ridge of a 5–9-week-old fetus.

embryonic stem cells: ES cells; cells having the potential to develop into any cell, tissue, or organ in a body, obtained from the inner cell mass of the blastocyst.

endocytosis: Incorporation of substances into a cell by phagocytosis or pinocytosis.

endogenous: Produced or synthesized within the organism (opposite of exogenous).

enzyme: A protein or part-protein molecule used as a catalyst in biochemical reactions.

epigenetic: The processes or interactions by which genes are not expressed in certain tissues.

ES cells: See embryonic stem cells.

Ethical Intuitionism: The ethical theory that justifies ethical truths through the immediate grasping of either a principle or the application of the principle in some given situation.

eukaryote: An organism composed of one or more cells containing visibly evident nuclei and organelles.

evolution: Change through time that results from natural selection acting on genetic variations present among individuals of a species; evolution results in the development of new species.

exogenous: Caused by factors or an agent from outside the organism.

exon: A segment of DNA that is transcribed into RNA and translated into protein, specifically the amino acid sequence of a polypeptide; characteristic of eukaryotes.

FISH analysis: Fluorescent *in situ* hybridization; a method of analyzing the DNA content within a cell using DNA probes.

frame-shift mutation: The insertion or deletion of a nucleotide pair causing disruption of the reading frame.

G_0 phase: Stationary or quiescent phase of the cell cycle.

G_1 phase: The first growth phase of the cell cycle, starting just after offspring cells form.

G_2 phase: The second growth phase of the cell cycle, beginning after DNA synthesis.

gamete: A specialized haploid cell, such as an egg or spermatozoa.

gel electrophoresis: Electrophoresis in which proteins or nucleic acids migrate through a gel (agarose or polyacrylamide) and separate into bands according to size.

gene: The fundamental physical unit of heredity that transmits a set of specifications from one generation to the next; a segment of DNA that codes for a specific product.

gene therapy: The insertion of normal or genetically altered genes into cells, usually to replace defective genes, especially in the treatment of genetic disorders.

genetic code: The "language" of the genes dictating the correspondence between nucleotide sequence in DNA (in triplets or codons) and amino acid sequence in proteins.

genetic drift: Changes in the gene pool of a small population due to chance.

genetic recombination: Presence of a new combination of alleles in a DNA molecule as the result of crossing over at meiosis, chromosomal alterations, or gene mutations.

genetics: The study of genes; the study of inheritance.

genotype: The genetic makeup of an organism.

germ-line cells: The lineage of cells that contribute to the formation of the next generation of organisms, cf. somatic cells, which contribute to the body of the organism but not to any descendants.

GFP: See green fluorescent protein.

glycoprotein: A conjugated protein in which the nonprotein group is a carbohydrate.

green fluorescent protein: A protein originally isolated from jellyfish that fluoresces green under UV light.

guanine: One of the four nitrogen bases in DNA or RNA; pairs with cytosine.

haploid: Having the gametic number of chromosomes or half the number characteristic of somatic cells.

heat shock proteins: Proteins synthesized in response to cellular stress.

hematopoietic stem cell: A blood precursor cell that can divide indefinitely and gives rise to all the different lineages of blood cell types.

hemoglobin: The major protein in red blood cells.

hemophilia: A sex-linked hereditary blood defect that occurs almost exclusively in males and is characterized by delayed clotting of the blood.

herpesvirus: A group of large DNA viruses.

heterozygous: Having two different alleles of a gene.

hexamers: An oligonucleotide comprising 6 nucleotides.

histone: A small protein, with a high proportion of positively charged amino acids, that binds to the negatively charged DNA and plays a key role in its folding into chromosomes.

homologous chromosomes: One of two copies of a particular chromosome in a diploid cell, each copy derived from a separate parent.

homozygous: Having two identical alleles of a gene.

inosine: An artificial nucleotide that binds with any of the bases.

intron: A segment of DNA that is transcribed into precursor mRNA but then removed before the mRNA leaves the nucleus.

inversion: A sequence of DNA or genes reversed from their normal order in a segment of a chromosome.

karyotype: The chromosomal composition of a cell or organism.

lentivirus: A type of retrovirus that can infect dividing and nondividing cells.

lymphocytes: White blood cells responsible for the immune response; constitute 20 percent to 30 percent of the white cells of normal human blood.

M phase: The mitotic phase of a cell cycle.

macromolecule: A large, complex molecule with a backbone formed from long carbon chains.

marker studies: Studies in which marker genes of no therapeutic value are inserted in genes to follow the fate of the transduced cells. Often used in the development of gene therapy as safety and feasibility studies.

meiosis: Two successive nuclear divisions (with corresponding cell divisions) that produce gametes (in animals) or sexual spores (in plants) having half of the genetic materials of the original cell.

messenger RNA: mRNA; the RNA complementary to one strand of DNA; transcribed from genes and translated by ribosomes into protein.

metaphase: The stage of mitosis and meiosis in which the chromosomes become arranged in the equatorial plane of the spindle.

mitochondria: Membrane-bound organelles, the size of bacteria, within the cytoplasm of a cell, involved in energy production.

mitosis: The event that leads to the production of two nuclei in one cell; usually followed by cell division.

mitotic spindle: The array of microtubules that serve to separate the duplicated chromosomes during mitosis.

monocistronic: An mRNA that encodes only one protein.

monogenic: Relating to or controlled by a single gene.

monosomy: Having a single copy of a chromosome in a diploid cell.

morula: The stage of very early embryo development, when the embryo appears as a mass of about 30 to 60 cells.

multiple alleles: The existence of several known alleles for a gene.

mutagen: A substance or form of energy that increases the rate of mutations in an organism.

mutation: A heritable change in the nucleotide sequence of a chromosome.

northern blotting: Transfer of denatured RNA that has been separated by gel electrophoresis to a membrane and detection by hybridization.

nucleic acids: DNA or RNA; a chain of nucleotides joined by phosphodiester bonds.

nucleoside: A compound (adenosine, guanosine, cytidine, uridine, or thymidine) that consists of a base combined with deoxyribose or ribose.

nucleotide: A subunit of DNA or RNA, composed of a 5-carbon sugar, a nitrogen base (adenine, guanine, cytosine, uracil, or thymine) and a phosphate group.

nucleus: In eukaryotic cells, the organelle that houses the chromosomal DNA.

Okazaki fragments: Short fragments of DNA produced on the lagging strand and joined together by DNA ligase.

oligonucleotide: A short chain of nucleotides.

operon: In a bacterial chromosome, a set of related protein-coding genes transcribed as a single mRNA.

operator: Short region of DNA in a prokaryote that controls transcription of an adjacent gene.

origin of replication: The nucleotide sequence at which DNA synthesis is initiated.

parvovirus: A small, single-stranded DNA virus.

PCR: See polymerase chain reaction.

Personal Worldview Imperative: All people must develop a single comprehensive and internally coherent worldview that is good and that we strive to act out in our daily lives.

phenotype: The expression of a genotype in the appearance or function of an organism.

phosphodiester bond: The linkage between nucleotides on the same nucleic acid strand.

phosphoproteins: Proteins that contain additional phosphate groups.

plasmid: A small cicular DNA molecule in bacteria that replicates independent of the genome.

point mutation: A change in a chromosome at a single nucleotide within a gene.

poly-A tail: The terminal part of mRNA that is composed of a polynucleotide chain consisting entirely of adenine residues.

polycistronic: A mRNA that encodes two or more proteins.

polymerase chain reaction (PCR): A method for rapidly producing large amounts of a given DNA segment, using DNA polymerase, by separating the double-stranded DNA, synthesizing a second strand with DNA polmerase, and repeating the process many times.

polynucleotide: A linear chain of more than 20 nucleotides.

polypeptide: A linear chain of amino acids linked by peptide bonds.

primary RNA transcript: Newly synthesized RNA, the final product of transcription.

primary structure: The sequence of nucleotides in an RNA or DNA strand, or amino acids in a protein.

primer: A short oligonucleotide (or RNA) that hybridizes with a template strand, providing a 3'-OH group for the initiation or extension of nucleic acid synthesis.

prokaryote: A cellular organism, usually bacteria, that does not have a distinct nucleus.

promoter region: The region of a chromosome containing a specific nucleotide sequence to which RNA polymerase attaches to initiate transcription of mRNA.

pronucleus: The haploid nucleus of a sperm or egg.

prophase: The first stage of mitosis characterized by the condensation of chromosomes (consisting of two chromatids), the disappearance of the nuclear membrane, and formation of mitotic spindle.

protein: One or more polypeptide chains of amino acids; most structural materials and enzymes in a cell are proteins.

proteolytic cleavage: Cutting of a protein to change its function, either activation or inactivation.

provirus: The form of a retrovirus when it is integrated into the genetic material of a host cell and by replicating with it.

reading frame: Any of the three possible ways of reading a sequence of nucleotides as a series of triplets.

recessive: The member of a pair of alleles that is not expressed, even though both alleles are present (opposite to dominant).

recombinant DNA: Whole molecules or fragments that incorporate parts of different parent DNA molecules, as formed by natural recombination mechanisms or by recombinant DNA technology.

recombinant DNA technology: A set of techniques for recombining genes from different sources and transferring the product DNA into cells where it is expressed.

recombinant virus: Virus produced by recombinant DNA technology to contain modified viral nucleic acid (DNA or RNA) within a virus capsid or membrane; used to introduce nonviral genes into a cell.

reductionism: The replacement of one phenomenon or one phenomenological account by another. In the philosophy of biology this often means the replacement of an upper level (i.e., phenotypic) phenomenom/ account by a lower level (i.e., genotypic) phenomenon/account. The implication in this move is that the upper level is *nothing but* an expression of the lower level *simpliciter.* Thus the lower level under this assumption is more primary than the upper level and therefore ought to be the principal source of study.

regulatory sequences: Genes that are involved in turning on or off the transcription of genes that code for amino acid sequences.

replication: The process of making a copy of the DNA in a cell nucleus.

repressor: A protein that binds to a region of DNA and prevents transcription of an adjacent gene.

restriction endonuclease: An enzyme that recognizes specific nucleotide sequences in DNA and cleaves the DNA chain at those points; used in genetic engineering.

retrovirus: An RNA virus that is replicated in a cell by first making a double-stranded DNA provirus that integrates into the host cell chromosome; used as a gene-therapy vector.

reverse transcriptase: An enzyme that transcribes RNA into cDNA; found in association with retroviruses.

reverse transcription: The process by which viral RNA (in retroviruses) is transcribed into DNA.

ribonucleic acid: RNA; a single-stranded nucleic acid similar to DNA but having the sugar ribose rather than deoxyribose, and uracil rather than thymine as one of the bases; the material coded by DNA to carry out specific genetic functions.

ribonucleoprotein: A nucleoprotein that contains RNA.

ribose: A 5-carbon sugar found in RNA molecules.

ribosomal RNA: rRNA; a class of RNA molecules found, together with characteristic proteins, in ribosomes.

ribosome: The subcellular structure, containing rRNA and proteins important in the synthesis of proteins from mRNA.

ribozymes: An RNA molecule with catalytic activity.

RNA: See ribonucleic acid.

RNA polymerase: An enzyme that catalyzes the assembly of the RNA molecule.

secondary structure: The characteristic folding of the polypeptide backbone of a protein due to the formation of hydrogen bonds; a spiral or zigzag arrangement of the polypeptide chain.

sex chromosomes: One of a pair of chromosomes that differentiates between and is partially responsible for determining the sexes.

Shared Community Worldview Imperative: Each agent must strive to create a common body of knowledge that supports the creation of a Shared Community Worldview (that is complete, coherent, and good) through which social institutions and their resulting policies might flourish within the constraints of the essential commonly held core values (ethics, aesthetics, and religion).

Shine-Delgarno sequence: A sequence of nucleotides in bacteria involved in the initial binding of mRNA to the ribosome.

signal sequence: The directions provided by the first few amino acids synthesized on the ribosomes for the transport of proteins to different parts of the cell.

Southern blotting: Transfer of DNA that has been separated by gel electrophoresis to a membrane and detection by hybridization.

S phase: The synthesis phase of the cell cycle during which DNA is replicated.

spliceosome: The protein complex involved in removal of introns from primary RNA transcripts.

splicing: The process by which portions of the primary RNA transcript (introns) are cut out and the ends are joined.

SSCP: Single-stranded conformational polyporphism analysis; a method for detecting mutations in a DNA sequence based on the tertiary structure of single-stranded DNA.

stem cells: A relatively undifferentiated cell with the capability of self-renewal and giving rise to to progeny that can undergo terminal differentiation.

STR: Short tandem repeat sequences; repetitive DNA sequences found in the DNA genome.

Taq polymerase: A heat-stable polymerase often used in the polymerase chain reaction.

telomere: The natural end of a eukaryotic chromosome.

tertiary structure: The 3D structure of a macromolecule, often a protein.

thymine: One of the four nitrogen bases in DNA; pairs with adenine.

transcription: The process of RNA synthesis from a specific DNA template.

transcription factors: Protein required to initiate or regulate transcription in eukaryotes.

transduction: The transfer of nonviral DNA by a virus to a cell.

transfer RNA: tRNA; the small RNA molecules that decode mRNA into protein during translation and transfer a specific amino acid to the growing polypeptide chain.

transformation: Genetic modification of a bacteria or cell by the uptake and incorporation of exogenous DNA.

translation: The assembly of a protein on the ribosomes, using mRNA to direct the order of amino acids.

translocation: Transfer of part of a chromosome to a different position especially on a nonhomologous chromosome.

triplet: The three nucleotide pairs that comprise a codon.

trisomy: Three copies of a chromosome in a diploid cell.

uracil: One of four nitrogen bases in RNA; pairs with adenine.

Utilitarianism: The ethical theory that suggests that an action is morally right when that action produces more total utility or happiness for the group as a consequence than any other alternative does.

vector: A virus or plasmid used to transmit genes into the genome of a cell or organism.

virtue ethics: The ethical theory that suggests that individuals should strive to cultivate virtues or excellences through habituation of their own actions and through the education of others toward the same. The object is to create a good personal character. Good actions will flow from a good character.

virus: A particle consisting of nucleic acid (RNA or DNA) enclosed in a protein coat, capable of replicating in a host cell.

VNTR: Variable number of tandem repeat sequence; highly repetitive DNA sequences found in genomic DNA.

western blotting: The transfer of a protein from a gel to a membrane and detection with antibody.

zona pellucida: A protective barrier formed during maturation of the oocyte, that limit the number of sperm that penetrate into the oocyte cytoplasm. The zona pellucida remains surrounding the fertilized egg until after the blastocyst stage of embryogenesis.

zygote: Diploid cell formed by the fusion of the egg and sperm.

Further Readings

Some Key Ethical Principles.

Ethical Intuitionism

Augustine, St. of Hippo. *The City of God.* Books 12–14, xxi. Trans. by M. Dods. New York: Modern Library, 1950.

Benedict, Ruth. *Patterns of Culture.* Boston: Houghton Mifflin, 1934, Chaps. 1–3.

Brandt, Richard. *A Theory of the Good and the Right.* Oxford: Clarendon Press, 1979.

Cudworth, Ralph. *Eternal and Immutable Morality.* London: J&J Knapton, 1688.

Moore, G. E. *Principia Ethica.* Cambridge, UK: Cambridge University Press, 1903.

More, Henry. *Enchiridion Ethicum.* London, 1662.

Price, Richard. *A Review of the Principal Questions and Difficulties in Morals.* London, 1758.

Prichard, H. A. "Does Moral Philosophy Rest upon a Mistake?" *Mind* 21 (1912): 487–99.

———. *Moral Obligation.* Oxford, UK: Clarendon Press, 1949.

Rawls, John. *A Theory of Justice.* Cambridge, MA: Harvard University Press, 1971.

Reid, Thomas. *Essays on the Active Powers of the Human Mind.* London, 1758.

Ross, W. D. *The Right and the Good.* Oxford: Oxford University Press, 1930.

Virtue Ethics

Adkins, A. W. H. "The Connection Between Aristotle's *Ethics* and *Politics*" in D. Keyt and F. D. Miller, eds., *A Companion to Aristotle's Politics.* Oxford: Oxford University Press, 1991, pp. 75–93.

Alderman, Harold. "By Virtue of a Virtue." *Review of Metaphysics* 36 (1982): 127–53.

Annas, Julia. *The Morality of Happiness*. Oxford: Oxford University Press, 1993.

Anscombe, G. E. M. "Modern Moral Philosophy." *Philosophy 33* (1958): 1–19.

Aristotle. *Nicomachean Ethics and Eudemian Ethics* from ed. Jonathan Barnes, *The Complete Works of Aristotle: The Revised Oxford Translation*. Princeton, NJ: Princeton University Press, 1984.

Aquinas, Thomas. *The Summa Theologica* and *Summa Contra Gentiles*, selections, ed. and trans. Anton C. Pegis. New York: Modern Library, 1945.

Baier, Annette C. *Postures of the Mind: Essays on Mind and Morals*. Minneapolis: University of Minnesota Press, 1985.

Becker, Lawrence C. "The Neglect of Virtue." *Ethics* 85 (January 1975): 110–22.

———. *Stoic Ethics*. Princeton, NJ: Princeton University Press, 1997.

Irwin, T. H. *Plato's Ethics*. Oxford: Oxford University Press, 1995.

MacIntyre, Alasdair. *After Virtue*. London: Duckworth, 1981, 2nd ed. 1985.

Louden, Robert B. "On Some Vices of Virtue Ethics." *American Philosophical Quarterly* 21 (1984): 227–36.

Murdoch, Iris. *The Sovereignty of Good*. New York: Schocken Books, 1971.

Roberts, Robert C. "Will Power and the Virtues." *The Philosophical Review* 93 (1984): 227–47.

Rorty, Amelié Oksenberg, ed. *Essays on Aristotle's Ethics*. Berkeley: University of California Press, 1980.

Stocker, Michael. "The Schizophrenia of Modern Ethical Theories." *Journal of Philosophy* 73.14 (1976): 453–66,

Slote, Michael. *From Morality to Virtue*. Oxford: Oxford University Press, 1992.

Wolf, Susan. "Moral Saints." *Journal of Philosophy* 79.8 (1982): 419–39.

Utilitarianism

Adams, Robert Merrihew. "Motive Utilitarianism." *Journal of Philosophy*, 73.14 (August 12, 1976): 467–81.

Austin, John. *The Province of Jurisprudence Determined*, ed. Robert Campbell, 5th edition, 2 vols. London: John Murray, 1885.

Bentham, Jeremy. *An Introduction to the Principles of Morals and Legislation*. Oxford: Oxford University Press, 1789.

Baier, Annette. "Doing Without Moral Theory?" in Stanley G. Clarke and Evan Simpson, eds., *Anti-Theory in Ethics and Moral Conservatism*. Albany: State University Press of New York, 1989.

Bailey, James Wood. *Utilitarianism, Institutions, and Justice*. New York: Oxford University Press, 1997.

Becker, Lawrence C. "Good Lives: Prolegomena." *Social Philosophy and Policy* 9.2 (1992): 15–37.

Gibbard, Alan. "Utilitarianism and Human Rights." *Social Philosophy and Policy*. 1.2 (spring 1984): 92–102.

Hutcheson, Francis. *A System of Moral Philosophy*. 2 vols. London: privately published by his son Francis, 1775.

Johnson, Conrad D. *Moral Legislation: A Legal-Political Model for Indirect Consequentialist Reasoning*. Cambridge, UK: Cambridge University Press, 1991.

Korsgaard, Christine. "Two Distinctions in Goodness." *Philosophical Review*, 88.2 (April 1983): 169–95.

Lyons, David. *Forms and Limits of Utilitarianism.* Oxford: Clarendon Press, 1965.

———. *Rights, Welfare, and Mill's Moral Theory.* Oxford: Oxford University Press, 1994.

Mill, John Stuart. *Utilitarianism.* London: Parker, Son & Bourn, 1863, rpt. 1979, Hackett Publishers.

Paley, William. *The Principles of Moral and Political Philosophy.* London, 1785.

Scheffler, Samuel. *The Rejection of Consequentialism: A Philosophical Investigation of the Considerations Underlying Rival Moral Conceptions,* rev. ed. Oxford: Oxford University Press, 1994.

Schneewind, J. B. *Sidgwick's Ethics and Victorian Moral Philosophy.* Oxford: Oxford University Press, 1977.

Schultz, Bart, ed. *Essays on Henry Sidgwick.* Cambridge: Cambridge University Press, 1992.

Shaw, William H. *Taking Account of Utilitarianism.* Oxford: Blackwell, 1999.

Sidgwick, Henry. *The Methods of Ethics,* 7th edition. London: Macmillan, 1907.

Slote, Michael. *Common Sense Morality and Consequentialism.* London: Routledge, 1985.

Smart, J. J. C. and Bernard Williams, *Utilitarianism: For and Against.* Cambridge, UK: Cambridge University Press, 1973.

Rawls, John *A Theory of Justice.* Cambridge, MA: Belknap Press of Harvard University Press, 1971.

Regan, Donald. *Utilitarianism and Co-operation.* Oxford: Clarendon Press, 1980.

Thomson, Judith Jarvis. "On Some Ways in which a Thing Can Be Good." *Social Philosophy and Policy.* 9.2 (1992): 96–117.

Deontology

Donagan

Donagan, Alan. *The Theory of Morality.* Chicago: University of Chicago Press, 1977.

Hegel, G. W. F. *Hegel's Philosophy of Right.* tr. T. M. Knox. Oxford: Oxford University Press, 1942.

———. *Hegel's Phenomenology of Spirit.* tr. A. V. Miller. Oxford: Oxford University Press, 1977.

Oakeshott, Michael. *Rationalism and Politics and Other Essays.* London: Methuen, 1962.

Gewirth

Gewirth, Alan. *Reason and Morality.* Chicago: University of Chicago Press, 1978.

———. *The Community of Rights.* Chicago: University of Chicago Press, 1996,

———. *Self-Fulfillment.* Princeton, NJ: Princeton University Press, 1999.

Beyleveld, Deryck. *The Dialectical Necessity of Morality.* Chicago: University of Chicago Press, 1991.

Boylan, Michael. *Gewirth: Critical Essays on Action, Rationality, and Community.* New York: Rowan and Littlefield, 1999.

Regis, Edward Jr. *Gewirth's Ethical Rationalism.* Chicago: University of Chicago Press, 1984

Kant

Immanuel Kant. *Groundwork of the Methaphysics of Morals.* tr. H. J. Paton. London: Hutchinson, 1948, rpt. New York: Harper and Row, 1956.

————. *Ethical Philosophy,* incl. *The Metaphysics of Morals.* tr. James Ellington. Indianapolis, IN: Hackett, 1983.

————. *Critique of Practical Reason.* tr. L. W. Beck. New York: St. Martin's Press, 1963.

————. *Lectures on Ethics.* tr. Louis Infeld. London: Methuen & Co., 1931; rpt. New York: Harper and Row, 1963.

Cummiskey, David. *Kantian Consequentialism.* Oxford: Oxford University Press, 1996.

Herman, Barbara. *The Practice of Moral Judgment.* Cambridge, MA: Harvard University Press, 1993.

Hill, Thomas. *Autonomy and Self-Respect.* Cambridge, UK: Cambridge University Press, 1991.

Korsgaard, Christine. *The Sources of Normativity.* Cambridge, UK: Cambridge University Press, 1996.

Rawls

Rawls, John. *A Theory of Justice.* Cambridge, MA: Harvard University Press, 1971.

Daniels, Norman. *Reading Rawls: Critical Studies on Rawls, A Theory of Justice.* New York: Basic Books, 1974.

The Science of Genetic Engineering

Alberts, Bruce, et al. *Molecular Biology of the Cell.* New York: Garland Publishing, 1994

Arms, K. and P. S. Camp, *Biology. A Journey into Life.* Saunders College Publishing.

Anderson, W. French. "Human Gene Therapy." *Nature.* 392 Supplement, pp. 25–30.

Ausubel, Frederick M., et al., eds. *Short Protocols in Molecular Biology.* John Wiley & Sons, Inc.

Campbell, K. H. S., J. McWhir, W. A. Ritchie, and I. Wilmut. "Sheep Cloned by Nuclear Transfer from a Cultured Cell Line." *Nature* 380 (1996): 64–66.

Cosset, F.-L. and S. J. Russell. "Targeting Retrovirus Entry." *Gene Therapy* 3 (1996), pp. 946–56.

Fisher, K. J., et al. "Recombinant Adeno-Associated Virus for Muscle Directed Gene Therapy." *Nature Medicine* 3 (1997), pp. 306–12.

Jain, Kewel K. *Textbook of Gene Therapy.* Seattle, WA: Hogrefe and Huber Publishers, 1998.

Glick, Bernard R. and Jack J. Pasternak. *Molecular Biotechnology: Principles and Applications of Recombinant DNA.* Washington, DC: American Society for Microbiology, 1998

Gurdon, J. B. and Alan Colman. "The Future of Cloning." *Nature* 402 (1999): 743–46.

Marshall, Eliot. "Improving Gene Therapy's Tool Kit." *Science* 288 (2000): 953.

Romano, Gaetano, et al. "Latest Developments in Gene Transfer Technology: Achievements, Perspectives and Controversies over Therapeutic Applications." *Stem Cells* 18 (2000): 19–39.

Trent, R. J. *Molecular Medicine: An Introductory Text.* New York: Churchill Livingstone, 1997.

Watson, James D., et al. *Recombinant DNA: A Short Course.* New York: Scientific American Books, distributed by W. H. Freeman, 1983.

Yan, Hai, Kenneth W. Kinzler, and Bert Vogelstein. "Genetic Testing—Present and Future." *Science* 289 (2000): 1890–92.

Ethics in Genetic Engineering

Andrews, Lori B. *The Clone Age: Adventures in the New World of Reproductive Technology.* New York: Henry Holt, 1999.

Areen, Judith. "The Greatest Rewards and the Heaviest Penalties." *Human Gene Therapy.* 3.3 (June 1992), pp. 277–78.

Brannigan, Michael C. *Ethical Issues in Human Cloning.* New York: Seven Bridges Press, 1999.

Cole-Turner, Ronald, ed. *Human Cloning: Religious Responses.* Louisville, KY: Westminister John Knox Press, 1997.

Epstein, Suzanne L. "Regulatory Concerns in Human Gene Therapy." *Human Gene Therapy.* 2.3 (fall 1991), pp. 243–49.

Fletcher, John C. and W. French Anderson. "Germ-Line Gene Therapy: A New Stage of Debate." *Law, Medicine & Health Care.* 20.1/2 (spring/summer, 1992), pp. 26–39.

Fletcher, John C. and G. Richter. "Human Fetal Gene Therapy: Moral and Ethical Questions." *Human Gene Therapy.* 7 (1996), pp. 1605–14.

Hendin, Herbert. *Seduced by Death: Doctors, Patients, and the Dutch Cure.* New York: W. W. Norton, 1996.

Juengst, Eric T., ed. "Human Germ-Line Engineering—Special Issue." *Journal of Medicine and Philosophy.* 16.6 (December 1991), pp. 587–694.

Kolata, Gina. *Clone: The Road to Dolly and the Path Ahead.* New York: William Morrow, 1998.

Lewontin, Richard, et al. "Confusion over Cloning: An Exchange" *New York Review of Books* (March 5, 1998): 46–47.

Mackinnon, Barbara, ed. *Human Cloning: Science, Ethics, and Public Policy.* Urbana: University of Illinois Press, 2000.

Neel, James V. "Germ-Line Therapy: Another View." *Human Gene Therapy.* 4.2 (1993): 125–33.

Nichols, Eve K. *Human Gene Therapy.* Cambridge, MA: Harvard University Press, 1988.

Nussbaum, Martha and Cass R. Sunstein, eds. *Clones and Clones: Facts and Fantasies about Human Cloning.* New York: W. W. Norton, 1998.

Palmer, Julie Gage. "Liability Considerations Presented by Human Gene Therapy." *Human Gene Therapy.* 2:3 (fall 1991), pp. 235–42.

Rantala, M. L., and Arthur J. Milgram, eds. *Cloning: For and Against.* Chicago: Open Court, 1999.

Tauer, Carol A. "Does Human Gene Therapy Raise new Ethical Questions?" *Human Gene Therapy.* 1.4 (winter 1990), pp. 411–18.

Thompson, Larry. *Correcting the Code: Inventing the Genetic Cure for the Human Body.* New York: Simon and Schuster, 1994.

Von Tongeren, Paul J. M. "Ethical Manipulations: An Ethical Evaluation of the Debate Surrounding Genetic Engineering." *Human Gene Therapy.* 2.1 (1991), pp. 71–75.

Walters, LeRoy and Julie Gage Palmer. *The Ethics of Human Gene Therapy.* New York: Oxford University Press, 1997.

Walters, LeRoy. "Ethics and New Reproductive Technologies: An International Review of Committee Statements." *Hastings Center Report.* 17 (3, Supplement, June 1987): S3–S9.

Walters, LeRoy. "Ethical Issues in Human Gene Therapy." *Journal of Clinical Ethics.* 2.4 (winter 1991), pp. 267–74.

Zohar, Noam J. "Prospects for 'Genetic Therapy'—Can a Person Benefit from Being Altered?" *Bioethics.* 5.4 (October 1991), pp. 275–78.

Interesting Web Sites

The following information provides a starting point for finding interesting material on the science and ethics of genetic engineering. Since much of the Internet experience is following associated links to other sites, these brief annotated offerings will be the first but not the last point in your exploration.

Some Key Ethical Principles

Basic Ethics in Action series that explores issues in normative and applied ethics.
http://www.prenticehall.com

The Hastings Center. An independent research institute that explores issues in ethics and bioethics.
http://www.thehastingscenter.org

The Kennedy Institute of Ethics at Georgetown University. This site also includes the SCOPE Note series. This is a valuable beginning to many issues in bioethics.
http://www.georgetown.edu/research/kie/

The European Network for Bioethics. This site relates to the very useful Biomedical Ethics Newsletter. Wide-ranging.
http://www.uni-tuebingen.de/zew/english/intro_enbe.html

General topics in medical ethics, from Ethics in America.
http://www.learner.org/exhibits/medicalethics/

Articles in biomedical ethics. A general selection.
http://www.uwc.edu/fonddulac/faculty/rrigteri/biomed.htm

About.com-Philosophy. A general site that links traditional perspectives to biomedical ethics.
http://philosophy.about.com/

Ethics Updates Home. This site describes moral theories and pressing moral problems (including those relating to bioethics).
http://ethics.acusd.edu/

The Science of Genetic Engineering

American Society for Gene Therapy Home Page.
http://www.asgt.org/

Office of Biotechnology Activities—policies on gene therapy, xenotransplantation, genetic testing, etc.
http://www4.od.nih.gov/oba/

National Library of Medicine—PubMed. A resource for searching the medical literature for published papers in any area of medicine.
http://www.ncbi.nlm.nih.go/pubmed/

MIT's Biology Hypertextbook—covers cell biology, recombinant DNA, and genetics.
http://esg-www.mit.edu:8001/esgbio/

Expert Reviews in Molecular Medicine at Cambridge University
http://www.emm.cbcu.cam.ac.uk

E.g., Gene therapy: potential applications in clinical transplantation, J. W. Fry and K. J. Wood
http://www.emm.cbcu.cam.ac.uk/99000691h.htm

Home page of French Anderson, one of the pioneers in gene therapy—with links to articles on the history of gene therapy, ethics, protocols, etc.
http://www.frenchanderson.org/

Wiley—The Journal of Gene Medicine Website. In this site you will find tables of contents for scientific journals that specialize in gene transfer research and clinical trials.
http://www.wiley.co.uk/genetherapy/

NOAH: New York Online Access to Health Home Page. This site answers basic questions about who should consider carrier and prenatal testing and what the benefits and risks are.
http://www.noah-health.org/english/illness/genetic_diseases/geneticdis.html#DIAGNOSING

Rare Genetic Diseases in Children: An Internet Resource Gateway supported by NYU.
http://mcrcr2.med.nyu.edu/murphp01/genether.htm

Vanderbilt Gene Therapy pages.
http://www.mc.vanderbilt.edu/gcrc/gene/try.htm

The Iowa Center for Gene Therapy. A review of current research.
http://genetherapy.genetics.uiowa.edu/

The Yale gene therapy program. A review of current research.
http://info.med.yale.edu/ycc/rs01f.htm

Institute for Human Gene Therapy, University of Pennsylvania. It discusses what is happening at the institute, and an update on the death of Jesse Gelsinger.
http://www.med.upenn.edu/~ihgt/

Ethics in Genetic Engineering

The National Human Genome Research Institute, National Institutes of Health. Home of the Human Genome Project and center of ongoing research in gene therapy and its ethical implications.
http://www.nhgri.nih.gov

Office for Human Research Protections.
http://ohrp.osophs.dhhs.gov/index.htm

Including "Conflict of Financial Interest and Science," a review of a meeting.
http://ohrp.osophs.dhhs.gov/coi/index.htm

Human Genome Project—ethical, legal and social implications.
http://www.ornl.gov/hgmis/medicine/genetherapy.html

Australian National Centre for Genome Research and Public Issues Program
http://www.csu.edu.au/learning/ncgr/gpi/Index_gpi.html

The Ethics of Cloning of Humans.
http://www.msoe.edu/~tritt/sf/cloning.humans.html

CHW Ethics in Medicine. This site provides the Roman Catholic perspective on cloning and genetic engineering.
http://www.chw.edu/community/ethics.asp

Genetics and Ethics links.
http/www.changessurfer.com/hlth/genes.html

The Genetic Information Research Institute. This site discusses the current research in genetic therapy and how it might impact our society.
http://www.girinst.org

Future Generations. A site devoted to discussions on eugeneics.
http://www.eugenics.net

Index